Collecting Cultures

Indigenous Archaeologies Series

The Indigenous Archaeologies Series consists of books on contemporary developments, debates, and methodological and theoretical advances in indigenous archaeology. This series presents the results of original research, conducted primarily in the Americas, Australasia, and southern Africa. Royalties from these books are donated to the World Archaeological Congress (WAC), to support the travel of indigenous people to WAC conferences.

The reach of this series goes beyond indigenous archaeology, as the ethical practice of archaeology has the potential to touch on general questions relating to social justice and human rights. The books in this series explore some of the ways in which archaeology can be made more socially responsible. The Indigenous Archaeologies Series is committed to the promotion and empowerment of indigenous peoples.

Series Editors
Claire Smith, Flinders University
Dorothy Lippert, Smithsonian Institution
Joe Watkins, University of New Mexico
H. Martin Wobst, University of Massachusetts at Amherst
Larry J. Zimmerman, Minnesota Historical Society

Books in the Series
1. Joe Watkins, *Indigenous Archaeology: American Indian Values and Scientific Practice*
2. Rodney Harrison and Christine Williamson, eds., *After Captain Cook: The Archaeology of the Recent Indigenous Past in Australia*
3. Alistair G. Paterson, *The Lost Legions: Culture Contact in Colonial Australia*
4. Sally K. May, *Collecting Cultures: Myth, Politics, and Collaboration in the 1948 Arnhem Land Expedition*

Collecting Cultures

Myth, Politics, and Collaboration in the 1948 Arnhem Land Expedition

SALLY K. MAY

ALTAMIRA
PRESS

A division of
ROWMAN & LITTLEFIELD PUBLISHERS, INC.
Lanham • New York • Toronto • Plymouth, UK

Published by AltaMira Press
A division of Rowman & Littlefield Publishers, Inc.
A wholly owned subsidiary of The Rowman & Littlefield Publishing Group, Inc.
4501 Forbes Boulevard, Suite 200, Lanham, Maryland 20706
http://www.altamirapress.com

Estover Road, Plymouth PL6 7PY, United Kingdom

British Library Cataloguing in Publication Information Available

Library of Congress Cataloging-in-Publication Data

May, Sally K.
  Collecting cultures : myth, politics, and collaboration in the 1948 Arnhem Land
Expedition / Sally K. May.
     p. cm. — (Indigenous archaeologies series)
  Includes bibliographical references and index.
  ISBN 978-0-7591-0598-0 (cloth : alk. paper) — ISBN 978-0-7591-1314-5 (electronic)
  1. Arnhem Land Expedition (1948) 2. Arnhem Land (N.T.)—Discovery and
exploration. 3. Aboriginal Australians—Australia—Arnhem Land (N.T.) I. Title.
  DU398.A7M36 2010
  919.429'5—dc22   2009017999

Printed in the United States of America

Contents

Preface and Acknowledgments   vii

Foreword by Stephen Loring   xi

1   Beginnings   1

2   Ethnographic Collecting   19

3   Preparing for Arnhem Land   35

4   Exploring the Great Unknown—Groote Eylandt   51

5   Exploring the Great Unknown—Yirrkala   69

6   Exploring the Great Unknown—Oenpelli   79

7   Collecting Arnhem Land   95

8   When We Have Put to Sea   107

9   Reflections on an Ethnographic Collection   123

10   A Series Most Promising   149

11   The Ongoing Impact   181

References   195

Index   217

About the Author   229

Cautionary Note

This book contains names and photographs of Aboriginal people from Arnhem Land, some of whom are now deceased. Care should be taken not to mention these names to people in Arnhem Land or neighboring regions as it may cause distress to some relatives. Where possible, permission has been obtained from direct family members to include their images.

Preface and Acknowledgments

This book began to take shape back in 2000 when I was completing my dissertation at Flinders University in South Australia. From that time, the making of this book became a process of detective work as I searched for evidence of the expedition and its collections. It has taken nine years to reach this point and I believe I have still only scratched the surface of the stories relating to this important expedition.

Just as the 1948 Arnhem Land Expedition was collaborative between Australia and the United States, so too has this research involved work in both countries. With this preface I hope you will gain a better understanding of the influences on my work and the unusual journey that has been undertaken in pursuit of information relating to the events of 1948. Thanks are due to a large number of people who offered support, encouragement, and advice during the course of this research.

Since 2001 research for this book was undertaken while I was working on other major research projects, including my PhD with the Centre for Cross-Cultural Research, Australian National University. Fieldwork relating to my PhD offered the opportunity to discuss the Arnhem Land Expedition with the remote Aboriginal communities they visited in 1948 and to begin to understand the impact that such an event had/has on their lives and communities. I am particularly indebted to the people of Oenpelli (Gunbalanya) for their friendship and collaboration in research over the last nine years. I would also like to thank the people of Groote Eylandt, Yirrkala, and Milingimbi Island for taking the time to discuss the events and collections of the 1948 expedition with me. Community reengagement with the collections is an ongoing process and I look forward to working with you all on this for years to come.

I was a little surprised (and delighted) to find that some of the Arnhem Land Expedition members were still alive, some sixty years after the expedition took place. One of the first expedition members I approached was cameraman Peter Bassett-Smith, and I thank Peter and his wife, Diana, for generously discussing their stories with me on several occasions. Expedition nutritionist Dr. Margaret McArthur and National Geographic Society photographer Howell Walker also took the time to discuss their experiences with me by phone and letter. I regret not having spent more time recording Margaret's and Howell's stories and experiences relating to this expedition before they passed away. Finally, expedition botanist Professor Raymond Specht has been a constant source of information and encouragement over the last nine years and I sincerely thank him for his assistance. Ray's stories have shed new and fascinating light on the events of 1948.

By chance a friend, Gary Jackson, introduced me to Gerry Blitner in 2007. This introduction led to some of the most important work undertaken for this book. Gerry, as an Aboriginal assistant to the expedition at Groote Eylandt, recalled clearly the events of 1948 and, more important, gave me an insight into the Aboriginal experience of the expedition—from impressions of expedition members, to the location of sites visited in 1948. In the months before Gerry's death in early 2008, Dr. Martin Thomas and I worked to record some of the stories of Gerry Blitner with the assistance of his daughters Annie and Irma. I thank Gerry, Annie, and Irma for all their time and enthusiasm during these intensive days of discussions and recording.

There are many other people who have assisted with this book and I would like to thank them by name. First, Associate Professor Claire Smith has encouraged me to finish this book since I completed my dissertation with her and Associate Professor Mark Staniforth in 2000. This book would not have been published without her encouragement and support. As already mentioned, Mark Staniforth co-supervised the original research for this book and guided my historical research in Australia and the United States, and I thank him for his time, feedback, and support during this busy year. This book is part of the World Archaeological Congress and Altamira Press Series Indigenous Archaeologies, and I thank the series editors Claire Smith, Martin Wobst, Dorothy Lippert, Larry Zimmerman, and Joe Watkins for commissioning this book. Since taking up my current position at the Research School of Humanities, Australian National University, I have been granted the time to complete this book and I am grateful for this opportunity and for my colleagues' support.

While conducting research in the United States I was fortunate to have the support of Professor Stephen Loring and Dr. Joan Gero. Thanks also to Professor Martin Wobst for his guidance and also to his daughter Natalia for their hospitality in Amherst. In Washington, D.C., I am indebted to the "Underwood Boys" (Jim, Nicco, Tim, and Ryan) for their hospitality and their comical insights into American culture.

Others who have assisted at various stages of research for this book include Ken Mountford, Anthony Murphy, and everyone at Injalak Arts and Crafts, Andrew Hughes (South Australian Museum), David Hunt (National Museum of Natural History, Smithsonian Institution), David Kaus (National Museum of Australia), David Rosenthal (National Museum of Natural History, Smithsonian Institution), Eileen Jellis (Art Gallery of Western Australia), Jacklyn Young (Queensland Art Gallery), Jan Robison (Art Gallery of South Australia), Jenny Tonkin (State Library of South Australia), Judith Ryan (National Gallery of Victoria), Ken Watson (Art Gallery of New South Wales), Kim Akerman (Tasmanian Museum and Art Gallery), Stan Florek (Australian Museum), and Barrina South (Australian Museum).

I would like to thank staff at the following institutions I visited during the course of my research: Australian Institute of Aboriginal and Torres Strait Islander Studies, Australian Museum Library, National Archives of Australia, National Geographic Society, National Library of Australia, National Museum of Australia Library, National Anthropological Archives (USA), Smithsonian Institution Archives, and the Smithsonian Institution Film Archives.

Recently, Dr. Martin Thomas, Dr. Sven Ouzman, Duncan Wright, Professor Paul S. C. Taçon, and Professor Claire Smith took the time to comment on part or all of the draft manuscript of this book and their suggestions were gratefully received. The National Geographic Society kindly allowed me to use their images for this book (including the front cover) and I am most grateful for this. I wish to thank Mitch Allen, Jack Meinhardt and Marissa Parks at Altamira Press for their guidance and their patience and for the opportunity to publish on a topic that is close to my heart. Finally, I would like to thank my family for their unwavering support of my work, and I dedicate this book to my dad, Rolly May.

Sally K. May
2009

Foreword

Our culture has a cornerstone, it's called respect.

—*Clarence Jackson (Galtín Asx'áak Daa naawú Tá Gooch), Tlingit elder and chairman of the Council of Traditional Scholars, on the occasion of the blessing of the gift of an ocean-going canoe to the Smithsonian on June 19, 2008.*

For the things themselves, the objects, there is no beginning, no end. Events, like a swirling mass of migrating birds, come together and then disperse, appear, depart, and then reappear, bound by the dictates of the weather of history and the tenacity of preservation. The extraordinary ethnological collections from the 1948 American-Australian Scientific Expedition to Arnhem Land, now partially housed at the Smithsonian Institution's National Museum of Natural History (at the state-of-the-art conservation facility, the Museum Support Center, in Suitland, Maryland), are as much a testimony to the complexities and sociopolitics surrounding an international natural history and anthropology-collecting expedition as they are a celebration of the practical, spiritual, and mythological bonds between the Aboriginal peoples of Groote Eylandt, Yirrkala, and Oenpelli (Gunbalanya) and their traditional homelands in Arnhem Land. The materials derived from the 1948 expedition to Arnhem Land are the most significant and substantial portion of the Smithsonian's ethnographic collections from Australia and the only collection from Australia to be systematically—scientifically—documented and acquired.

In this book Sally K. May charts the convolutions—part personalities, part sociopolitics, part science—that led to the formation of a cooperative scientific expedition to Arnhem Land. The Arnhem Land expedition was in many respects among the last of the large interdisciplinary exploring expeditions that began with the likes of Charles Darwin's voyage aboard the *Beagle* (1831–1836), and that culminated in the mid-twentieth century with the exploits of collector-scientists like Herbert Lang and James Chapin of the American Museum of Natural History's Congo Expedition (1909–1915) and Roy Chapman Andrews in China and Mongolia in the 1920s. These natural history and anthropology-collecting expeditions, popularized by newspapers and such publications as *National Geographic*, shaped public opinion about the character of scientific research, specifically the role of natural history museums, and provided the legacy of collections that today testify to the diversity and evolution of life on earth.

From its founding in 1846 the Smithsonian Institution has had a strong Americanist agenda, especially in matters pertaining to the indigenous cultures of North America. The very first publication of the fledgling institution, *Ancient Monuments of the Mississippi Valley* (1848), by Ephraim Squier and Edwin Davis, was a critical assessment of the Native American remains and earthworks of the American Midwest. Following the American Civil War, western expansion and the acquisition of new territories in the west and the north engaged the attention of all branches of the American government. Succumbing to the belief that the American Indians were a vanishing race, Smithsonian anthropologists in the Bureau of Ethnology (established by an act of Congress in 1879) under John Wesley Powell (the geologist and explorer who led the first party to explore the Colorado River through the Grand Canyon in 1869) conducted ethnographic, archaeological, and linguistic research among Indian tribes in the western United States, Canada, and Alaska. Coincidently, Smithsonian archaeologists and physical anthropologists began to amass what was to become the world's largest museum collection of human remains (most of which were derived from North American tribal groups). Powell initiated an impressive publication series to document the research of his intrepid naturalists and anthropologists. The annual reports and bulletins of the Bureau of American Ethnology form the intellectual bedrock of American anthropology.

From its inception, Smithsonian anthropology has had a prominent materialist bias, a heritage derived from the proclivities of the Smithsonian's second secretary, Spencer Fullerton Baird, who served from 1878 until his death in 1887. Baird, an accomplished ornithologist, arrived at the Smithsonian in 1850 as assistant to the founding secretary, Joseph Henry. It was Baird who played the prominent role in transforming the fledgling institution into a national museum with strong interest in natural history. Throughout the latter half of the nineteenth century, the scientific mission of the Smithsonian, including the nascent disciplines of ethnology and archaeology, served as a handmaiden to the growth of national identity through the collection, description, and categorization of the natural history of the American hemisphere. Gradually the Smithsonian expanded its collecting efforts beyond the immediate confines of the Americas as the United States, though too late to follow the European colonial experience, sought to assert its stature on the international arena. The legacy and zeal of Baird's naturalists were such that the natural history collections of the Smithsonian have grown in size and significance to become one of the largest such repositories and research centers in the world today, housing more than 125 million natural science specimens and cultural artifacts.

Under Spencer Baird and John Wesley Powell, Smithsonian anthropology had a decidedly strong focus on collecting material culture, under the assumption that cultures, like natural organisms, could be neatly categorized and described by their appearances and attributes. Several prominent early Smithsonian anthropologists were primarily trained as naturalists and brought their collecting zeal and recognition of the importance of provenience to their acquisition of ethnological materials. Linguistics was another sphere of interest to Smithsonian anthropologists, but here too accumulated vocabularies and word lists were often acquired under a salvage premise: that the native speakers were doomed to extinction and the Smithsonian archives represented the best means of preserving their linguistic diversity. Smithsonian anthropology has long prided itself on the breadth and significance (the relatively early acquisition and the incomparable documentation) of its anthropological collections.

Until about twenty years ago the Smithsonian's Department of Anthropology enjoyed a mostly quiet, reflective place in American anthropology, comfortable with its sobriquet as the "Nation's Attic" and somewhat at a distance from the discordant notes of an emergent, politically active, and socially engaged anthropology and from the radical transformations in the discipline of

archaeology beginning in the early 1970s. This aloofness has gradually dissolved under the impetus of the passage of the 1989 National Museum of the
American Indian Act and the 1990 Native American Graves Protection and
Repatriation Act (NAGPRA). These precedent-setting legislative acts required
the Smithsonian to return human remains as well as certain classes of artifacts
(funerary objects, sacred objects, and objects of cultural patrimony) to the descendant communities from which the materials were appropriated. These
legislative initiatives radically transformed the institution's relationship with
Native Americans, opening up the collections and the archives to Native
American researchers, archivists, elders, and artisans. While contentious at
times, the intellectual environment brought about by the repatriation revolution has made the Smithsonian a far more receptive place for indigenous research and scholarship and has broadened the mandate of the anthropology
department to become more inclusive and more nuanced in its responsibilities for the stewardship of the collections it controls. It was this climate of
repatriation predicated on responsibility and respect that inspired the Arctic
Studies Center (ASC), as a separate program of the Smithsonian's anthropology department, to take a conspicuous leadership role in reaching out to and
working with native communities in Alaska, Canada, and Greenland.
Through consultation and collaboration, the ASC facilitates access of northern residents to museum collections and archives, conducts community-
based archaeological and ethnohistorical research, and supports efforts to
celebrate and preserve the cultures and knowledge of northern Indigenous
peoples through exhibitions and educational programs.

Since 1992 the Arctic Studies Center has partnered with Inuit and Innu
communities in northern Labrador on a series of community archaeology
projects that seeks to involve the full spectrum of northern community members in the creation and articulation of their history. With the passing of this
generation of elders—the last people to be born in snow houses and tents and
to grow up pursuing a subsistence-based lifestyle on the land—so passes the
last best link to the hunting, fishing, and foraging way of life that is humanity's
common heritage. With them passes much knowledge and wisdom, the special
rapport between human beings, the land, and animals that has been eroded by
village life and nearly extinguished by the urbanization and technology of the
modern world. Country-based archaeology and history initiatives, informed
by the moral authority of participating seniors and older people with country

experiences, have sought to instill in young people knowledge about the accomplishments of their ancestors, foster pride in Innu and Inuit identity, and directly involve communities with the construction of their past.

Somehow something of this northern research practice and paradigm reached the ears of Claire Smith and the organizers of the Fulbright Symposium, "Indigenous Cultures in an Interconnected World," held at the Museum and Art Gallery of the Northern Territory in Darwin, Australia, on July 24–27, 1997. Together with a colleague, Daniel Ashini, an Innu activist and later president of the Innu Nation, I traveled to Darwin to participate in the symposium and discuss the nature of our collaborative research. Hosted by the University of New England (Armidale, New South Wales [NSW]), the Australian Institute of Aboriginal and Torres Strait Islander Studies (Canberra, Australian Capital Territory [ACT]), the Northern Territories Museum and Art Gallery, and the Jawoyn Association (Katherine, Northern Territory [NT]), the symposium addressed key issues relating to Indigenous art and archaeology, repatriation and intellectual property rights, globalization, the impacts of economic development, and the survival of Indigenous cultures. Unlike many formal conferences—with interaction between speakers limited to paper presentations and perhaps a question or two—the open forums and discussion format of the Darwin symposium greatly facilitated, as archaeologists are wont to say, exchange and interaction. Indigenous participants and researchers from around the world had the opportunity to share their perspectives on governments, anthropologists and anthropology, social and economic development, cultural tourism and proprietary rights, and traditional lands and resources. It was readily apparent to all conference attendees that global economic and communication systems had radically altered the lifeways of even the world's most remote and marginalized communities. But far from signaling a diminution of cultural traditions and values, these facets of globalization held tremendous potential for supporting and encouraging cultural survival and even fluorescence as new economic and political perspectives could be brought forward, and new alliances between communities, researchers, and activists forged. The Fulbright Symposium at Darwin was a catalyst for many to pursue a more activist and socially conscious agenda that linked Indigenous community members with other groups in distant lands who shared similar social and economic threats to their lands and cultural heritage.

At the conclusion of the Fulbright Symposium some of us were fortunate enough to travel in Arnhem Land, visiting Pularumpi on Melville Island and the communities of Maningrida and Bulman, where we spent a brief time in a bush camp on the traditional lands of the Ngkalabon people. Having sought the permission of traditional landowners, we were escorted to rock-art sites at Naritjbambulan, Barunga, and Mataranka. Although a brief and fleeting introduction, it was apparent to those of us who have lived and worked with northern communities in the Canadian arctic and sub-arctic, Alaska, and Greenland that many of the issues confronting Indigenous communities in both Northern and Southern Hemispheres—pertaining to concepts of land tenure and ownership, the maintenance and continuity of traditional knowledge and controls over intellectual property, distinct artistic traditions, and notions of education and social services—had pronounced similarities. But most apparent, in Arnhem Land and in the Arctic, is the profound and pervasive notion of *respect* that infuses traditional Indigenous approaches to their land and their community: respect for the knowledge of older community members steeped in country experiences and traditional life ways, respect for the animals and resources the country provides, respect for the spiritual relationships and boundaries that link human beings with their environment and with the living world that surrounds them. Such lessons are timely indeed as the world tumbles into the maelstrom of resource extraction, overharvesting, global warming, and urbanization.

In January 1999, after the fourth World Archaeological Congress in Cape Town, South Africa, two Australian Indigenous delegations—one that included Peter Manabaru and Jimmy Wessan, accompanied by Ken Isaacson, Richard Hunter, and Claire Smith, and a second that included Irene Fisher, Eileen Cummings, and Tara Dodd (from the South Australian Museum)—arrived in Washington, D.C. Eager to repay the many courtesies and considerations that had been extended to me in Arnhem Land, I arranged for the delegations to visit the Smithsonian's Museum Support Center so that they might have an opportunity to examine the ethnographic materials from Australia and especially the materials acquired by the 1948 Arnhem Land expedition.

There is a profound silence in the remote shadowy corners of the "pod," the cement and steel building that serves as the museum's collection repository. Light, temperature, and humidity controls and dust-scouring filters and hermetically sealed doors create an imposingly sterile atmosphere that keeps time in abeyance. The building is a time machine, for here, thanks to the collecting acumen of scholars and anthropologists who thought to acquire these things from distant lands and peoples, reside astonishing things, many things that but for the miracle of preservation and conservation might have vanished nearly altogether. At times the atmosphere in the pod can be electric with excitement as you wait, heart beating and mind racing, to see what treasures will be revealed in the next steel cabinet. At other times it is sobering, almost somber, as you realize that the people who made these objects—both humble, domestic things and astonishing things crafted for celebration and worship—have long passed away. Something of both these sentiments was palpable as we looked upon the collections from the 1948 Arnhem Land Expedition. For half a century the collection, including baskets, tools, and an astonishing array of bark paintings, had lain quiet and dark, nearly forgotten, in their cabinets. How remarkable that the first visitors to seriously examine the material from Arnhem Land would be Indigenous Australians, a fact that seems to confirm many of the suppositions about the increasing involvement and awareness of Indigenous communities in anthropological research that were prominently discussed at both the Fulbright Symposium at Darwin and the World Archaeological Congress in Cape Town.

Having traveled more than halfway around the world, the Australians were confronted by objects made by individuals from communities adjacent their own. Their response, a strange mixture of awe, uncertainty, appreciation, and respect, was a potent distillation of the sentiments of the Smithsonian curators, anthropologists, and collections management staff that showed such diligence in caring for the collections. The Smithsonian's Department of Anthropology and the National Museum of the American Indian recognize that they share an extraordinary responsibility, along with other large colonial institutions that house much of the world's patrimony, to facilitate access to the collections to the descendants of the people from whom the materials were derived. This will be both a great challenge and a great boon to museum anthropology in the future. The visiting elders, observing the respect and care "their" artifacts received, noted with satisfaction that their curation had assured preservation of materials no longer in use. In their inspection of the collection, Peter Manabaru and Jimmy Wessan provided information about the subjects of bark paintings and discussed the sacred significance of some of the objects.

Sensing that we all needed some fresh air the day following our visit to the Museum Support Center, we made an excursion to the Bombay Hook National Wildlife refuge on Chesapeake Bay to view the wintering flocks of waterfowl. However, it was a stop at Wye, Maryland, to see the four-hundred-year-old Wye Oak that most impressed the visitors. The ancient tree was likened to a place of dreaming where obvious care and respect (cables supporting the weight of branches, grounding wires to insure against lighting strikes, and a protective fence to keep visitors off the roots) had been lavished on it, leading the elders to concede that the local "white fellas" yet retained some awareness of the importance of significant things. The visit to see the Wye Oak was prompted by the memory I had of being shown a tree by a billabong near Bulman that our Ngkalabon guide pointed out as having great significance for the role it played in an Ancestral or "Dreamtime" story.

The inspiration and insight resulting from such visits are among the greatest delights of museum work. The Indigenous peoples of Australia confront many of the same challenges faced by communities throughout the north. It is exciting to know that in both places the wisdom and respect of honored elders (older people with country skills and knowledge) provides an impetus for an increasingly vocal, informed, and active cadre of Indigenous scholars to conduct anthropological research for themselves, their communities, and their descendants.

Postscript

On July 29, 2008, Sally K. May accompanied a delegation of traditional Indigenous landowners from Arnhem Land to Washington, D.C., to participate in the return of the remains of at least thirty-three individuals "collected" during the 1948 Arnhem Land Expedition and stored in the research collections at the National Museum of Natural History. Accompanying Dr. May was Donald Gumurdul and Alfred Nayinggul from Oenpelli (Gunbalanya), Joaz Wurramara and Thomas Amagula from Groote Eylandt, and Lori Richardson, Assistant Director of the International Repatriation Program (Commonwealth Government of Australia) and herself an Aboriginal and Torres Strait Islander woman. The human remains from Groote Eylandt and West Arnhem Land (Red Lily Lagoon, Arguluk Hill, and Injalak Hill) were formally returned to the community representatives from Gunbalanya and Groote Eylandt in a quiet ceremony at the Australian Embassy. In participating in the collection return the Smithsonian became the first major American museum to return Indigenous remains to Australia. Surprisingly, however, the Smithsonian retained the remains of at least thirteen other people collected during the expedition, citing the official government-to-museum memorandum of agreement toward the disposition of human remains and archaeological material recovered in the course of the expedition. Australian-government spokesperson and Indigenous Affairs Minister Jenny Macklin has affirmed the Australian government's commitment to helping Indigenous representatives from Arnhem Land to bring these remains home as well.

Curiously, the return of a portion of the human remains from Arnhem Land has been adamantly portrayed by the Smithsonian's Department of Anthropology as a "loan return" rather than a "repatriation," a mere administrative formality brought about as a result of the diligence of Dr. May's research and the concern of the Indigenous communities of Arnhem Land and the Australian government through the work of the Department of Families, Community Services and Indigenous Affairs (FACSIA), and the Australian Embassy in Washington, D.C. Since the establishment of the Smithsonian's Repatriation Office in 1991, the office has adopted a strict "letter-of-the-law" approach to the repatriation of human remains, one tenet of which has been an adamant resistance to engaging in any foreign repatriation claims. Prior to the codification of policy by law, the department was involved in two high-profile repatriation cases, one concerning the return of several *Ahayu:da*—carved wooden ceremonial offerings—to the Zuni in 1987 and, in 1991, the return of the remains of approximately a thousand individuals of Alutiiq and Koniag descent to the Alaskan native village of Larsen Bay on Kodiak Island. Decisions for both of these repatriations—or returns—were predicated on moral and ethical grounds, not on legal mandates, which at the very least established a precedent for a more nuanced, expansive, and responsive approach to resolving the differences between anthropological institutions and descendant communities.

The resurgence of an awareness and interest in the collections of the 1948 Arnhem Land Expedition is a poignant example of the foresight and dedication of the researchers who made the collection, the stewardship of museum curators and conservators who have overseen its care and preservation, and the excitement and passion of researchers and descendant community members who find in the collection clues, memories, and testimonials to an extraordinary tradition and legacy. Through the miracle of preservation these artifacts come back to haunt us. Our duty as curator, anthropologist, researcher, community member, or visitor is to celebrate both the traditions and ancestors from whence the collections were derived as well as respect and acknowledge the different perspectives and interests of the many parties who have an interest in the collections.

Stephen Loring
Smithsonian Institution
Arctic Studies Center, Department of Anthropology
October 2008

1

Beginnings

Some of the most powerful and memorable moments in people's lives come from encountering different cultures. It is sobering to stand face to face with people whose lifestyles are profoundly dissimilar to your own. Such cross-cultural encounters can reveal the very best and the very worst in individuals and the cultural beliefs by which they judge and engage others and, indeed, themselves. In February 1948, a team of Australians and Americans came together in Australia to begin, what was then, one of the largest scientific expeditions ever to have taken place in this country—the American-Australian Scientific Expedition to Arnhem Land (henceforth, the Arnhem Land Expedition). Today it remains one of the most significant, most ambitious, and least understood expeditions ever mounted.

These seventeen men and women came as researchers and in supporting roles and together journeyed across the remote region known as Arnhem Land in northern Australia for eight months. From varying disciplinary perspectives, and under the guidance of expedition leader Charles Mountford, they investigated the people and the environment of Arnhem Land. In addition to an ethnographer, archaeologist, photographer, and filmmaker, the expedition included a botanist, a mammalogist, an ichthyologist, an ornithologist, and a team of medical and nutritional scientists. Their first base camp was Groote Eylandt in the Gulf of Carpentaria. Three months later they moved to Yirrkala on the Gove Peninsula and three months

FIGURE 1.1
Our camp and personnel at Oenpelli, October 1948. Collection of Frank Setzler, National Library of Australia, nla.pic-an2820731.

following that to Oenpelli (now Gunbalanya) in west Arnhem Land (see figure 1.2). The journey involved the collaboration of vastly different sponsors and partners (among them the National Geographic Society, the Smithsonian Institution, and various agencies of the Commonwealth of Australia). In the wake of the expedition came volumes of scientific publications, kilometers of film, thousands of photographs, tens of thousands of scientific specimens, and a vast array of artifacts and paintings from across Arnhem Land—this latter collection being of specific focus in this book. The legacy of the 1948 Arnhem Land Expedition is vast, complex, and, at times, contentious.

This book will take you on a journey spanning countries, governments, museums, and remote Australian Aboriginal[1] communities. What makes the events of 1948 even more remarkable are the cross-cultural encounters taking place—between Aboriginal and non-Aboriginal participants, and between American and Australian scientists and their organizations. Some of the friendships formed during this nine-month expedition lasted a lifetime. This is illustrated in the correspondence between many expedition members that

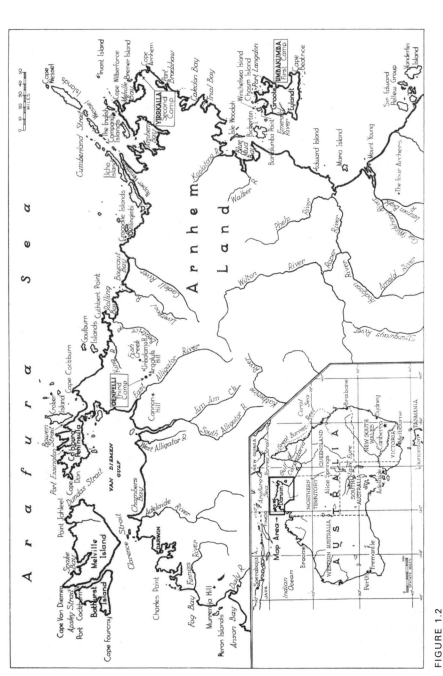

FIGURE 1.2
Map of Northern Territory, Australia showing regions visited during the 1948 Arnhem Land Expedition (after Mountford 1956: xxii).

continued for decades. As deputy-leader of the Arnhem Land Expedition Frank Setzler (to expedition medical doctor Brian Billington, December 31, 1948) writes:

> Australia begins to seem like a dream, and a very pleasant one. My reactions now are somewhat comparable to those I had when I first reached Australia. I am sorely missing that good old Australian beer!! To say nothing of steak and eggs for breakfast. And don't think I haven't told my friends about it. Susan [Mrs. Setzler] has been so pleased with my having lost 30 lbs that I am practically on a starvation diet. I am afraid she'll send me back to Arnhem Land if I start putting on a few pounds.

Other relationships descended rapidly into lifelong academic argument, as illustrated by letters from expedition archaeologist Frederick "Fred" McCarthy (to archaeologist Frank Setzler, April 28, 1949):

> Monty [Charles Mountford] has been in Sydney for two months but has not been in to see me. I gave a lecture to our Pacific Islands Society on Arnhem Land and who should be in the audience but Monty—he ignored me during the supper afterwards. A nice type.

While on the surface science would seem to be the core motivator for this expedition, in truth politics were central to its success in attaining funding and international collaborators. The leader of the expedition, Charles Mountford (see figure 1.3), was an amateur filmmaker and ethnographer working for the Commonwealth of Australia. He was also an honorary associate in ethnology at the South Australian Museum. Mountford must be credited with conceptualizing the expedition and providing the impetus for it to occur for years before 1948.

In 1945 and 1946 Mountford toured the United States showing films of Aboriginal life in Australia, which he had produced earlier in his career (see chapter 3, "Preparing for Arnhem Land," for further details). So why was a self-proclaimed ethnographer being paid by the Commonwealth of Australia to tour the United States showing films of Aboriginal life? The simple answer is—propaganda. The primary motivation for employing and supporting Mountford at this time was to gain favorable publicity for Australia and to encourage good relations between Australia and the United States following

FIGURE 1.3
Charles Mountford recording an interpretation of a bark painting from an unidentified Groote Eylandt man during the Arnhem Land Expedition. Photograph by Howell Walker, National Geographic Society (after Mountford 1949:750). Courtesy National Geographic Society.

World War II. As Dr. Alexander Wetmore of the Smithsonian Institution wrote in relation to the Arnhem Land Expedition, "We look forward with keen interest to this work, particularly to the close association that it brings between representatives of our two governments. We may, I trust, consider this a beginning to an even closer cooperation in future scientific matters than has existed heretofore" (Wetmore, December 3, 1947: 2).

Scientists and explorers in the United States liked Charles Mountford's films and following a lecture to 4,000 members of the National Geographic Society, the money and resources for future fieldwork started to flow:

> I have read Mr. Mountford's research proposal with much interest and it has my hearty approval. In fact, I should favor increasing the grant to $10,000 or more if this would increase the effectiveness of the expedition. (Briggs, April 20, 1945)

So while Mountford actually asked for less money, the National Geographic Society offered $10,000 to mount a scientific expedition in Australia and other organizations soon took note.

The official research proposal submitted by Mountford (March 5, 1945) to the National Geographic Society included study in four main areas: the art of the bark paintings, the art of the body paintings, the general ethnology of the people, and music in secular and ceremonial life. Yet, the real reasons for this expedition taking place can only be understood by revealing the *unpublicized* aims of the expedition. These aims were outlined in a private letter from Charles Mountford to the president of the National Geographic Society, Gilbert Grosvenor, on January 28, 1947:

1. Establish a good neighbor policy and scientific cooperation between the United States of America and Australia.
2. Provide publicity for Australia through the publication of three, if not four, illustrated articles in the *National Geographic Magazine*. (Circulation 1,250,000. Estimated Readers 5,000,000).
3. Study and record the aborigine's pattern of life in relation to the terrestrial and marine fauna and flora.
4. Investigate seasonal movements and shelter of the aborigines, and, by examination of their foods determine how well, or otherwise, they are able "live off the land."

5. Make a nutritional health survey of the natives and their food as a guide for future administration.
6. Collect and identify the plants, birds, animals and fish in the various environments of Arnhem Land.
7. Carry out a food fish survey along the coast of Arnhem Land.
8. Determine the food resources of land and sea as data for future military operations (this was urgently needed, but not available, during the last war).
9. Produce, for the National Film Board, five coloured cine films on the ethnology and natural history of Arnhem Land.[2]

Clearly, international politics was just as important as science for the Arnhem Land Expedition.

With the involvement of other institutions, including the Australian Museum and the United States National Museum (Smithsonian Institution), the small expedition grew to seventeen people from a variety of disciplines, nationalities, and, indeed, cultural experiences. As Mountford (January 28, 1947: 3) states, "With the pooling of the resources of so many Departmental bodies and scientific institutions, this should be the best equipped scientific party ever sent into the field for the study of Australian natural history and ethnology." In chapter 3, "Preparing for Arnhem Land," I explore this complex history in more detail and introduce the players in this story.

This book is based on the substantial documentary evidence available. It is, therefore, an historical account, but it is also based on ethnographic accounts gleaned from discussions with the surviving expedition members, the surviving Aboriginal participant, and both groups' descendents. Yet, this is not just a history book. Instead, it is imbued with archaeological, anthropological, and museological methods and motivations. This interdisciplinary approach offers us another way to understand cross-cultural encounters—through the items that were collected.

As Susan Pearce (1992: 24) suggests, "Objects . . . have lives which, though finite, can be very much longer than our own. They have the power, in some sense, to carry the past into the present by virtue of their 'real' relationship to past events." One of the other key issues explored in this book is how this expedition—in the greater scheme of things—acts as a metonym or a microcosm of larger issues relating to cross-cultural encounters and the collection of material culture from Aboriginal communities in the late 1940s. How can the phenomenon of exploration, politics, collecting, and cross-cultural encounters be understood and nuanced from the field notes and particular artifacts that were collected by expedition members? For the Arnhem Land Expedition, exploring the factors that led to the expedition, and of the fieldwork itself, can go some way toward answering this question. An analysis of aspects of the expedition collections (in this case the ethnographic collection[3] and, in particular, the painting collections) can take us one step further.

So, what exactly did expedition members collect? The answer is over 50,000 archaeological, ethnographic, and natural history specimens. These included approximately 13,500 botanical specimens, 30,000 fish, 850 birds, 460 mammals, and over 2,000 ethnographic artifacts (Mountford 1975: 231). In just eight months, these researchers formed some of the most significant Australian collections of the twentieth century.

In November 1948, after eight months in the field, when the last of the Arnhem Land Expedition members were safely back in Darwin and thinking ahead to their journeys home, they would have been reflecting on their collections. It is the distribution and life history of these artifacts that forms the core of the discussion in chapter 8, "When We Have Put to Sea." In this chapter I focus in on the ethnographic collection drawn together during these eight months in Arnhem Land. This collection includes dozens of different artifact types such as fibre objects, spears, children's toys, and, arguably the most famous aspect of the collection, the paintings. This particular ethnographic collection offers us the opportunity to explore diverse aspects of both Aboriginal and non-Aboriginal culture and, particularly, the cross-cultural encounters that took place during this expedition. Today, these Arnhem Land Expedition artifacts turn up in the most unusual places (small regional museums in England, Sotheby catalogs, and so forth). Because of poor recording keeping, and some slippery international trading, a complete census of the artifacts the expedition members acquired during their eight months in Arnhem Land is impossible.

The Arnhem Land Expedition took place during a year of particular international significance with, for example, apartheid becoming official in South Africa, Israel being declared an independent state, and the Soviet Union beginning its blockade of West Berlin. Meanwhile, this Australian expedition was being promoted as the most important scientific research to take place in years. Newspaper reports, radio interviews, and films all documented the importance with which this expedition was regarded, as the following newspaper clipping demonstrates:

Smithsonian Scientists Move into New Camp in Australian Jungle
The Australian-American scientific expedition has moved into its second camp to continue a study of primitive Northern Australia. The party's new base is . . . situated at Gove, in Melville Bay, a former RAAF base. From the new base, the Australians and Americans will trudge through the stinking mud of the nearby Paperbark Swamp, home of the giant crocodile. In this swamp, 11 years ago, a trapper shot a crocodile 26 feet, four inches long. (*Evening Star*, July 19, 1948)

Following the fieldwork (which will be discussed in chapters 4, 5, and 6), the complete scientific results were published in four volumes (Mountford 1956, 1960; Mountford and Specht 1958; Specht 1964). The National Geographic Society published four articles on the expedition, namely David Johnson's "The Incredible Kangaroo" (1955: 487–500), Charles Mountford's "Exploring Stone Age Arnhem Land" (1949: 745–82) and "Australia's Stone Age Men" (1963: 385–92), and Howell Walker's "Cruise to Stone Age Arnhem Land" (1949: 417–30).

Aside from these books and articles, few publications have explicitly dealt with the Arnhem Land Expedition. The exception is Colin Simpson's discussion of his brief visit to one of the expedition base camps (see *Adam in Ochre* 1951). Most of the expedition members used artifacts collected during this expedition as subjects for their later publications; for example, Frederick McCarthy published a variety of articles during the 1950s based on the Arnhem Land Expedition collections—"Arnhem Land Baskets" (1955: 368–71), "Aboriginal Rain-Makers and Their Ways" (1952: 302–5), "Purse-Net Fishing in Arnhem Land" (1953: 21–23)—and Frank Setzler with McCarthy, "A Unique Archaeological Specimen from Australia" (1950: 1–5).

While the Arnhem Land Expedition may have been well publicized, the processes of collection and the distribution of the artifacts are not well documented. In fact, for such a large and significant collection, it is acutely lacking in context. It is one of the aims of this book to address this issue. Research to date includes a 1992 cataloging consultancy report for the National Museum of Australia. In this report Craig Elliott (1992) documented some of the methods of collection and the original and present distribution of some of the artifacts. His main focus was the National Museum of Australia's portion of the collection that stems from the artifacts acquired by the Australian Institute of Anatomy (AIA) following the expedition. Chris Jones's (1987) graduate diploma dissertation on the collection of toys is one of only four other works to be concerned with artifacts purely from the Arnhem Land Expedition. The other three are Stan Florek's (1993: 117–24) "F. D. McCarthy's String Figures from Yirrkala: A Museum Perspective," Margo Neale's (1998: 210–17) article for the Queensland Art Gallery concerning the "bastard" bark paintings received by this institution, and my own Flinders University dissertation from 2000 titled "The Last Frontier? Acquiring the American-Australian Scientific Expedition Ethnographic Collection 1948."

Other researchers have included Arnhem Land Expedition artifacts as part of a larger study such as Claudia Haagen's 1994 "Bush Toys." Judith Ryan (1990) also discusses bark paintings from the expedition in context with other paintings held in the National Gallery of Victoria. Since the reviews of the "Records of the American-Australian Scientific Expedition to Arnhem Land" ceased to emerge in journals in 1957 (for example, anonymous 1957; Berndt 1958; Bouteiller 1957; Elkin 1961; Gruber 1962; Kaberry 1962; Kabo 1958; Worsley 1957), Annie Clarke (1998) is the only researcher to have written on these works. Her paper was concerned with the language of these publications and, particularly, with analyzing whether gender could be explored through the language used in the publications of two expedition members, archaeologist Frederick McCarthy and nutritionist Margaret McArthur.

The documentation surrounding the Arnhem Land Expedition is enormous, especially considering the unpublished field journals and correspondence kept in museums and libraries in Australia and the United States. Despite this, no history of the Arnhem Land Expedition, except that written by Mountford in 1956, has been published and some of the studies concerning the collection or parts of the collection are unpublished or, in the case of the Elliott (1992) report, partially confidential.

In the chapters 9 and 10, "Reflections on an Ethnographic Collection" and "A Series Most Promising," I take this book in a more analytical direction. The first of these chapters explores the ethnographic collection acquired during the Arnhem Land Expedition in relation to two key areas: the collectors and the character of their institutions. The second narrows this focus to the collection of paintings labeled by McCarthy (May 17, 1948) as "a series most promising."

Charles Mountford used the term "ethnographic" to describe the nonexcavated cultural objects collected during the Arnhem Land Expedition. Ethnographic collections acquired for and stored by museums offer the opportunity to draw out contextually aware inferences about human behavior. Ian Coates (1989: 1–2) states that "collections . . . are often seen as providing objective information or 'facts' about societies from which they were acquired." The Arnhem Land Expedition challenges this view due to the nature of the collection process as well as the formation of criteria for the selection of materials to collect. Charles Mountford's commissioning of bark paintings with specific stories is an excellent example of this process. While most museum or gallery visitors, including researchers, would assume that the paintings were produced with little or no direct influence from the collector, in fact, many of the Arnhem Land Expedition paintings were commissioned pieces. Rather than diminishing the cultural value of these paintings, this situation forces us to acknowledge that collecting is a complex and multifaceted process and to rethink Aboriginal attitudes toward these collectors at the time and how their responses may manifest in the collections that were formed.

It may be this lack of context and, in turn, contextual understanding that has led researchers such as Altieri (in Aagaard-Mogensen 1988: 157) to state that "of all the institutions developed during the nineteenth century perhaps none has received such uniformly bad press by contemporary pundits as the museum." This "bad press" has, to some extent, often been due to museums failing to place their artifact base in their emic and etic context or to acknowledge their own cultural influences on their collections. This lack of context and understanding has often made ethnographic collections relatively ineffective for researchers interpreting aspects of the cultures from which they were acquired (Clifford 1997). Collections such as the Arnhem Land Expedition ethnographic collection represent moments of culture contact and are, therefore, ideal for exploring cross-cultural encounters. The extent to which individuals, institutions, and the numerous biases they harbor have influenced this collection is a focus of this book. The Arnhem Land Expedition ethnographic collection, in effect, is more representative of a cross-cultural encounter than purely of the Aboriginal cultures from which the artifacts were acquired. As such, the book does not analyze the material collections to interpret Aboriginal culture. On the contrary, this book focuses on what we can learn about relationships and the anthropological and archaeological disciplines through these material items and associated literature.

There is a key difference between study of a collection (i.e., how a collection came to be a supra-artifact) and a study that proceeds from a collection (i.e., comparative studies of, for example, stone artifacts), which is more the archaeological norm. This book explores the collection as a supra-artifact rather than the latter. There are four primary themes evident in studies on ethnographic collections of Australian Aboriginal artifacts. In general, collections and the studies that chronicle them have been considered the raw material for research. First, there are technical works in which collections are used to test and develop new analytical techniques (e.g., Barton 2007; Buhmann, Robins, and Cause 1976; Kealhofer, Torrence, and Fullagar 1999; Morris 1987). Second, some research uses collections to answer specific questions about the manufacture and/or use and meaning(s) of a particular kind of artifact (e.g., Block 1987; Glassow 1980; Harrison 2004; Jones 1987; Torrence 1993; Wright 1979). Third, there are catalogs that aid in the dissemination of information concerning the material held (e.g., Florek 1993; MacGregor 1997; McCarthy 1974). Finally, with the development of explicit museum theory since the early 1980s, the phenomenon of museums and their collections as artifacts and assemblages has demanded increasing recognition. This recognition seeks to contextualize museums and their collections by investigating the historical backgrounds and circumstances under which the collections were acquired (see, for example, Coates 1989; Cooper 1975; Hunter and Donovan 2005; Katz 2003; Mulvaney 1983). The metanarrative of this book places the Arnhem Land Expedition ethnographic collection in historical context.

There are a number of reasons why the Arnhem Land Expedition's ethnographic collection was chosen as a focus for a book concerned with myth, politics, and collaboration in ethnographic collections. The first motivation was that very little work had been undertaken on any of the historical sources or the material culture since the publication of the records of the expedition in the 1950s and 1960s. The collections were brought to my attention in 1999 by archaeologist Claire Smith while I was studying for my honors degree at Flinders University in South Australia. Smith was herself made aware of the collections by Stephen Loring, a staff member at the National Museum of

Natural History, Smithsonian Institution. The Smithsonian holds a significant proportion of the materials collected in 1948. As he discusses in the foreword to this book, Loring was aware that little research had ever been undertaken on the collection and realized that the museum could use some historical information on this important asset.

No complete catalog of the ethnographic artifacts has ever been produced. Rather, as discussed in chapter 8, "When We Have Put to Sea," the artifacts were immediately split into smaller groupings to be distributed throughout Australia and the United States. The lack of a complete catalog and subsequent division of the full collection has meant that any research into the artifacts has been of isolated portions of the entire collection. Yet, this is not so different to archaeological method—as we regularly study fragments of a larger whole. At the same time, it is important to remember that there was never meant to be one complete ethnographic collection from the Arnhem Land Expedition. In fact, each expedition member was collecting artifacts they and/or their institutions desired relatively independently.

The Arnhem Land Expedition collections held by the National Museum of Australia, the South Australian Museum, and the Smithsonian Institution commonly represent a large percentage of each institution's material from Arnhem Land. In the case of the National Museum of Natural History (Smithsonian Institution) approximately 339 of their 762 ethnographic artifacts from Australia were acquired during this expedition (David Rosenthal, personal communication, July 17, 2000). This represents 45 percent of their entire Australian ethnographic collection, yet very little research has ever been conducted to supply this and other institutions with contextual information about the materials' acquisition.

Another motivation for focusing on this particular expedition was that the ethnographic collection offered an opportunity to explore collection strategies and their influence on ethnographic collections in Australia and overseas during the 1940s. This collection represents a large sample size of 2,144 specimens from a short time period. The collection of nearly 500 bark paintings, which is the focus of chapter 10, "A Series Most Promising," also represents a complete census from the communities visited. I was fortunate to have abundant documentation to assist with the analysis of collection strategies. These include diaries, letters, government reports, films, sound recordings, and photographs. These sources tell us some of the thoughts, movements, and ideals of the collectors. The existence of an ethnographic collection itself tells us something of the changes in ethnography, ethnology, and archaeology from the 1940s through today where we would likely classify these objects differently.

Throughout much of this book I critique the methods used by the collectors to acquire cultural knowledge and materials from Aboriginal people. One of the widely promoted collections from this expedition was the paintings that, as will be explained in chapter 9, "Reflections on an Ethnographic Collection," were separated and distributed widely. If we consider just the painting collection for a moment, we realize that it makes up over 22 percent (n = 484) of all the ethnographic material collected, and it is undeniable then that this was a particular area of interest for the expedition members and a deliberate bias in their collecting.

Just as the expedition members did in 1948, by choosing to focus on paintings in this book I am drawing your attention to one type of ethnographic artifact at the expense of the others. The abundance of paintings in these collections, and my decision to focus on them, is largely a consequence of Charles Mountford's own inclination toward this aspect of Aboriginal material culture, above all others. Namely, the large number of paintings is a reflection of the mindset of the collector as well as the culture of study. Considering paintings represent over 22 percent of all ethnographic material collected by the expedition, my choice of these artifacts seems to be carrying on a tradition of selecting for artistic and highly visual or conspicuous artifacts.

Perhaps here you will come to understand the need to offer some justification for my choices. First, the decision to analyze one category of artifact from the 1948 expedition was made two months into my research. When visiting the National Museum of Natural History (Smithsonian Institution) in Washington, D.C., I saw the extent of their collections and realized that any records I could make of the *whole* collection would be limited and cursory. It was always my aim in undertaking this research to move beyond general empirical descriptions of the artifacts and into some penetrating analysis. I, therefore, made the decision to concentrate on one type of artifact and while still analyzing the whole ethnographic collection in general terms, I would specifically examine the paintings. The paintings thus have become a metonym for the wider Arnhem Land Expedition collections as well as the practices and methodologies of the collectors.

It may be suggested that it is not the choice of one artifact type that leads to informed critique but rather how this choice was made. Why did I choose paintings and not stone artifacts, fibre objects, spears, or some other type? Is my choice of paintings as much determined by notions about the "importance" of art as opposed to some notion of the "dry" nature of other artifacts? The answer to this question is twofold. First, I knew from detailed investigations that at least 484 paintings were acquired during this expedition. These paintings constitute the largest single ethnographic artifact category collected during the expedition. This, by any standard, is a significant collection and when considered as a single collection rather than as a fragmented entity housed in over ten different institutional collections, it provides a considerable sample size from which to seek some larger meanings. It also became clear that the collectors had acquired every painting from the communities visited—a complete census. This is rare.

Second, at the very beginning of this study it was obvious that museums and art galleries holding artifacts from the Arnhem Land Expedition were interested in finding out more about paintings, perhaps more than any other artifact type. I think this desire for knowledge had a deeper meaning than simply museum and gallery staff being interested in the "artistic" artifacts. After all, there were figurines, necklaces, carved model canoes, and more in the collections, which are also artistic in the broadest sense, but most people were not as eager for information about these.

It could be argued that painting is an artifact category that is theoretically more informed than many others because it straddles several disciplines; the insights from which act as a mutually constraining and enabling web of argumentation (Wylie 1989). I thought there must be another reason for this interest and considered that, at least in the not-so-distant past, paintings (particularly bark paintings) represented to many people a fusion of art and artifact. In the 1940s, people's perceptions of bark paintings were living on the thin line between these two distinctions and I propose that even today museums and galleries are not always sure how to treat them. It is not my aim here to give an outline of what constitutes art and why bark paintings do or do not fit into this mold—though this will be touched upon in later chapters. Rather, the unique situation of these paintings demanded recognition and, along with the other factors such as some existing knowledge of the area, Aboriginal community concern for these paintings, and a large sample size, I was confident in my decision to make them the major material culture focus of this book.

Paintings aside, the political, economic, and extended cultural influences behind this collecting were enormous and important for understanding the attitudes toward non-Aboriginal people in 1940s. Another important reason for the focus on the ethnographic collection is that when considering the expedition, it is clear that a substantial quantity of material was acquired from the Aboriginal people of Arnhem Land in a relatively short time (2,144 ethnographic artifacts in eight months). These artifacts were collected during a period when Aboriginal people were increasingly living in government-supported, church-run missions, or similar kinds of authoritarian establishments (for further information see Berndt and Berndt 1954; Cole 1972, 1975, 1980; Dewar 1995; Hamby 2005; May 2005, 2006; Mulvaney 2004; Rose 1960; Thomson 1949; Trudgen 2000).

The government of the Commonwealth of Australia, as well as other non-Aboriginal parties, was implicitly and explicitly forcing Aboriginal people to alter their life ways. The acquisition of Aboriginal artifacts was, therefore, undertaken in circumstances when power relations between collector and Aboriginal producer were particularly unequal. Aboriginal men, women, and children offered up their products to collectors in exchange for tobacco, food, or small amounts of money (see, e.g., Mulvaney and Calaby 1985; Ryan 1990; Spencer 1928; Taylor 1996).

The final chapter of this book, "The Ongoing Impact," discusses the return of information about the Arnhem Land Expedition to the descendants of the Aboriginal people who lived through the 1940s in an attempt to unite ethics as theory with archaeology as practice. We can today attempt to make amends for the intrusiveness of past research and its consequences. Yet, the ongoing impact is not as simple as returning old photographs to communities. It is about acknowledging that for Aboriginal Australians, there remains a cultural link with the objects, or, to paraphrase Howard Morphy (1998: 37), in journeying to other places Aboriginal objects can carry with them their links to land, history, and identity. This connection is significantly stronger when the skeletal remains of their ancestors are the objects of collection, as they were during the Arnhem Land Expedition. Furthermore, our understanding of objects as objects is often a willful misreading of Aboriginal notions of material culture.

It is hoped that this book will assist future research on the collections by Aboriginal communities, other researchers, and other interested individuals and groups. It may also assist communities to reconnect with their material culture including sacred objects and the remains of their ancestors. It is also hoped that it will bring the Arnhem Land Expedition collections to the attention of researchers with an interest in material culture from this period.

This book, unashamedly, does not explore all aspects of the Arnhem Land Expedition. For example, it does not discuss the internationally significant scientific work of the mammalogist, botanist, ichthyologist, ornithologist, biochemist, nutritionist, or medical doctor. The scope, nature, and impact of each scientist's work could fill volumes and deserves more attention than I can give it in this book. This book does not explore many aspects of the other visual evidence from the Arnhem Land Expedition—films, sound recordings, and photographs, except where they relate directly to the topic at hand. Such evidence has the potential to provide great detail about the material lives of people in Arnhem Land in 1948. I look forward to reading future publications and watching films on these aspects of the collections.

At first glance a person looking at the history of the Arnhem Land Expedition may think that its story begins and finishes with the pitching of tents in March 1948 to their striking in November 1948. This is not the case. This expedition spanned two continents and nearly two decades from the birth of the idea in 1945 to the publishing of the last volume of records in 1964. In 2008 the Arnhem Land Expedition celebrated its sixtieth anniversary and it is hoped that this book might bring the expedition, its members, and their collections to the attention of another generation of people: not just archaeologists, anthropologists, or historians but also the Aboriginal people to whom the success of the expedition is due. The Arnhem Land Expedition is a remarkable story as it represents the myth and politics of collecting in the immediate aftermath of World War II. I have no doubt it will continue to inspire diverse groups to remember, to reflect, and to engage with this extraordinary inheritance.

NOTES

1. Throughout this book I use the term "Aboriginal" as a generic term referring to the first nations of mainland Australia. The term "indigenous" is used when referring to Aboriginal and Torres Strait Islanders.

2. These aims have been left as written by Mountford in the original document; they are deliberately unedited.

3. Charles Mountford used the term "ethnographic" to describe the nonexcavated cultural objects collected or, in other words, artifacts, not found in archaeological associations. I have retained this phrasing for the sake of continuity.

2

Ethnographic Collecting

Museums have appropriated culture in many ways. All of our collections were made with political agendas—albeit unconscious ones—in mind, and all bear the indelible marks of the contexts from which they arose, once we choose to look for them.

(Pearce 1994: 1)

Collecting was central to the aims and the success of the Arnhem Land Expedition and throughout this chapter I question the motivations of the men and women of the Arnhem Land Expedition to collect artifacts of another culture. What made the gaining of these collections so important that governments were willing to donate many thousands of dollars and highly educated men and women were willing to give up years to the cause? The answer has wider implications than this expedition alone.

Before presenting the Arnhem Land Expedition as a case study in ethnographic collecting, it is important to understand that this cross-cultural encounter and the nature of its collections are part of a wider movement influenced by contemporary beliefs relating to the nature of Aboriginal and non-Aboriginal Australian (or, for want of a better word, "Western") cultures. Why, in 1948, was collecting from Australian Aboriginal people such an important endeavor? Two issues of importance are the notions of collecting or salvaging specimens of Aboriginal cultures and the impact of Social Darwinism on collecting in Australia. While the desire to collect may generally be considered uncomplicated, on closer examination it is always found to have aspects that have ingress to other, nonmuseological aspects of life.

I begin this chapter with a discussion of the phenomenon of collecting with specific reference to collecting material culture from indigenous groups around the world. I then follow this discussion with an exploration of the role of museums in collection formation both in terms of the history of museum collecting and the nature of academic exploration of these issues. This book, however, is about an ethnographic collection and, as such, I explore the intricacies and individualities of ethnographic collecting and, in particular, collections formed in Australia. Finally, an emerging academic and theoretical discussion of collecting by indigenous scholars closes this chapter and, in turn, marks the beginning of the Arnhem Land Expedition histories in chapter 2, "Preparing for Arnhem Land."

THE DESIRE TO COLLECT

Werner Muensterberger (1994: 4) gives a general definition of collecting as "the selecting, gathering, and keeping of objects of subjective value." He then goes on to ask, "Is it an obsession? An addiction? Is it a passion or urge, or perhaps a need to hold, to possess, to accumulate?" (Muensterberger 1994: 3). It is important to remember that humans have felt the desire to "collect" for thousands of years, if not more, and at each of these stages they have collected for diverse reasons. Elsner and Cardinal (1994: 2) also comment that the history of collecting is a narrative of how humans have tried to accommodate, to appropriate, and to extend the taxonomies and systems of knowledge they have inherited, and he adds, "Social order is itself inherently collective: it thrives on classification, on rule, on labels, sets and systems." In this way, collecting extends to empires collecting countries and populations, early modern Europe secular authorities collecting slaves, churches collecting souls, and archaeologists collecting artifacts and contextual knowledge.

Australia has been a playground for antiquarian collectors since the eighteenth century. In Australia they found a continent, unknown to most of the world until the 1600s, brimming with potential for discovery. In 1929 the Australian explorer Captain George Hubert Wilkins wrote of Australia's "quaint eccentricities" including the "old-man Kangaroo," which he notes as standing on its hind legs and measuring ten feet tall. And, of course, there are the "two unique and extraordinary creatures, the egg-laying mammals or monotremes—the platypus and the echidna." When the first examples of these creatures were taken to Europe they were so unusual that they were believed to be fakes (Wilkins 1929: 6).

Why did the outside world care about Aboriginal Australia? From first contact, the indigenous people of Australia occupied a unique place in social theory. In Australia, the world believed that a people lacking almost all of the attributes of civilization or humanity had been found. Most wore no clothes, they were believed to have no domesticated animals or crops, and they were largely regarded as relics from some earlier period of humanity. Despite extensive evidence to the contrary, these attitudes took a long time to fade and some would argue that they still survive in parts of Australian society today. The collection of material culture from Australian Aboriginal groups illustrates these changes in attitude. The objects were curiosities from an unknown land.

The 1948 Arnhem Land Expedition was late in terms of exploration in Australia. While expedition members dubbed themselves as "exploring the great unknown," in fact, these areas, while remote, were far from unknown. They had been subject to study since the earliest explorers began their attempts at documenting the social and cultural lives of the indigenous people in the 1800s. So why did they want to collect from Arnhem Land in 1948? How is this linked to wider shifts in philosophical understandings of the human condition?

Nietzche (1974: 24) once described the common view of Australia in the late eighteenth and nineteenth centuries as one of a "palaeontological penal colony" because the Western world viewed this continent as a museum where the past could still be seen in a natural state. As will be discussed later in this chapter, the gathering of artifacts from cultures for the purposes of display and study was seen in the nineteenth century as a sophisticated form of hunting (O'Hanlon and Welsch 2000). Just as they considered hunting to be the primary reason for the production of artifacts, so was it their reason for collecting (Griffiths 1996: 19–20). Griffiths (1996: 21) argues the popularization of natural history during this time was inseparable from frontier experience, imitations of war, hunting prowess, evolutionary morals, social status, and other so-called manly pursuits. In eighteenth and nineteenth century Australia this was carried to the extreme with Aboriginal people being hunted themselves, alongside of their material culture (Reynolds 1987, 2006).

As mentioned earlier, much of the scientific world at this time assumed that there was a universal model of human society and human nature (Hurst Thomas 2000). The history and collecting of the Arnhem Land Expedition is the central concern of this book and it is not useful to detail the many, varied, and shifting social theories proceeding to this particular event. Instead, I focus on the social theories evident in and inspiring the collecting in Arnhem Land. In 1949 expedition leader Charles Mountford (1949: 745–82) wrote an article titled "Exploring Stone Age Arnhem Land," and he concluded this article with the following sentence:

> Calmly, slowly, the aborigines returned to their halcyon life in Arnhem Land where haste had no place, where time never mattered, where tribal folk didn't reckon in days or years or even centuries. (Mountford 1949: 782)

The title and his concluding remarks are just two examples of Mountford's attitudes toward Aboriginal people in Australia. They reveal the continuation of Social Darwinian views of society by some researchers at least into the 1950s. Terms such as "Stone Age," "prehistoric," and "primitive" proved to be powerful metaphors for the "uncivilized" and conveyed to the world an image of a static and moribund culture.

It is important to understand that "modernity," in basic terminology, refers to modern society or industrial civilization. It is particularly associated with (1) a set of attitudes toward the world and the idea of the world as open to transformation by human intervention; (2) economic institutions, especially industrial production and a market economy; and (3) a range of political institutions, including the nation-state and mass democracy (Giddens and Peirson 1998: 94). Modernity allows for many different theories of human nature to coexist. Two such theories are Darwin's theory of natural selection (Darwin 1859) and the theory of unilineal progress (Hurst Thomas 2000; Pearce 1995: 123). Though these two theories were formally contradictory, they came to be seen as synonymous and in the context of colonialism they are known collectively as Social Darwinism (Griffiths 1996: 10; Hofstadter 1944; Kaye 1986). In brief, Social Darwinism was Darwinian competitiveness applied to society rather than nature; the man credited with popularizing the notion was English philosopher Herbert Spencer (1820–1903). Spencer developed the concept of evolution as the progressive development of the physical world, biological organisms, the human mind, and human culture and societies. He is best known for coining the phrase "survival of the fittest" in his book *Principles of Biology* (1864), after reading Charles Darwin's *On the Origin of Species* (1859).

In essence, modernity was concerned with the development of meta-narratives, overarching theories through which objective realities and truths could be defined (Foucault 1970: 226; Layton 1997: 186). Foucault (1970: 162) states that the critical question concerned the reasons for resemblance and the existence of genus. At the very core of this idea rested the belief that objective reality existed and could be perceived and quantified—scientific knowledge and understanding arrived at by the operation of human reason upon the observed world (Layton 1997: 186).

The interpretation of this was simple—humanity was improving through natural selection. It was improving biologically, culturally, emotionally, and intellectually. The logical next step was that Western society would thrive, and the world's "primitive" cultures would slowly disappear or change their cultural practices to become "Western." As Wilkins (1929: 4) argues, "It appears that Nature has preserved in Australia types that have perished elsewhere in the evolution of animal life, but these types must perish as surely as the Dodo and primitive Man have perished." These beliefs impacted upon the collection of material culture from the so-called "primitive" people of the world.

As a consequence of changing social theories such as Social Darwinism changes were also occurring in collection practices and museum practices. By the mid-nineteenth century, collections of curiosities were giving way to the modernist scientific museum study based on classificatory principles. The three-age system is one example of this change taking place. The three-age system refers to the periodization of human prehistory into three consecutive time periods, named for their respective predominant tool-making technologies: the Stone Age, the Bronze Age, and the Iron Age. Such a system was revolutionary for its time as it shifted disorganized cabins of artifacts into classified and ordered systems (Rowley-Conwy 2007).

People collected and arranged their artifacts to support these social theories with tangible scientific evidence (Foucault 1970: 162; Griffiths 1996: 10; Pearce 1995: 123). Consequently, alongside of the classification of human culture was the classification of their material culture. Evolutionary theory prompted new ethnological displays and the most influential British curator was General Augustus Henry Lane-Fox Pitt-Rivers (1827–1900), who was one of the first people to establish an archaeological and ethnological museum in Britain (Hudson 1987: 31):

> Pitt Rivers . . . collection drive was linked with an overarching philosophy of man and material culture in which Darwinian ideas, applied to objects, yielded a scheme whereby artefact types developed one from another according to a process of natural selection. (Pearce 1992: 8)

It is important to note that Pitt-Rivers believed that historical sequences could be reconstructed using actual objects to show different cultural levels achieved by human groups and to illustrate notions of progress (Pearce 1992: 8). He was a Darwinist and believed in a direct correlation between the evolution of species by natural selection and the progress of human society. He compared the prehistorian to the paleontologist and extinct fauna to primitive humans (Hudson 1987: 31). Meanwhile, archaeologists and anthropologists were beginning to accumulate large museum collections, which were backed by interpretive ideas about typology deriving from Pitt-Rivers' classificatory schema, eighteenth-century biology, and, later, Vere Gordon Childe's ideas on the relationship between material evidence and human cultures (Pearce 1992: 8).

The artifact during this period became a piece of primary evidence in a Western view of natural and cultural development and was, therefore, placed upon an ascending evolutionary ladder, just as human beings were (Clifford 1988: 228; Griffiths 1996: 22). It is also relevant that the producers of Western knowledge—Victorian Europe—had a formal belief in the "Great Chain of Being" that asserted Victorian Europe's physical and intellectual superiority (Fagan 1998; Lovejoy 1964). Such superiority was Eurocentric and measured by the presence and absence of certain types of objects such as the wheel, monumental architecture, and writing. This science of classification is, in Gould's words (in Elsner and Cardinal 1994: 2), "a mirror of our thoughts, its changes through time and is the best guide to the history of human perceptions." Elsner and Cardinal (1994: 2) continued with this idea that if classification is the mirror of collective humanity's thoughts and perceptions, then collecting is its material embodiment.

It is within these ideas that the political rationality, a term stolen from Foucault, of modernist collecting emerges (Bennett 1995: 89). Foucault (in Bennett 1995: 90) argued that the emergence of new technologies that aim at regulating the conduct of individuals and populations is characterized by their own specific rationalities and generates their own political problems and relations.

Linda Tuhiwai Smith (1999: 86) argues that many indigenous cultures were seen as occupying one of several, more primitive stages, through which humanity had passed before reaching its apogee in the form of Edwardian and Victorian Europe. This was the case in Australia where Aboriginal groups were argued to show the scientific world the most simple and fundamental systems of social organization. These groups were placed on the lowest rung of the evolutionary ladder as biological and cultural relics "slipping into extinction" (Griffiths 1996: 10; Trigger in McBryde 1985: 11–16). Even Darwin (1871: 521) commented in his publication *Descent of Man* that "at some future period not very distant as measured by centuries, the civilized races of man will almost certainly exterminate, replace the savage races throughout the world."

The situation for Aboriginal Australians and Native Americans has many similarities. David Hurst Thomas (2000: xxxi) argues that this new evolutionary benchmark confirmed the conventional frontier wisdom: "Noble he might be, the American Indian was properly grouped with the inferior races—all afflicted with darker skins, flawed behavior, and second-rate biology." In line with the scientific beliefs of the time, Native Americans (like Aboriginal Australians) were believed to represent not just a separate racial type but a distinctive level of social development—"a holdover from an earlier, inferior stage of human evolution" (Hurst Thomas 2000: xxxi). With most human "races" occupying one or the other rung on this evolutionary ladder or "great chain of being," those on the top rungs felt they could look down and view the past in authoritative contemplation. While looking they could reach down and take souvenirs of this past for their mantelpiece—perhaps gloating at evidence of their superiority via others' supposed inferiority?

HUNTING THE HUNTER-GATHERERS

The gathering of artifacts from other cultures for the purposes of display and study was seen in the nineteenth century as a refined and educated form of hunting (O'Hanlon and Welsch 2000). Naturalists and antiquarians were inspired by the thrill of the chase. Whether they were chasing nature or culture, the thrill existed and, as mentioned previously, just as they considered hunting to be the primary reason for the production of artifacts, so was it their reason for collecting. Natural history became an outdoor school of character formation. Pearce (1995: 126) would seem to agree stating that natural history collecting "afforded an intellectual outlet for the middle class . . . and gave collectors the feeling of being at the cutting edge of their time."

From roughly the eighteenth century into the early nineteenth century, two specific types of collecting were common. The first concentrated upon art and natural history and manifested itself in important museums to which the general public was allowed. The second concentrated upon historical and exotic material with its exhibition being commercially organized. Between these two aspects lurked the major private collectors, often with a foot in both of the aforementioned aspects of collecting (Pearce 1995: 124; Pearce 1998).

As discussed later in this book, most collectors saw the cultural groups from which they were collecting as endangered. With some exceptions, the full implications of natural selection and Social Darwinism were not confronted until the twentieth century and many would argue that they are still being addressed today (Griffiths 1996: 11; Hurst Thomas 2000).

It is worth reiterating here that collections are, more often than not, associated with modern museums. It is for this reason that the museum is central to this discussion of collecting. The aim here is not to give a history of museums but rather to give an insight into the role of this institution in ethnographic collecting. Vergo (1989: 1) states that the museum can be traced back to the Ptolemaic *mouseion* at Alexandria, which was thought to be a mix between a library, a place for scholars, for historians, and for philosophers. Similarly, museums have emerged in varying forms and this variability is important as we try to situate Australian museums and collectors in an international setting (see, for example, Clunas 1991; Goswamy 1991; Yamaguchi 1991). It is usually assumed that the museum as a modern institution came to the Renaissance cities and courts of Italy around the middle of the fifteenth century and then spread to other continents (Pearce 1992: 1–2; Vergo 1989: 1–2). It is important to consider that in some countries, such as Australia, the distinction between museums and art galleries is relatively clear, while in others it is not. Both institutions are very much shaped by their particular historical conditions or, as Duncan (1995: 3) argues, "the politics of their ruling founders or the collecting habits of their patrons."

MUSEUMS AND COLLECTING

History

There has been a gradual expansion of interest in human history from ancient epics and writings of historians (such as Herodotus), to the collecting of literature in libraries (such as the Great Library at Alexandria), to the ecclesiastical collections in the Middle Ages, to the baronical collections of the Renaissance, and to the creation of specialist museums in the eighteenth century (Alexander, in Aagaard-Mogensen 1988: 8). These meeting places represented important situations where leisured individuals could amass knowledge and become increasingly concerned with curiosities of the natural and cultural world. Such early museums and collections were thus profoundly undemocratic. Curiosities were collected in cabinets, which eventually grew into whole rooms, buildings, and institutions.

In the eighteenth and nineteenth centuries there developed an interest in the sorting and arranging of material in the museum context. Eilean Hooper-Greenhill (1989: 63) has argued that the upheavals of the French Revolution created the conditions of emergence for a new "truth," a new rationality, out of which came a new functionality for a new institution, the public museum. In other words, the public museum was established as a means of sharing what had previously been private (Bennett 1995: 89). Bennett (1995: 93) disagrees, stating that museums constituted socially enclosed spaces to which access was largely restricted. He also argues that, although the timing of the public museums revolution varied from country to country, by the mid-nineteenth century the principles of the new form were apparent everywhere. Everyone, at least in theory, was welcome (Bennett 1995: 93). In short, the public museum is an institution whose distinguishing characteristics were clarified during the first half of the nineteenth century (Bennett 1995: 92; Knell 2004).

The public museum was shaped with two deeply contradictory functions—that of being an elite temple of the arts, as well as a utilitarian instrument for democratic education. Later a third function was added—that of being an instrument of discipline (Hooper-Greenhill 1989: 63). Foucault (1977) also discusses the idea of museums as an instrument of discipline and he argues that the development of modern forms of government is traced in the emergence of new technologies that aim to regulate the conduct of individuals and populations. As such, these technologies are characterized by their own specific rationalities: they constitute distinct and specific modalities for the exercise of power (Foucault, in Bennett 1995: 90). Other museum theorists such as Goodman (in Aagaard-Mogensen 1988: 140) have appeared to be devoted to the idea of the museum as a disciplinary institution, stating "A museum functions much like other institutions as a house of detention, a house of rehabilitation, or a house of pleasure; or in the vernacular, a jailhouse, a madhouse, or—a teahouse."

The change to a public museum was not simply a matter of the state claiming ownership of cultural property on behalf of the public or of the museum opening its doors to all enfranchised citizens. It was also about the new organizational principles governing the arrangement of objects within the museum. Museum displays came to be governed by new scientific principles with stress being laid upon observable differences and similarities rather than hidden resemblances (Bennett 1995: 95–96).

Public museums felt the need to distinguish themselves from their antiquarian predecessors. As science appeared to emerge from ignorance into truth so did the museum attempt to emerge from chaos into order (Bennett 1995: 2). It is important to remember that collections of artifacts (objects made, adapted, or used by human beings) were acquired and classified using the same methods earlier applied to natural specimens—the classification of humans and their artifacts was prefigured and determined by classifying natural phenomena (Pearce 1992).

The role of museums, collectors, and collections in the modern view of moral improvement was increasingly that of an educator. Pearce (1992: 3) argues that museums, collectors, and collections were seen as playing their part in the development of reliable and orderly citizens, which the Victorian establishment desired to see. They gave these moral qualities, such as respectability and domesticity, tangible forms stemming from Layton's (1997: 186) idea of constructing a better society in which to live. Museums held the actual evidence and true data, which the meta-narratives depended upon for verification (Pearce 1992: 4).

E. Doyle McCarthy (1984: 105) would seem to agree with this argument, reasoning that "since the beginning of the modern era the prospect of a limitless advance of science and technology, accompanied at each step by moral and political improvement, has exercised a considerable hold over Western thought." Museums could project these contemporary worldviews simply by arranging the collected material in particular patterns or, in other words, they could make intelligible a scientific view of the world (Pearce 1992: 4). Murray (1904, in Bennett 1995: 96) early in the twentieth century argued that the distinguishing factors of the modern museum were the principles of specialization (e.g., geology museums, natural history museums) and classification, two scientific principles. This was different to premodern museums, which were designed to invoke surprise and wonder by exhibiting rare and exceptional artifacts (Bennett 1995: 96).

Research

Literature concerning the so-called old museology is abundant. Authors deal with subjects such as museum administration, conservation, registration, sponsorship, and so on. It is certainly not the aim of this book to discuss these texts in any detail. Rather, my interest lies with what Peter Vergo (1989) called "new museology." These studies may, in turn, provide insights into today's society, what we value today, and what researchers feel justified in researching.

Arguably the most prolific museum theorist is Susan Pearce (1992, 1994, 1998, 1999) who qualifies her research by stating that "the making of a collection is one way in which we organize our relationship with the external physical world, and so the effort to understand them is one way of exploring our relationship with the world." Pearce (1994: 1) suggests that museums have an obligation to try and understand themselves so that they can understand more clearly what messages they are giving and how these are received. It would appear that theory dealing with museums has largely developed from this feeling of obligation. Its development as a field, however, comes relatively recent compared with other similar fields of investigation.

Material culture studies, and museums, languished for most of the middle decades of the twentieth century, until around 1975 when ideas about the meanings of objects and how they can be studied underwent a radical shift as did the broadly structuralist and poststructuralist ideas developed earlier (Pearce 1992: 8). Macdonald (in Macdonald and Fife 1996: 1) has argued that this sudden interest in museums may have stemmed from the practical problems that museums have been and are continuing to face in recent decades. She states that museums face an unremitting questioning about whom they are for and what their role should be and she admits that the contradictory and ambivalent position museums are in today makes it desirable for further research to be undertaken. In short, the colonial gave way to the postcolonial and this affected museums. It forced introspection and museums had to accept themselves as part of the fabric of a human story rather than objective commentators.

Peter Vergo's (1989: 3) call for a radical reexamination of the role of museums and Lars Aagaard-Mogensen's (1988: 5) similar assertion that a set of intellectual views and assessments of the museum today is long overdue seem to have attracted scholars over the past twenty to thirty years. Texts such as *Theorizing Museums* by Macdonald and Fife (1996), *The Birth of the Museum* by Bennett (1995), *The Representation of the Past* by Walsh (1992), *A Cabinet of Curiosities* by Weil (1995), and Karp and Levine's (1991) *Exhibiting Cultures: The Poetics and Politics of Museum Display* to name but a few, have pushed museum theory (including reevaluations of long-held beliefs) into the spotlight.

> Not until long after the foundation of the first museums did anyone think of them as a phenomenon worthy of study; and it is more recently still that museology . . . has come to be recognised as a field of enquiry in its own right. (Vergo 1989: 3)

Vergo introduced the idea of a new museology in his 1989 text *The New Museology*. He offered the idea that a new museology exists because of discontent with the old museology, which concentrated upon methods in museums. He argued that the new museology should be concerned with the purposes of museums or they themselves would be dubbed "living fossils" (Aagaard-Mogensen 1988: 5).

One of the more "alternative" texts emerging out of the last twenty years of the twentieth century is Robert Lumley's (1988) anthology *The Museum Time Machine* that appears as a critical study in the context of the old museology. While in more recent years texts such as Muensterberger's (1994) *Collecting: An Unruly Passion* and to a lesser extent Elsner and Cardinal's (1994) *The Culture of Collecting* have looked at the psychological aspects of collection forming. Just like this book, both these texts are concerned with the appropriation of collections of artifacts by museums, how they were acquired, and who acquired them. While a discussion of the collector has appeared only in passing throughout this chapter, the role and intricacies of collectors is a key element of this book and is a focus of later chapters.

ETHNOGRAPHIC COLLECTIONS

Bennett (1995: 96) notes that Jomard, curator at the Bibliothèque Royale, argued as early as the 1820s for an ethnographic museum that would illustrate "the degree of civilisation of peoples . . . who are . . . but slightly advanced." General Pitt-Rivers is further credited with developing display principles appropriate to Jomard's objective. Pitt-Rivers (in Daniels 1975: 171) stressed that his collection was not simply to surprise an audience but to instruct an audience. For this reason he displayed typical objects rather than those that were considered rare. Bennett (1995: 96) states that it was not until the end of the century that these principles became widely dispersed. This was thanks partly to Otis Tufton Mason (1838–1908), the first full-time curator of ethnology at the United States National Museum (Smithsonian Institution). In the late 1870s and early 1880s, Mason developed new strategies for organizing and cataloging this institution's ethnology collection and installed this newly cataloged collection into new buildings that were opened in 1881 (Coen 1983).

Ethnographic collections at this time were being formed in an attempt to capture an image of a culture in terms of its objects as opposed to presenting a level of description of cultural practices. The influence of the typological system developed by Pitt-Rivers deserves greater consideration as it enlightens us about important changes in museological practice prior to the Arnhem Land Expedition. Pitt-Rivers became interested in anthropology in the 1850s as a result of a detailed study he made of the history of firearms for the British Army. Throughout the 1860s he built up a large ethnographic collection and wrote on the principles of classification (Griffiths 1996: 20, 68; Trigger 1989: 197).

During the latter half of the nineteenth century Pitt-Rivers arranged his collections in order to illustrate his research into the principles and the course of human cultural evolution (Chapman 1985: 39). As Balfour (in Myres 1906: v) states, "He [Pitt-Rivers] was led to believe that the same principles must probably govern the development of the other arts, appliances and ideas of mankind." Pitt-Rivers' drive to collect was linked with an all-encompassing philosophy of human beings and material culture in which Darwinian ideas yielded a scheme whereby artifact types developed one from another. This development was due to processes of natural selection and constituted the empirical evidence by which a culture could be assigned a rung on the Great Chain of Being. To prove his thesis and to illustrate its truth Pitt-Rivers began collecting extraordinary numbers of artifacts and the museum that bears his name, to this day, retains a largely typological collection.

Glyn Daniels (1975: 171) suggests that Pitt-Rivers and Flinders Petrie were the two key players responsible for the transformation of the archaeological outlook from one of curiosity to one that was "frankly sociological." This revolution moved archaeology away from a study of art treasures (a nineteenth-century legacy from the late-eighteenth-century study of classical antiquities) and from a contemplation of *art* objects to the contemplation of *all* objects (Daniels 1975: 171). At the same time, Pitt-Rivers placed little emphasis upon the context of the material he collected. The collections were, consequently, arranged according to the assumptions of a static culture with no consideration of differences in form due to age, location, or variations in function.

PERSPECTIVES ON COLLECTING IN AUSTRALIA

In this chapter I have barely scratched the surface of the literature surrounding museological practice in the eighteenth, nineteenth, and twentieth centuries. It was my aim to present the key people and events from these periods in order to contextualize the Arnhem Land Expedition, the collector's aims and motivations. It is obvious that much has been written on the actions of museums in the past 200 years but only recently have the views of indigenous peoples come into focus in academic writings, and it is even more recently that indigenous scholars have themselves given voice to these concerns and been heard. It is timely then to end this discussion of museums and collecting by turning to some recent explorations of the impact of collecting on indigenous groups.

Social Darwinism with its tendency to lead to classification of indigenous groups demonstrates the political implications of such theories. As Duncan (1995: 3) argues, the issue of what museums do to other cultures, including minority cultures within their own societies, has become urgent as postcolonial nations attempt to redefine their cultural identities and as minority cultures seek cultural recognition. In reaction to the modernist views of an ordered and ranked world, the development of postmodernism and the movement toward the so-called decolonization of the museum has meant that beliefs in universal notions of progress became undermined (Hodder 1999: 149; Lyotard 1984: 37). Crimp (1987: 62) argues that the museum constitutes a specific form of the enclosure and restriction of cultural material. He argued as early as the 1980s that museums must break with this enclosing nature in order to become once more socially and politically relevant (Crimp 1987: 62).

Indigenous peoples of the world have often been frustrated with the way their histories and ways of life have been represented and interpreted in museums (Brown 1995: 52–53). This is not surprising given that until recently most museums—for example, in Australia—did not employ indigenous people to assist with the development of exhibitions and the interpretations of their cultures. Virginia Dominguez (1987: 132) has argued that the implicit hierarchical nature of *otherness* has invited practices of representation that amount to strategies of domination through appropriation, an argument echoed in the work of Linda Tuhiwai Smith (1999). In the final chapter of this book I turn to the ongoing impact of the Arnhem Land Expedition for the Aboriginal people visited in 1948. In particular, their reengagement with the material culture and skeletal remains that were removed in the name of science will be discussed alongside of the shifting power relations relating to collections of Aboriginal material culture in museums today.

This chapter has introduced some of the key societal changes relating to the treatment and the classification of indigenous cultural groups by museums around the world. I have aimed to contextualize the later discussions relating to history, collecting and displaying artifacts from the Arnhem Land Expedition. More important, these shifting theories directly impacted upon the collectors who visited Arnhem Land in 1948—from their motivations for joining the expedition, to their selection of artifacts to collect, and more. The past, as it is materially embodied in museum collections, is a product of the present that organizes and presents it. It is within this context we will consider the Arnhem Land Expedition—a mid-twentieth-century expedition that had as its major aim the collection of Australian Aboriginal ethnographic material.

Preparing for Arnhem Land

I've lived in this country close on forty years . . . but these scientists can come in from Washington or Sydney and show me things I never knew were here . . . Like the botanist, Ray Specht, asks me have I seen a certain kind of tree. I reckon I know which he means—seen dozens of 'em. Then he asks me, "what sort of flower has it got?" Well, I scratch the old head, and I tell Ray I'm damned if I think that tree's got a flower at all. "All trees have got flowers," he says. Now I never knew that . . . I tell you, an old bushy like me has learnt a lot from being with this expedition!

—*Bill Harney, in Simpson 1951: 40*

A number of years ago some alluring questions were posed to me regarding this particular cross-cultural encounter: how did collectors of Australian Aboriginal material culture decide on what to collect, from whom, and where? What was the mechanism of exchange and the form of intercultural encounter that took place around these collecting activities? Furthermore, could the phenomenon of exploration, politics, collecting, and intercultural relations be understood from the field notes and collections? For the Arnhem Land Expedition, it is clear that a discussion of the buildup to the fieldwork—the preparations—can go some way toward answering these questions. As I have argued earlier in this book, the Arnhem Land Expedition was a large and ambitious project that escalated over the years between 1945 and 1948. I argue that politics (and particular international relations and Aboriginal affairs) dominated this expedition more than any other scientific expedition attempted at this time in Australia. I have chosen to illustrate these issues and the complex aims of the expedition by focusing on four main players: Charles Mountford, Arthur Calwell, Frederick McCarthy, and Frank Setzler. These four men represent distinctive organizations and, at the same time, had their own personal reasons for joining the expedition and, for three of these men, for focusing on specific research areas while in the field.

The earliest aims of the expedition were to observe the everyday life of Aboriginal people in Arnhem Land, to determine where they originally came from, to learn how they coped with their own environment, and to collect specimens of their material culture (Mountford 1949: 745). These, however, were just the explicit and official aims of the expedition with each institution and individual having their own reasons for traveling to Arnhem Land. Charles Mountford, as leader of the Arnhem Land Expedition, is the single most important character in this story.

> The story of Charles Mountford's lifelong devotion to the culture of the aboriginal people of Australia is one of the romances of scholarship. He found his vocation to record a great heritage of our land early in his career, and has been faithful to it ever since despite many setbacks, difficulties and even hardships. (Joseph Burke in Mountford 1976: v)

Charles Mountford was born May 8, 1890, into a family of Scottish and English descent that had come to South Australia within ten years of the colony's proclamation. Most of his family were farmers and general laborers who lived in rural South Australia. Charles Mountford insisted to his biographer Max Lamshed that "we were poor, but it was a uniform poverty. Everyone was in the same boat, so we didn't notice it" (Lamshed 1972: 10). He also recalled that his first experiences with Aboriginal Australians came from the visiting swaggies[1] who would share stories of their interactions with "the blacks" around the table in the evenings (Lamshed 1972: 13).

> "They were," Mountford says, "rather like a colonial counterpart of the troubadours, bringing news from the outside world which isolated homes would never have had otherwise. Some of them went regularly into country where there were still Aborigines, and often there was mention of 'the blacks' as they yarned about where they had been and what they had done." "I remember how this talk in-

terested me," Charles Pearcy Mountford recalls. "I would sit in a corner taking it all in when the men got round the fire—until father noticed me and sent me off to bed." (Lamshed 1972: 13)

After moving to the city of Adelaide, Charles Mountford spent most of his teen years selling stereoscopes. This was followed by work as a stable boy, a blacksmith's striker, a conductor on a horse-drawn tram (and later on the electric trams). By the age of twenty, Mountford was beginning to think that being a tram conductor was not a life-long career for him and so he took a correspondence course in mechanics and engineering. After applying for a variety of jobs he eventually secured a position in the engineering department of the postal service. He spent the next eight years working in this position and, on the side, furthering his education at the South Australian School of Mines and Industries (now the University of South Australia). In 1914 Charles Mountford married Florence Purnell, and they had two children, Ken and Anna (Lamshed 1972: 16–23).

In 1920 Charles Mountford was promoted to mechanic-in-charge at the Darwin post office and it is here in Darwin that his collecting activities really began. Not far from his home there was an Aboriginal compound where white locals would take their visitors to show them the terrible conditions. Mountford came to know some of the old men living in this compound, and these men and other such contacts would bring objects to Mountford's workplace to sell. He is said to have gained a reputation as a person interested in buying and as someone who treated Aboriginal people with friendship and respect. He is also said to have been invited to attend ceremonies in the Darwin and outer Darwin region (Lamshed 1972: 23–27).

Two-and-a-half years later and with his health suffering, the Mountford family was transferred back to Adelaide. Charles Mountford was thirty-three years old and a senior mechanic. In 1925 his life changed dramatically with the death of his wife. He began spending a time with his father and together they travel the countryside looking for distraction and adventure. On one of these outings the father and son located some rock engravings and the younger Mountford was soon tracing and photographing images for the South Australian Museum. The South Australian Museum ethnologist and archaeologist Norman Tindale encouraged Mountford's interest, and they collaborated on a short paper addressing the find to the Royal Society of

South Australia (Lamshed 1972: 28–30). Tindale would give Mountford a few pounds now and then to encourage him to continue searching for and recording rock art around South Australia but Mountford needed little encouragement.

This was an exciting period in Charles Mountford's life, particularly the time between 1936 and 1942. During this period, the University of Adelaide sponsored anthropological expeditions to Central Australia. Mountford, who was still working as a senior mechanic for the general post office in Adelaide, was assigned the position of leader for many of these expeditions. He also had the role of secretary for the Commonwealth Board of Enquiry, set up in 1935 to investigate charges of ill treatment of Aboriginal people at Hermannsburg Mission Station. T. G. H. Strehlow, another famous collector, worked with Mountford during this investigation. On these trips the remarried Mountford began what were known as his "art classes," a practice he continued for most of his career. Mountford would hand out sheets of drawing paper and colored crayons to Aboriginal people he met and ask them to draw "blackfellow way." Afterward he would try to record the associated story for the painting, with varying success. On one trip to the Warburton Range he collected more than 400 individuals' drawings.

During this time in the field, Charles Mountford produced two significant color documentary-style films, *Tjurunga* (1942) and *Walkabout* (1942). These two films happened to catch the attention of the then federal Minister of Information, Arthur Calwell. Seeing the films' potential for good publicity, Calwell offered Mountford a position in his department, organizing his release from the post office and sending him on a lecture tour to promote Australia in the United States as part of the "Australian overseas information programme" (Mountford 1975: 225; Mountford 1956: ix). After all, it was a time of war and many believed Australia needed good publicity to assist in ensuring continued military support from the United States (Elliott 1992: 4).

After numerous presentations of his films in the United States, it became apparent that Arthur Calwell was not the only person interested in Aboriginal affairs. On February 2, 1945, Charles Mountford found himself presenting to 4,000 enthusiastic members of the National Geographic Society in Constitution Hall, Washington, D.C. Among the large crowd were members of the National Geographic Society Research Committee. Following the successful presentation, they approached the ethnologist and suggested he submit a proposal for a scientific research expedition (Mountford 1975: 225; Mountford 1956: ix). Charles Mountford's subsequent proposal outlines his intentions for Arnhem Land fieldwork, in particular his desire to record and collect Australian Aboriginal art:

> Knowing that the simple art of these people would be the first aspect of their culture to disappear, I have concentrated on the investigation and recording of all phases of their art. (Mountford, March 5, 1945: 2)

Charles Mountford claimed that his previous fieldwork was "most successful."

> Already I have collected with their interpretations about fifteen hundred sheets of their primitive symbolism made entirely by these aborigines. This research has saved the art of the Central Australian from extinction. (Mountford, March 5, 1945: 2–3)

As discussed in the opening chapter of this book, Charles Mountford's official proposal to the National Geographic Society included study in four main areas: the art of bark paintings, the art of body paintings, the general ethnology of the people, and music in secular and ceremonial life (Mountford, March 5, 1945). His proposal was enthusiastically accepted by the National Geographic Society who offered to increase the funding to $10,000 if it would "increase the effectiveness of the expedition" (Briggs, April 20, 1945).

By 1945, Charles Mountford had spent twenty years unofficially researching the art, legends, and so-called domestic life of the Indigenous people of Australia, particularly in South and Central Australia (Mountford, March 5, 1945). He had attained a certain level of knowledge relating to the rock engravings of these areas and the everyday life of the Pitjantjatjara, Adnjamatana, Yankunytjatjara, and Aranda people, but he still had no formal training. This came much later in life. Charles Mountford was clearly the key protagonist pushing for the Arnhem Land Expedition to take place; however, he had an influential friend in Australia—Arthur Calwell.

> Politics is no career for the faint-hearted. It is an exacting, thankless, full-time, and sometimes dangerous occupation. . . . If I had to make the choice again, I would still choose a political career, although I do not know that I would advise it for others. (Calwell 1978: 3)

FIGURE 3.1
Portrait of Arthur A. Calwell, 1945 by Max Dupain, 1911–1992, National Library of Australia, nla.pic-vn3621575.

Arthur Calwell (see figure 3.1) was born on August 28, 1896, to a police officer father and devoutly Roman Catholic mother in Victoria (Calwell 1978: 14). His mother encouraged his interest in politics from an early age. As Calwell recalls:

I was always interested in politics as a boy, and at the age of twelve I made up my mind that I would listen to a debate in the national Parliament, which was then at the top of Bourke Street in Melbourne. I made my way to Parliament House after school, passed the attendant at the door and sat down in the public gallery. There I had my first and only glimpse of Alfred Deakin, the Prime Minister. Deakin walked into the chamber with dignity. I was impressed as he strode to a back bench and glanced appraisingly around the House. Then he lay down on the back bench and went to sleep. (1978: 29–30)

After entering public service at the age of sixteen, Calwell worked as a clerk in the Department of Agriculture. He attended rallies and political speeches and identified strongly with the ideas of socialism. He later worked in the Treasury before being elected to Federal Parliament in 1940. He was a member of the Australian Labor Party from 1913 to 1973 and represented this party for thirty-two years in the House of Representatives (Calwell 1978: 38). Arthur Calwell was described in 1951 as "shock-haired, firm-jawed, emotional, sensitive, ebullient, incisive" by a journalist who also asserts that Arthur Calwell "is known far more through the word that has been printed about him than through the word he has conceived" (*Australasian Post*, July 5, 1951: 8–11).

Calwell is most remembered today for his post–World War II role in promoting the "White Australia Policy" while he was minister for immigration for the Chifley government from July 13, 1945, to December 19, 1949 (Kunz 1988). He firmly believed that Australia should be preserved for the white races of the world and this was reflected in his immigration policies. As Calwell stated, "No matter where the pressures come from, Australian people will continue to resist all attempts to destroy our white society" (1978: 117). Yet, before being given the newly created Minister for Immigration portfolio, Arthur Calwell was already Minister for Information. Following World War II, the Australian government created the Department of Information to promote good cultural and scientific relations with their wartime ally, the United States (McArthur, Billington, and Hodges 2000; McArthur, McCarthy, and Specht 2000: 215). While the government needed to ensure continued military support from the United States, they were also interested in encouraging Americans to immigrate to Australia (Elliott 1992: 4; Kunz 1988: 12; Lamshed 1972: 187). As Arthur Calwell stated only six years before the Arnhem Land Expedition:

When I see the splendid specimens of American manhood walking the streets of Australian cities and recollect that America has been for more than a generation a melting pot for European nations, I am satisfied with the result of the amalgamation. It would be far better for us to have in Australia 20,000,000 or 30,000,000 people of 100 per cent white extraction than to continue the narrow policy of having a population of 7,000,000 people who are 98 per cent British. (Calwell, May 1942: 845–46)

Arthur Calwell was appointed Minister for Information on September 21, 1943, and remained in this position until December 19, 1949. It was during this time that Calwell "discovered" Charles Mountford and exploited the anthropological and filmmaking skills of this man to pursue the aims of his portfolio. Calwell saw the 1948 Arnhem Land Expedition as a wonderful opportunity for promoting scientific relations with the United States.

Arthur Calwell arranged for the Commonwealth Government to support the expedition by paying Mountford his usual wage plus expenses and transport (Mountford, March 5, 1945: 4). The Minister for Air offered air transport, the Minister for the Army made food and equipment available, and the Minister for Health arranged for three scientists from the Australian Institute of Anatomy to join the expedition and study Aboriginal health and nutrition. The Minister for the Interior also placed his organization in the Northern Territory at their disposal (Mountford 1956: xxi). Arthur Calwell's influence was responsible for the size and publicity associated with the Arnhem Land Expedition.

Arthur Calwell was also at the forefront of funding discussions and personnel negotiations with the Australian minister Sir Frederic Eggleston in Washington, D.C., secretary of the Smithsonian Institution Alexander Wetmore, and the National Geographic Society (Mountford 1956: xxi; Mountford 1975: 225). As news broke of the impending expedition, other organizations and institutions seized upon Charles Mountford's initial plan to include one or two other researchers (Wetmore 1945: 1; Mountford 1975: 226). The end result was a seventeen-member expedition—one of the largest scientific expeditions ever to have taken place in Australia. As Mountford bragged, "This should be the best equipped scientific party ever sent into the field for the study of Australian natural history and ethnology" (January 28, 1947: 3).

Charles Mountford was clear in his unofficial aims for the expedition, as discussed in the opening chapter to this book. These aims were clearly influenced by the aims of Arthur Calwell—for example, to "Establish a good neighbour policy and scientific cooperation between the United States of America and Australia" and to "Provide publicity for Australia through the publication of three, if not four, illustrated articles in the *National Geographic Magazine*" (Mountford, January 28, 1947).

> Let me say that I regard this present trip as one of great importance in further-ing friendly relations between scientists and government officers in Australia with the Smithsonian Institution. We must do everything that we can to pro-mote the welfare of the work and the relationships that should exist between the Smithsonian and Australian workers. These, for various reasons, have been more tenuous in the past than I have liked. (Wetmore, July 9, 1948)

Clearly, international politics was just as important as science for the Arn-hem Land Expedition. Arthur Calwell remained Minister for Information un-til December 19, 1949, as part of the John Curtin, Francis Forde, and Ben Chifley governments. In 1960 he became leader of the Federal Parliamentary Labor Party (the Opposition) but failed to overcome the Menzies government in the polls. He held this position until 1967 when he was succeeded by Gough Whitlam. Calwell survived an assassination attempt in 1966 following his speech at an election campaign meeting in Sydney. He had devoted the major part of his speech to "the immorality and the horrors of the war in Vietnam" (Calwell 1978: 5). Arthur Calwell died on July 8, 1973.

Frank Setzler was one of four researchers from the Smithsonian Institution who came to Australia for the 1948 Arnhem Land Expedition—the others were mammalogist David H. Johnson, ornithologist Herbert G. Deignan, and ichthyologist Dr. Robert Miller. Frank Setzler was born in Freemont, Ohio, in 1903 and attended Ohio State University before receiving his doctorate from the University of Chicago. He was assistant field director of the Ohio State Museum and Indiana state archaeologist before joining the National Museum (later the National Museum of Natural History, Smithsonian Institution) in 1930 as assistant curator in archaeology (*Washington Post*, February 20, 1975). By 1937 he was head curator. In the United States he was considered an au-thority on North American archaeology; however, it was the Arnhem Land Expedition that brought him to the attention of a much wider audience.

Frank Setzler was originally unable to join the expedition due to health problems but due to a delay was able to join the group (Wetmore, December

24, 1946). This one-year delay was due to the Smithsonian Institution unexpectedly needing staff intended for the Arnhem Land Expedition for "commitments in connection with the Bikini tests" (Calwell, February 28, 1947). In other words, the scientists intended for the Arnhem Land Expedition were required for research relating to nuclear weapons testing in the Pacific. Without the Americans the government of Australia believed it would not achieve the desired publicity. As Charles Mountford wrote to Gilbert Grosvenor, National Geographic Society,

> When Dr. Alexander Wetmore was able to send only two land naturalists, my minister considered that the reduced number and scope of the American staff was insufficient a basis for the publicity he desired to give the expedition, and therefore suggested its postponement until next year. (January 28, 1947)

As a representative of the Smithsonian Institution, Frank Setzler was there to help improve relations (primarily scientific relations) between his institution, the U.S. government, and the government of Australia. This is illustrated in the following letter written by Dr. Alexander Wetmore of the Smithsonian Institution:

> We look forward with keen interest to this work, particularly to the close association that it brings between representatives of our two governments. We may, I trust, consider this a beginning to an even closer cooperation in future scientific matters than has existed heretofore. (December 3, 1947)

It is not difficult to see why Frank Setzler was chosen as deputy leader of the Arnhem Land Expedition. It was good politics to have both an American and an Australian as leaders. Frank Setzler was officially asked to take the deputy leader's position by Charles Mountford in 1947. Mountford (October 20, 1947) stated that he desired a "smooth-working, harmonious time together" and that he would greatly value Setzler's cooperation. As I will describe later in this book, this relationship was at times anything but harmonious.

Prior to his departure Frank Setzler was urged by Charles Mountford (December 28, 1947) to read Lloyd Warner's *A Black Civilisation* (1937), and in the following abstract he describes how he foresees his research progressing:

My program will consist of an ethnographic study of the material culture of the aborigines of Arnhem land as well as an archeological survey and excavations of such prehistoric sites as may exist. Due to the tropical conditions, archeological sites may be limited to shell heap deposits on the numerous islands along the coast and adjoining seashore, or in caves and rock shelters farther inland. In the field of physical anthropology an attempt will be made to obtain palm prints for a study of dermatoglyphics and to make "taste blindness" tests as well as the customary photographs and measurements of the natives. Facial masks will be made for use in constructing habitat group exhibits for the U.S. National Museum. By use of recording instruments an attempt will be made to mechanically record the various corroborees (ceremonies) and languages for future studies of the various dialects spoken among the various linguistic groups. (Setzler, January 6, 1948)

Frank Setzler was advised on his research program by Alexander Wetmore (January 8, 1948) who made it clear that his investigations were to be "concerned with the anthropological aspects of the studies" and that this should include both "ethnological investigations and researches in archeology as opportunity permits." As a side project, Wetmore suggested that he should make facial and other casts of the "Aborigines."

The events of the Arnhem Land Expedition are the subject of later chapters in this book, but Frank Setzler's initial reaction to the Aboriginal people of Groote Eylandt is worth mentioning at this point as it demonstrates something of this archaeologist's understanding of Aboriginal cultures prior to his arrival. Setzler recalled being taken off guard by the Aboriginal children of this small island who he found playing "cowboys and Indians." Expedition members later learned that the islanders had been shown American movies during World War II, courtesy of an American air base on the island (*Washington Post*, February 20, 1975). Setzler retired in 1961 and moved to Culver, Indiana. He died there in 1975 and was survived by his wife, Susan Perkins Setzler, and two sons, Frank and Paul.

Frederick McCarthy's involvement with the Arnhem Land Expedition was the Australian Museum's sole link with this event. McCarthy worked for the Australian Museum from 1920 until 1964, starting at the young age of fourteen. His first job at the museum was as a library clerk and he remained in this position—registering and cataloging books—for ten years. Attenbrow and Khan (1994: 5) tell us that from 1928 he worked part-time in both the library and the Department of Birds and Reptiles, and in 1932 he was upgraded to full-time assistant in this department. Not long after this, McCarthy moved to the Department of Ethnology as assistant curator and was, at the same time, undertaking formal anthropological training under Professor A. P. Elkin at Sydney University. McCarthy eventually took over as curator of anthropological collections in 1941.

In this role, McCarthy had undertaken archaeological and anthropological fieldwork and had published his findings relating to rock art and stone artifacts as well as general archaeological excavation reports. Most of these articles were published in *Records of the Australian Museum* or *Mankind*. McCarthy was significantly more qualified than either Frank Setzler or Charles Mountford in the fields of Australian archaeology and anthropology.

Charles Mountford had originally approached the United States National Museum (Smithsonian Institution) in the hope that they would provide an anthropologist for the expedition but they were unable to fulfill this request. Mountford had specifically asked for Dr. Homer Garner Barnett (1906–1985), Dr. Gordon Randolph Willey (1913–2002), or Dr. Philip Drucker (1911–1982) but each was engaged in other research projects (Wetmore, December 24, 1946). In 1948 the Australian Museum released McCarthy from his position (with full pay) for six months (later extended) because it believed it would be beneficial for McCarthy and for the museum. Walkom (January 19, 1948) outlined the reasons, "The field experience and the contact with the natives would be very valuable to him in his anthropological work, and there is no doubt that the museum collections would benefit greatly as a result of his field work in a region where such field work is not often possible."

McCarthy saw his aims in the field as very similar to Charles Mountford's:

> The opportunity to visit Arnhem Land as a member of this Expedition, and as a museum anthropologist, was accepted eagerly because it presented a wide scope of anthropological research in a great and little known Reserve which is now one of the few remaining areas in Australia where the real nomadic life of the Australian aborigines can be studied first-hand. Here, we believed, could be seen being made and used some of the fascinating ritual and utilitarian objects exhibited in our museums. Moreover, we would have an opportunity to study the physique, character and social life of the native people of Arnhem Land. (McCarthy n.d.a: 1)

Professor A. P. Elkin, chairman of the Scientific and Publication Committee of the Trustees for the Australian Museum, was very pleased with Fred McCarthy's inclusion and offered to assist the museum with any anthropological matters while McCarthy was in the field (Walkom, January 19, 1948). Elkin was one of the scientists who expressed dismay at the choice of Charles Mountford as leader of the Arnhem Land Expedition. The anthropologist wrote directly to the secretary of the National Geographic Society, Dr. Gilbert Grosvenor, pleading with them to take a trained social anthropologist on the expedition. Elkin expressed a view held by many Australian researchers that Charles Mountford was not a genuine ethnologist due to his lack of formal training: "Mr. Mountford, who is a good photographer, especially of still subjects, and who has done valuable work in the recording and copying of native art, is not a trained social anthropologist, much to his own regret" (Elkin, May 30, 1945). Dr. Grosvenor asked an insulted Mountford to assist him in writing a reply to Elkin. Their reply included the announcement of Charles Mountford's leadership role and Elkin was instructed to contact the leader directly regarding any problems (Lamshed, 1972: 120–22).

Ronald and Catherine Berndt joined Professor Elkin in his concerns about Mountford's qualifications (*Advertiser*, February 28, 1948). Their major criticism stemmed from Mountford's promotion of Arnhem Land as "the great unknown" (Mountford, in *Herald* July 20, 1945; *West Australian* January 12, 1948; *Mail* March 13, 1948; *Sydney Morning Herald* March 20, 1948; *Mail* July 17, 1948). They and other researchers had been working in these areas in recent years. The Melbourne *Sun* (March 9, 1948), for example, ran a story concerning the expedition titled, "U.S. Allies for Assault on Last Frontier." It was also significant that it was Charles Mountford's films and not his expertise as a researcher that led to his invitation to lead the Arnhem Land Expedition. Moreover, A. P. Elkin attacked Charles Mountford's lack of formal credentials and his style of writing (storytelling) not only before this expedition but also on many other occasions. For example, in 1938 Charles Mountford applied to the Carnegie Trust for fieldwork funds that were granted, but later withdrawn, following intervention by Professor Elkin (Lamshed, 1972: 73). It has been suggested that Elkin arranged for Howard Coates, a Native Affairs Department patrol officer, to tail the party. Coates kept Elkin abreast of Charles

Mountford's work in the field. The anthropologist was said to be delighted with the problems encountered by the fieldworkers (to be discussed later in this book) and laughed at the leader's research stating, "I see Mountford is busily discovering things that have been known for years" (Elkin, in Wise 1985: 205).

Charles Mountford saw these attacks as having been motivated by jealousy and suggested in his diaries that Elkin wanted to lead the expedition (Mountford n.d.a: 12). Charles Mountford's biographer and friend Max Lamshed (1972) suggested that Mountford did not worry himself about these matters; nevertheless, he was conscious of his lack of training and rarely referred to himself as an anthropologist but rather a fieldworker:

> I have not had the academic training in philosophy for that [cultural interpre-
> tation]. Without such training, it would be presumptuous, as well as dangerous,
> to venture into such a field. I am content to have gathered and verified the ba-
> sic material so that others working now, or those who will come after, may use
> it to further their studies on the origin and development of primitive man
> (188).

On March 18, 1948, the members of the Arnhem Land Expedition stood to be photographed by the side of a Royal Australian Air Force plane at a small airport on the outskirts of Adelaide (figure 3.2). It was very early in the morning and they were bid farewell by the media and by a small number of people they had come to know during the preceding three weeks of their promotional tour of Brisbane, Sydney, Canberra, Melbourne, and Adelaide. Five of the group—David Johnson, Herbert Deignan, Robert Miller, Howell Walker, and Frank Setzler—had also made the long journey from the United States before undertaking this tour. Together, these fourteen individuals (later to be joined by three others) had very little idea of what they would face in Arnhem Land. On the way to Darwin they stopped in Alice Springs to refuel and finally arrived in Darwin at 5 P.M. The tons of equipment took two weeks to arrive by land and the expedition members waited at a tourist camp in Nightcliff and visited Delissaville (Belyuen), where they informally began some research, sound and film recording, and collected a number of specimens and artifacts. There was no more time for preparation: the Arnhem Land Expedition had begun.

FIGURE 3.2
Arrival at Parafield Airport (Adelaide) from Melbourne, March 1948. Left to right: Dave Johnson, Herbert Deignan, Raymond Specht, Frederick McCarthy (behind), Charles Mountford, Keith Cordon (behind), Frank Setzler, Peter Bassett-Smith, Bessie Mountford, Howell Walker, and Bob Miller. Photograph courtesy of Raymond Specht.

NOTE

1. "Swaggies" or swagmen are generally itinerant laborers who carry their personal belongings in a bundle as they travel around in search of work.

4

Exploring the Great Unknown—Groote Eylandt

Whether he believed it or not, Charles Mountford promoted the 1948 Arnhem Land Expedition as a journey into the unknown and one aimed at enlightening the world on the last Australian frontier (see, e.g., *Herald* July 20, 1945; *West Australian* January 12, 1948; *Mail* March 13, 1948; *Sydney Morning Herald* March 20, 1948; *Mail* July 17, 1948; *Herald* November 18, 1948). Indeed, for Mountford and nearly all of the other expedition members, it was an exciting, once-in-a-lifetime opportunity to explore regions and cultures that were entirely foreign to them.

In February 1948, the expedition members arrived in Darwin after weeks of promotional activities in Australian capital cities. Throughout the next three chapters, I focus on their eight months of fieldwork in Arnhem Land, with an overview of the activities at each base camp (Groote Eylandt, Yirrkala, and Oenpelli), and focus on the nature of ethnographic research and collecting at each of the base camps. These chapters are not a complete history of the fieldwork activities of the Arnhem Land Expedition; elements of its history are drawn together to assist in exploring the processes involved in the shaping of the Arnhem Land Expedition ethnographic collection.

Charles Mountford only ever gave one reason for his selection of base camps for the Arnhem Land Expedition. He declared that each base camp represented different environments and, we can assume from this, he believed different environments would produce diverse research outcomes. He also

51

FIGURE 4.1
Aboard flight from Adelaide to Darwin. Left: Bessie Mountford, Margaret McArthur, Brian Billington, Peter Bassett-Smith, Charles Mountford (standing), Frank Setzler (standing). Right: Frederick McCarthy, Kelvin Hodges, Herbert Deignan, John Bray, Raymond Specht, Bob Miller, Dave Johnson. Photograph courtesy of Raymond Specht.

clearly chose base camps close to major settlements, presumably to assist with logistics. Time in the field was divided fairly evenly between three main camps—Umbakumba on the northern side of Groote Eylandt, Yirrkala in northeast Arnhem Land, and Oenpelli (today known as Gunbalanya) in western Arnhem Land (see figure 1.2). Another camp had been planned for the Roper River; however, due to major delays in arriving at their first camp, it was abandoned (Mountford 1956: xxiii; Mountford 1975: 226). While Um-bakumba, Yirrkala, and Oenpelli were the major base camps, a number of side trips were made by expedition members, including visits to Milingimbi Is-land, Chasm Island, Bickerton Island, and Winchelsea Island. In chronologi-cal order I discuss the key events taking place at each base camp with a focus on the nature of ethnographic collecting.

After two weeks in Darwin waiting for their supplies to arrive overland from Adelaide, the team made its way to the first base camp, Umbakumba. As mentioned in the previous chapter, the expedition had the support of the armed forces in Australia and, given the extraordinary amount of equipment the researchers were carrying, this support was essential. Arrangements had been made for the Royal Australian Air Force (RAAF) to transport personnel and equipment from Darwin to each new base camp. It was soon discovered, however, that even the RAAF did not have the capability to carry the huge load of expedition equipment, and additional transport had to be arranged. In haste they found that a 400-ton, flat-bottomed, wooden barge named *Phoenix* was available to carry excess equipment and staff to Groote Eylandt.

While many of the team arrived at Groote Eylandt aboard the RAAF Catalina flying boat, the unfortunate expedition members who decided to make the journey by sea were stranded when a storm pushed the *Phoenix* onto a reef near the mouth of the Liverpool River. The barge did not sink but was stuck, with some serious damage and an injured crew member, on the reef for five weeks as the crew attempted to save expedition equipment and food. One of the stranded expedition members was National Geographic Society photographer Howell Walker who later documented this journey in the article "Cruise to Stone Age Arnhem Land" (Walker 1949: 417–30). Of course, poor communication meant that the expedition members who had arrived on Groote Eylandt via aircraft had little knowledge of their colleagues' whereabouts. They also had little food and lacked the necessary equipment for their scientific work to begin. As a reporter for the *Daily Mirror* wrote:

> Starving Scientists
>
> A Catalina left Darwin at daylight today with emergency supplies for the American-Australian Scientific Expedition on Groote Eylandt, as the launch which was to have followed the expedition with supplies broke down. Until the aeroplane arrives the scientists will have a first-class chance of studying native food-stuffs. (April 16, 1948)

On June 12, 1948, expedition cameraman Peter Bassett-Smith penned the following song about the situation:

"The Phoenix Never Came In"
An expedition left the north one day,
Flew by Catalina far away,
All the stores were to have gone ahead

On the barge Phoenix, instead.
But the Phoenix never came in.

While on Groote Eylandt they were near starvin'
She hadn't even left Darwin.
Oh! The Phoenix never came in.

All was well on a clear blue sea,
Eggs for breakfast, caviar for tea!
Super service made the voyage fine,
On that Capricornian Line,
But the Phoenix never came in.

They all thought that Neptune had got-em,
When on a reef she rested on her bottom.
Oh! The Phoenix never came in.

Planes began to hover round and round
To see if she had really gone aground.
Off they went with just a shout of glee,
Saying she could put to sea.
But the Phoenix never came in.

For ten days the radio was talking,
While natives for help had been walking.
Oh! The Phoenix never came in.

Caulked at Milingimbi, on she sped,
At four knots she was full speed ahead.
Called at Elcho, up the Cadell Strait,
Going like a new V eight.
But the Phoenix never came in.

In spite of her great helter skelter,
At Cape Wilberforce she had to shelter.
Oh! The Phoenix never came in.

Then one night under a tropic moon,
A shadow crept into Little Lagoon,
All awoke hearing a mighty shout
That the Phoenix was about.
But the Phoenix never came in.

Though for stores everyone had been wishin'
It was only the boat from the Mission.
Oh! The Phoenix never came in.

At Umbakumba they had watched for days,
Peering out into a briny haze.
Half the camp had given up all hope of
Ever getting any dope.
But the Phoenix never came in.

Though when she was finally unloaded,
To work everybody felt goaded,
And they wished she had never come in.

Groote Eylandt was selected as the first base camp for the expedition because it was thought to offer the chance to study an island environment with
a generally arid, sandy hinterland in close proximity to the mainland coast
(Mountford 1956: xxiii). Camp for the expedition members was set up next to
Fred Gray's so-called "native settlement" in Umbakumba. This situation
would have undoubtedly assisted the researchers to become acquainted with
local Aboriginal people through the settlement's manager Fred Gray (Mountford 1956: xxiii). Setzler recorded that the younger Aboriginal men were keen
to assist the expedition with tasks such as moving equipment but that the
older men "preferred to wait and see what this white intrusion might signify"
(Setzler, January 13, 1950: 8).

Fred Gray worked as a trepang fisherman around the coast of Arnhem
Land before establishing a native settlement at Umbakumba. Gray never intended to establish a settlement on Groote Eylandt. Historical documents suggest that while working on the island he became concerned about the negative
impact cross-cultural interactions were having on the local Aboriginal people.
He asked the Church Missionary Society (CMS) to step in and oversee interactions between staff of the Flying Boat Base and the local Aboriginal people
stating that "there is definite contact between the aboriginals and the men
from the Base and the position . . . in my opinion is unsatisfactory" (Gray, August 24, 1938, in Dewar 1995: 82). When the CMS announced they could not
afford to staff the area for two years, Gray considered this inadequate and applied for permission to take up residence, and so began the Umbakumba "native settlement."

The settlement had many similarities to a religious mission and Gray himself was later criticized for exploiting Aboriginal people who had little concept of money and were paid in-kind with food, tobacco, and cloth rather than receiving a wage for their work (Dewar 1995: 82–84; Rose 1968: 135). At the same time, the joining of the Arnhem Land Expedition with Fred Gray's settlement proved to be practical as payment scales for many artifacts and for work were already set (Elliott 1992: 88).

In addition to the original transportation problems, the expedition members found that the shortwave radio, their only connection with the outside world, did not work (Mountford 1975: 227). Charles Mountford spent much of the first five weeks trying to resolve these many problems. At one stage he embarked on a lengthy walk from Umbakumba to the mission station on Groote Eylandt as well as searching for the *Phoenix* in Fred Gray's thirty-three-foot launch. He, like many other expedition members, did little research or collecting during this time. The real work program began when the team was finally reunited—five weeks later. Plans to visit the Roper River were abandoned, and this allowed them to spend a total of fourteen weeks on Groote Eylandt, despite the delays.

Expedition nutritionist Margaret McArthur was lucky enough to arrive by air into Groote Eylandt and did not let equipment delays prevent her from beginning her research. By the time the *Phoenix* arrived, she had already set up a nutrition camp at Hemple Bay. Later she was to work with expedition botanist Raymond Specht and Native Affairs officer Howard Coates on Bickerton Island. She aimed to investigate food-gathering techniques and nutrition of the local people while Specht concentrated on the botany of the area (Mountford 1956: xxv).

Raymond Specht's diary records give an interesting insight into camp life during the expedition's time on Groote Eylandt. He writes:

> Apart from two excellent cooks (helped by two Aborigines) who do wonders with tinned food, we have many other amenities. We each have a tent that serves as a laboratory as well. A native does the laundry. We have an open invitation to visit and use the Gray's homestead whenever we like. The Grays have put themselves out for us. They have even put electric light down to our mess tent, as well as water. Our work has definitely upset their routine; Fred Gray, in typical English style, doesn't deny it, but passes it off with a smile. His wife, Marjorie, who migrated from England two years ago to marry her boy-friend (after 20 years),

appreciates the company. Her "desert island disks"—gramophone records including "I'm all so alone in a strange land"—haunts us at night. (April 22, 1948)

Fred McCarthy and Frank Setzler conducted archaeological work on Winchelsea Island and they managed to collect a significant number of ethnographic objects including bark paintings (see figure 4.2). McCarthy recorded rock art around Groote Eylandt and its neighboring islands (see figure 4.3). Setzler concentrated on archaeology and he "took advantage of every opportunity to examine and if possible excavate carefully as many sites as possible" (McCarthy and Setzler 1960: 216). His excavations, often with the assistance of McCarthy and local Aboriginal men (see figure 4.4), emerged with diverse artifacts and human remains. While the exact number is not known, individual human bones collected during the Arnhem Land Expedition are recorded

FIGURE 4.2
F. M. Setzler, left, and F. D. McCarthy eating dinner in their tent on Winchelsea Island where we excavated several Malay graves, June 4, 1948. Collection of Frank Setzler, National Library of Australia, nla.pic-an24312850.

FIGURE 4.3
Frederick McCarthy and an unidentified Aboriginal man from Groote Eylandt record-
ing rock art on Chasm Island during the Arnhem Land Expedition. Photograph by
Howell Walker, National Geographic Society (after Mountford 1949:782). Courtesy the
National Geographic Society.

as numbering 241 and were collected or excavated by Setzler and McCarthy
across Arnhem Land (see chapter 11).

In addition to collecting human remains, Setzler took eight plaster casts of
Aboriginal people from the Umbakumba community using the Negaocol
technique (see figures 4.5 and 4.6).[1] Two casts were of hands while six were of
faces (Setzler n.d.: 1). The archaeologist desired these casts in order to produce
life-size molds of Australian Aboriginal people to display in the Smithsonian
Institution. Setzler humorously outlined his method for obtaining face casts
in a presentation to the National Geographic Society in 1950:

> After becoming acquainted with some of the men and observing their craving
> for tobacco, I was able to induce Kumbiala to undergo a warm mud bath treat-

FIGURE 4.4
Three arbitrary levels in Trench A of large shell heap around sacred well on Milingimbi Island in the Crocodile group, Arnhem Land, Australia, August, 1948. Collection of Frank Setzler, National Library of Australia, nla.pic-an24313031.

ment. This mulage had to be dissolved in a double boiler, then allowed to cool so as not to burn, but applied as warm as possible. The first coat was put on with a stiff brush in order to fill the pores . . . after removing the masks, the natives' faces, as you will probably notice, will be a shade lighter and their pores lose years of accumulated dirt. (January 13, 1950: 10)

These casts remain in the National Museum of Natural History (Smithsonian Institution).

Setzler was a busy man on Groote Eylandt as he also took palm and finger prints of more than one hundred people (with the assistance of Bessie Mountford), tested the taste buds of sixty families, collected hair samples, photographed people, collected ethnographic artifacts, produced biological

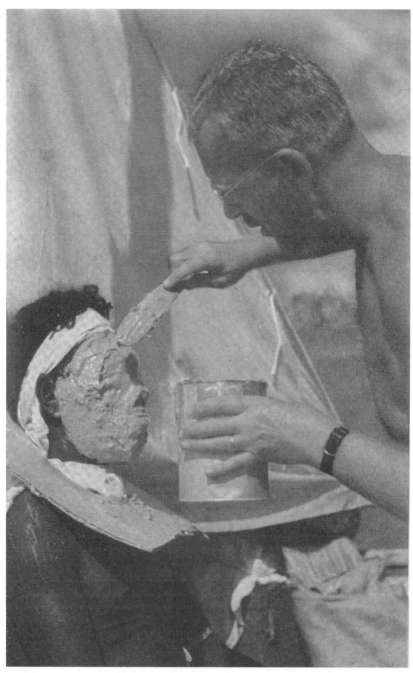

FIGURE 4.5
Frank Setzler making a cast of Kumbiala's face during the Arnhem Land Expedition. Photograph by Howell Walker, National Geographic Society (after Mountford 1949: 781). Courtesy the National Geographic Society.

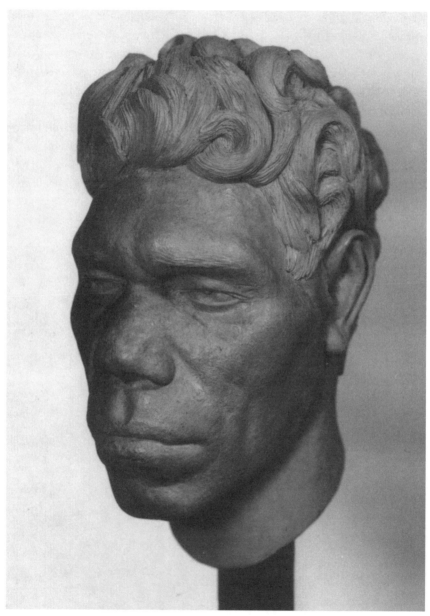

FIGURE 4.6
Completed face cast of Kumbiala from Groote Eylandt, held at the National Museum of Natural History, Smithsonian Institution, Washington, D.C.

reports on Aboriginal activities and took soil samples for pharmaceutical companies (Setzler n.d.: 2). For an archaeologist, many of these research activities were not standard practice with some leaning more toward physical anthropology or even medical research. As discussed in chapter 11, it is largely the type of work Frank Setzler undertook that is today considered by Aboriginal communities as the most intrusive and is of ongoing concern.

Two members of the Australian Institute of Anatomy's medical unit (medical doctor Brian Billington and biochemist Kelvin Hodges) established a workstation at Umbakumba and at the Angurugu Mission on Groote Eylandt. Robert Miller, David Johnson, and Herbert Deignan (see figure 4.7) collected fish, mammals, and birds respectively.

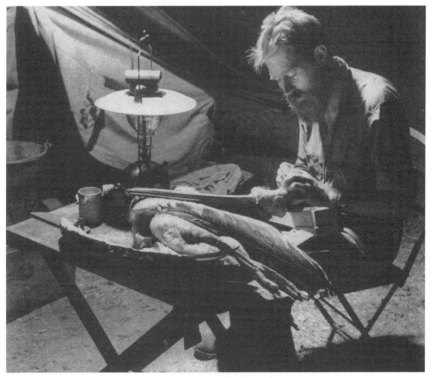

FIGURE 4.7
Herbert Deignan, expedition ornithologist, photographed by Howell Walker during the Arnhem Land Expedition (after Mountford 1949: 746). Courtesy National Geographic Society.

While much of his time was taken up with logistics and team management, Mountford did manage to film some cultural activities during his stay on Groote Eylandt. To assist in filming, he negotiated to have cultural songs and dances held near base camp. He negotiated this by offering to supply food to the participants. This also pleased Fred Gray who objected to people leaving their settlement to attend ceremonies (Mountford n.d.b: 387).

The filming and sound recording of Aboriginal cultural activities during the Arnhem Land Expedition was complicated. Expedition assistant Gerald "Gerry" Blitner was an Aboriginal man from the Roper River area working on Groote Eylandt in 1948. He recalled (in Thomas 2007b) that the Aboriginal men on Groote Eylandt considered Mountford "too pushy" and that he expected too much too soon. Evidence of Mountford's filming of Aboriginal people during earlier expeditions gives us some insight into his aims and ethics. One important aspect was his discovery that by handing out rations he maximized the assistance that could be gained. In 1940, for example, at the Granites in the Tanami Desert, he "again had charge of feeding the Aborigines . . . the chore gave him a chance to win over the women with tidbits, so that they were persuaded to discard their filthy Western garments . . . when he wanted them to pose for standard photographs" (Lamshed 1972: 53). During the same year, Mountford berated a group of Aborigines for wearing clothes while walking across the area he was filming (Lamshed 1972: 107).

When interviewed sixty years after the Arnhem Land Expedition, Gerry Blitner recalled the events of 1948 vividly, and his memories provide us with crucial evidence as to how some Aboriginal people on Groote Eylandt felt about, and how they experienced, the Arnhem Land expedition (see Thomas 2007b; May 2007). Blitner was born to an Aboriginal mother known to him only as "Sarah" and a German father, Frederick Charles Blitner, around 1920. As a child he spent time at Vandalin Island (his mother's traditional country) and the Roper River Mission and narrowly escaped being forcibly removed from his parents by the Commonwealth government. He recalls his mother smearing mud on his body to make his skin look darker as "she wanted [him] to look full blood." Blitner was moved to the Emerald River Station on Groote Eylandt when he was still only a young boy and was raised with other so-called "half-caste" children by the local missionaries. At this time he was expected to learn many rules, and the missionaries were strict with most aspects of his life. He states, "Today when I look back at things I find that the missionaries overlooked the fact that we were people not animals." At the same time he developed strong cultural and social ties to the local Aboriginal population on Groote Eylandt, ties so strong that his remains were taken to this island upon his death in 2008.

Blitner worked closely with Fred Gray for many years and seems to have been relied upon for a wide range of work including as a key assistant and translator for the Arnhem Land Expedition. He recalls, "As soon as the party all landed we had all the tents up and all the water system up there with pipes, and running it along there, making it easier for them, and then they started, and oh boy, that was biggest humbug" (Thomas 2007b; May 2007).

Charles Mountford made a strong impression on Gerry Blitner. He states, "And PC Mountford, oh, I . . . was told by a couple of the people he was a self-proclaimed anthropologist and he acted that way. He acted, sort of, [as] a tyrant, you know, he wanted it all his way, his way, his way, and he kept on" (Thomas 2007b; May 2007). As an assistant and translator for the expedition, Blitner was privy to local Aboriginal criticism relating to Mountford's work. For example, Blitner recalls Charlie, Quartpot, and Banjo, three local Aboriginal men, complaining about Mountford being too demanding and asking too many questions. Blitner was aware of the discussions taking place whereby Aboriginal community members were debating what they would tell Mountford and what aspects of their culture they would share with him. He remembers warning Mountford that the ceremonies were not "play dances" and that he must "appreciate the Aboriginal sense of it all" (Thomas 2007b; May 2007].

It is within this setting that Mountford formed an impressive collection of bark paintings and other ethnographic objects while camped on Groote Eylandt. It is important to note that the Groote Eylandt materials are also the best documented, with artists' names and interpretations often recorded. The collection strategy employed by Mountford at each base camp was to establish a tent where Aboriginal people could bring items they wanted to trade. Fred McCarthy recalled this in an interview with Craig Elliott in 1992. McCarthy states:

> All of the bark paintings were taken to Mountford's sort of shop. It was a big tent and the people took their bark paintings and things to him and he talked about them and paid them whatever he [pause] I don't know what he paid them. But he also got interpretations of them from the people. (Elliott 1992: 88)

McCarthy's diaries fill in some of the gaps as he states that 10/- to 1 pound was paid for each bark painting, 4/- to 10/- for spears, 5/- to 10/- for baskets, 10/-

to 15/- for mats and painted skulls cost 1 pound each (McCarthy August 8, 1948).

The bark paintings in the expedition collection, and, in fact, most of those housed in various universities and museums, have never been part of a wet-weather shelter, but have been made at the request of the investigator (Mountford 1956: 8).

Mountford went one step further than simply buying bark paintings. On more than one occasion he suggested topics for the artists to paint. The first painting Mountford collected, for example, was commissioned. He asked an artist named Minimini (see figure 4.8) to produce a painting of the "southeast wind mamarika (mamari:k)" (Mountford n.d.c: 176). Minimini is the well-known artist Minimini Numalkiyiya Mamarika and appears to have been one of the most prolific artists for Mountford in 1948. Minimini's clan was Warnindilyakwa (Yirritja moiety) and he spoke Anindilyakwa, as did most Aboriginal people on Groote Eylandt. His work is represented in other collections including the 1941 University of Melbourne Groote Eylandt collection. In May the ethnologist recorded, "Today, I asked for bark drawings dealing with astronomy, spirit children and gurumuka, the spirit of the dead. They were certainly tough subjects, but brought some interesting results" (Mountford n.d.d: 274). In this last case, the artist referred to as "Tatalana" is said by Mountford to have misunderstood the request and painted a different subject, annoying the collector.

FIGURE 4.8
Five of our native informants with the artist Minimini at the extreme right, Fred Gray's boys, Umba Kumba, Groote Eylandt, Australia, June 1948. Collection of Frank Setzler, National Library of Australia, nla.pic-vn3721470.

Other examples include "Nanawanda" being asked to draw the spirit children and after two days producing a bark painting depicting a man, his wife, and family. Mountford described this as "a most decorative sheet, but of little value for a greater knowledge of the origin of the spirit children" (Mountford n.d.d: 274). As I will discuss later in this book, these actions by the Groote Eylandt artists suggest an element of resistance or miscommunication relating to collecting by Charles Mountford in 1948 and tell us a great deal about the nature of these interactions. Following the expedition, Mountford (1956: 13) continued to declare that "the method which I adopted was to ask the men to make bark paintings for me, seldom suggesting a subject." His own diaries would seem to suggest otherwise.

It is also important to understand that Mountford already suffered from significant hearing loss and wore a hearing aid during his time on the expedition (personal communication John Mulvaney 2006; personal communication Raymond Specht 2006b). This, combined with the artists' broken English suggests that the recorded interpretations may be unreliable. Despite these difficulties, Raymond Specht (2006a) recalls that "the main artists—Nangapiana on Groote Eylandt, Mauwulan at Yirrkala, Kumutun at Oenpelli—were very tolerant and pleased to explain their art."

COMPETITIVE COLLECTING?

"The process of selection lies at the heart of collecting, and as we shall see, the act of collecting is not simple; it involves both a view of inherited social ideas of the value which should (or should not) be attached to a particular object and which derive from the modern narratives . . . and impulses which lie at the deepest level of individual personality" (Pearce 1992: 7).

As no prior contract about the division of the collections existed, collecting in the field became difficult and competitive even at the first base camp (Jones 1987: 13). At the heart of these difficulties was suspicion. Two months into the expedition Mountford and expedition archaeologist Fred McCarthy discussed the collection of bark paintings and the leader's suspicions about McCarthy. That night McCarthy recorded the discussion in his journal:

> I had a long discussion with Mountford in which I forced the issue regarding the number of bark ptgs [paintings], which he had limited to 15, that I was to get, and cleared the air regarding his suspicions about Elkin. It ended favorably for

me and now I can have as many ptgs [paintings] as opportunity permits. I have 22 to date. (McCarthy, May 19, 1948)

Two days before this meeting, McCarthy (May 17, 1948) recorded in his diary that the Groote Eylandt artists were producing up to five bark paintings a day for him and that his series was looking very promising.

So why was Mountford suspicious of McCarthy's relationship with A. P. Elkin? Mountford suspected that McCarthy, a former student of Elkin (see figure 4.9), was spying for the influential anthropologist and had been specially selected by him for the expedition. Mountford states in his field diary, "It is certain that Elkin recommended this chap [McCarthy], then persuaded Moy [Mr. Moy] to send him and writhe me. The levities will then be able to keep Elkin informed about the party" (Mountford n.d.e: 19). There is no evidence to suggest that this was the case. Mountford also suspected that Howard Coates (a

FIGURE 4.9
A. P. Elkin pictured with Bill Harney and other researchers at Maranboy 1948, National Library of Australia, nla.pic-vn3708017.

Native Affairs officer) had been suggested by Elkin (Mountford n.d.f: 17). While Mountford was probably wrong about McCarthy, Coates may have, in fact, been reporting to Elkin on the expedition and Mountford's research, though this is hearsay (Elliott 1992: 5).

From the shores of Umbukwumba to the great Ung-oo-roo-koo,
This place's so full of scientists, there's no room for me or you
They were eating lots of tucker, and sitting in their tents,
And waiting for the Phoenix in the cause of si-i-ence.

(From "Shores of Umbukwumba," by Fred Gray, 1948)

The expedition's stay at Groote Eylandt was successful in terms of research and collecting. Gerry Blitner's memories of working with Mountford during this period provide an enlightening insight into the nature of Mountford's techniques for obtaining information and artifacts. As Blitner (Thomas 2007b) recalls, "I couldn't stand some of the stuff what Mountford kept on trying to initiate, you know . . . he was after sacred things, very sacred." Alongside of this, collecting ethnographic artifacts had become competitive because Charles Mountford, Frank Setzler, and Fred McCarthy each held an academic interest in this study area. While the other disciplines were represented by sole researchers (e.g., ichthyology), ethnography was the realm of these three dominant characters and demarcation issues would cause each of them stress throughout the expedition and following. Foreseeing this issue, the three men held a meeting on April 11, 1948, and discussed plans for their work at the next two base camps. It was concluded that Mountford would concentrate on art and legends, Setzler would focus on archaeology, physical anthropology, and collecting material culture, while McCarthy would be concerned with archaeology, collecting material culture, and the quite specific areas of food and calendar issues, art, and string figures (McCarthy April 11, 1948). Naturally, many of these research areas overlapped, causing ongoing tension. The great collecting arguments had begun and they had not even made it to their second base camp.

NOTE

1. Casts were made of the following Aboriginal men and women (names spelled as recorded by Setzler): Thurinja, Minimi, Machana, Korbija, Kumbiala, Tamakidja, Tabaminja, and Nakaramba.

5

Exploring the Great Unknown—Yirrkala

Under intense media coverage, the expedition moved from its first base camp to its second, Yirrkala, on Thursday July 8, 1948. Yirrkala is located in the northeast corner of Arnhem Land (see figure 1.2) and was chosen by Mountford because it offered the scientists an opportunity to study life on the coast as well as among eucalyptus forests and freshwater billabongs. In 1948 Yirrkala was a Methodist Overseas Mission station, having been established in 1935. Today more than a dozen different Aboriginal clan groups (including Djapu, Gumatj, Rirratjingu) call Yirrkala home and collectively refer to themselves as Yolgnu.

After leaving Groote Eylandt, the Catalina planes made three trips carrying expedition personnel and equipment (including now a significant collection of ethnographic objects). The infamous *Phoenix* had been sent ahead to Yirrkala three weeks earlier with supplies and equipment and this cargo was waiting for them when they arrived (Setzler, July 12, 1948). The cargo then had to be transported from the Gove Airstrip to the base camp at Yirrkala, about five miles away. As Frank Setzler noted in a letter to Alexander Wetmore at the Smithsonian Institution, "For once everything clicked and we are well established, the last loads will be carried off the Mission boat by means of a dinghy and a dugout canoe this afternoon" (Setzler, July 12, 1948).

The day after expedition members arrived at Yirrkala, Wetmore was sitting in his office in Washington, D.C., drafting a letter to Frank Setzler that would prove quite pertinent. He writes:

The affairs of the Australian Expedition have been much on my mind in the last few weeks. . . . The party now has been long enough in the field, and has had sufficient of the usual mishaps incident to travel in remote places so that care needs to be used in the personal relationships of the leaders with the men. Let me say that I regard this present trip as one of great importance in furthering friendly relations between scientists and government officers in Australia with the Smithsonian Institution. Mountford I am sure has had his difficulties, due probably in part to "politics" among his own countrymen. Our arrangements for the work were made with him and we ought to back him up in all of his operations as far as we may. I have the feeling that he has been put in a very difficult situation due to the delay in transport of supplies and equipment for which he can hardly be blamed personally. I know you are Deputy Leader and I know will work wholeheartedly with him. I count on your doing so. (July 9, 1948)

The following day the expedition received a wireless message from Darwin informing them that Arthur Robert Driver, the administrator of the Northern Territory from 1946 to 1951, Elvin Seibert, the American consul from Adelaide, and Kevin Murphy, the deputy administrator of the Department of Information would be landing at Gove at 9:30 A.M. with the intention of visiting the expedition camp (Setzler, July 12, 1948). The expedition members quickly showered, shaved, and drove to the airstrip to meet the dignitaries. After arriving back at camp, Murphy and Driver requested a private audience with Mountford and Setzler:

It soon developed that Murphy and the Dept. of Information were very much fed-up on the various delays and poor arrangements that had been made thus far. He emphasised certain difficulties which had arisen between Monty and Mr. Gray as well as the Dept. of Native Affairs, at Groote. He stressed the making of four colored films which Monty was primarily to make, etc. etc. (Setzler, July 12, 1948)

The result of this meeting was that Mountford was asked to relinquish leadership of the scientific aspects of the expedition to Setzler. Mountford was told to concentrate on producing films for the Department of Information rather than undertaking anthropological research. Setzler was reluctant but did not immediately refuse the new position offered to him, something that Mountford never forgave him for (Mountford, July 29, 1948). Setzler considered the offer overnight and the next morning discussed it with his American colleagues who quickly advised him to refuse (Setzler, July 12, 1948). Setzler sent the following telegram shortly after:

> Mr. Kevin Murphy, Department of Information. Canberra.
> After conferring with my American colleagues I find it impossible to accept position. Regards. Frank Setzler. (July 12, 1948)

He received the following reply:

> Dr. Setzler
> Care Arnhem Land Expedition Radio
> Thanks for your telegram *stop* my only concern is that you and your colleagues be given ample opportunity for profitable scientific research *stop* to this end am sending [Bill] Harney as guide confident that his knowledge of terrain will give you what you want *stop* need be no alteration in your position best wishes.
> Murphy (July 14, 1948).

Mountford was pleased but most probably shamed and hurt by the actions of his own Department of Information, as well as by Setzler's hesitation in supporting him. Even so, Setzler noted in a letter to Wetmore one week later that Mountford "seemed like a new man since then and is devoting most of his time to directing the films" (July 18, 1948). While it may not seem immediately obvious, these events were crucial for the collecting of ethnographic material. Mountford was forced to make a decision at this point. He could stop collecting ethnographic objects and concentrate on making films, as his employer wished him to do. Or, he could continue collecting and minimize the work involved by not recording any contextual information for the objects, thus allowing more time for filming. He chose the latter.

Another important outcome of this political intervention was the inclusion of William "Bill" Harney in the expedition group (see figure 5.1). Harney had been living in the region for many years and had extensive knowledge of the fauna and flora as well as experience living with Aboriginal people. He was a

FIGURE 5.1
Bill Harney (back row, far right) with members of the Second National Geographic Expedition to Melville Island in 1954. National Library of Australia, nla.pic-vn3705155.

talented storyteller and singer and seems to have greatly lifted the spirits of expedition members (Mountford 1956: xxvii). Raymond Specht recalls that Harney's arrival was very much welcomed by expedition members. He states, "Fortunately at this time, the Native Affairs Officer, Bill Harney, replaced Howard Coates who had proven a disaster in liaison with Aborigines and Expedition members on Groote Eylandt and Bickerton Island" (2006b). It is unknown whether this lack of success by Coates was related to his friendship with A. P. Elkin. Also at Yirrkala, Keith Cordon returned home due to sickness in his family, John Bray took over as transport officer, and Reginald Hollow arrived to work as cook.

The stories Bill Harney tells us
   Just split our sides with mirth
With his twinkling eyes and waving arms and
   Somewhat ample girth.

Of the sisters and the dog fights and
  Many more like that
We hope that he's not talking through his old felt hat.
(Extract from the song "Bob the Bagman," by Robert Miller, written during
the Arnhem Land Expedition)

Mountford and McCarthy record working with, and collecting paintings from, artists such as Mawalan Marika, Wondjuk Marika, and Narritjin Maymuru during their work at Yirrkala. Yet, Mountford's recordkeeping remained poor at Yirrkala and we learn little about the artists and their lives from the 1948 archives. The same methods of ethnographic collecting were undertaken throughout the expedition and Mountford remained primarily around the base camp for the three months they were camped at Yirrkala.

It was a different story for other expedition members who scattered themselves around the islands and mainland sites of Arnhem Land. McArthur, Miller, Setzler, McCarthy, and Harney all traveled to Port Bradshaw where they conducted their independent research. Margaret McArthur established a nutrition camp with two Aboriginal companions, causing Mountford great concern. McArthur claimed that she could get a truer picture of the local people in their natural environment if she were by herself (Mountford 1956: xxvii; see figure 5.2). Mountford did not think it was appropriate for a woman to be alone in Arnhem Land but, nonetheless, gave her permission to go (Mountford 1975: 229). Even as late as 1948, McArthur's ability to work independently in remote regions of Australia was considered daring and, to some, inappropriate for a woman.

Scientist "Gamer" Than Ned Kelly
  Melbourne, Tuesday—Miss Margaret McArthur, young Canberra nutrition expert, who spent three weeks among savage Arnhem Land aborigines, was "gamer than Ned Kelly," Mr. D. C. White said today. Mr. White has returned to Melbourne after serving on the patrol vessel *Kuru* which landed Miss McArthur on the Arnhem Land coast. (*Herald*, September 22, 1948)

There was growing tension between Fred McCarthy and Charles Mountford and, in mid-July McCarthy recorded the following in his diary:

I told him [Mountford] that I was fed up with the bloody expedition on the basis of the constant jealousy of all the work that I was doing and the constant

FIGURE 5.2
Margaret McArthur weighing food for nutrition research during the Arnhem Land Expedition. The women are said to be from the Fish Creek region, near to Oenpelli. Photograph by Howell Walker, National Geographic Society (after Mountford 1949: 766). Courtesy National Geographic Society.

arguments about the number of and the distribution of the specimens. (July 18, 1948)

McCarthy also recorded the following event in his Yirrkala diary:

Wondjuk [Marika], my worker, painted our wallaby totem for me but Mountford [cornered] him on his way to my tent, took the painting and photographed it and got the story and next day had the audacity to tell me that he had had it done for me . . . why must he be always lying in this cheap way to defend his activities? (August 26, 1948)

Mountford doggedly pursued his main interest—Aboriginal myth, art, and symbolism during the expedition and the jealousy referred to by McCarthy was probably the result of their work overlapping. Raymond Specht recalls one such incident: "It was a pity that Fred McCarthy's interest in the rock art of Chasm Island trespassed on Monty's field—but Monty organized Fred's visit to Chasm Island!"(2006b).

McCarthy (July 19, 1948) also recorded that Mountford continued to suspect Setzler of wanting to take over as leader. This tension is probably a factor in McCarthy's and Setzler's desire to work away from the base camp. Raymond Specht (2006b) points out that Mountford had never organized such a large team of specialists but that he did encourage all to do their separate research sometimes in locations distant from base camp, although he also suggested that "it was a pity that he did not hold occasional inter-disciplinary discussions" (Specht 2006b).

On their return from Port Bradshaw, Setzler and McCarthy traveled to Milingimbi to carry out archaeological research while the others concentrated their study around the camp. Setzler and McCarthy also collaborated at this time in collecting ethnographic artifacts. After they had finished their archaeological work for the day, their tents became a shop similar to Mountford's, and local men and women were able to bring in their materials for trade. It is not recorded whether, like Mountford, they paid for the objects with cash but we do know they were trading tobacco, razor blades, combs, and mirrors to obtain the 191 ethnological specimens including bark paintings. The men were popular and people came from more distant places such as Cape Stewart on the mainland to trade their goods. McCarthy (n.d.a: 8) recorded that the people were eager to trade, and the number of artifacts obtained over a three-week period was substantial.

> After our excavations . . . we would return to our abode to find several Milingimbi natives and sometimes those from the mainland, such as Cape Stewart, waiting to barter their implements, baskets, even their highly prized ceremonial objects, for that dark brown stick of tobacco. As the allotted period of three weeks came to a close our house looked like a museum store room. (Setzler n.d.: 6).

At Milingimbi, Reverend Hannah and later Reverend Arthur F. Ellemor are said to have assisted the visiting researchers. Reverend Ellemor assisted by obtaining what Setzler and McCarthy did not have time to collect or record. He collected interpretations of designs and carved pipes for the pair (Ellemor, June 21, 1949). While Setzler and McCarthy were visiting Milingimbi, Mountford arranged for Reverend Ellemor to collect a number of bark paintings for his own collection (Mountford 1956: 267). This was an interesting arrangement considering men from his expedition were on the island collecting anyway. It could reflect that the individuals were collecting, at that stage, for their own institutions and, hence, the competition for bark paintings. Another consequence of this arrangement was that a missionary with different biases and experience was given the task of acquiring interpretations of these paintings from the Aboriginal community.

As discussed in chapters 9 and 10, some of the other ethnological material collected by Setzler on the mainland included weapons and hunting implements. McCarthy's focus, on the other hand, was on domestic objects, as well as weapons and hunting implements. He also collected canoes, musical instruments, log coffins, burial objects, and string figures (Florek 1993). Mountford continued to collect ethnographic objects and, after Groote Eylandt, paid less attention to recording their contextual information. He, significantly, often neglected to record the artist's name. His diaries show some attempts at recording the interpretations of the paintings but a great deal of information is missing. Interestingly, once the supply of bark for painting was exhausted at Yirrkala (and later at Oenpelli), Mountford (1956: 13) supplied the artists with sheets of rough-surfaced dark grey and green paper.

Yirrkala seems to have been the most comfortable camp for the group and large collections were made by all expedition members. The research group remained at Yirrkala until the middle of September 1948 when arrangements were made to move their equipment and personnel to Oenpelli, 600 miles away, in the forty-ton steel landing barge *Triumph* (Murphy, July 15, 1948, in Setzler, July 18, 1948; Mountford 1949: 745). As was becoming usual for the expedition, trouble ensued when *Triumph*'s engines failed and other means of transport to Oenpelli were necessary. Rescue came from the RAAF, the launch *Kuru*, and the lugger *Victory* (Mountford 1975: 230).

Silent Men Back from the Silence of Arnhem Land

    After five months' work in the remote regions of the Northern Territory, members of the American-Australian Arnhem Land Expedition returned to Darwin yesterday in a R.A.A.F. Dakota. With prolific growths of beard and hair almost to their shoulders, some of the party looked almost as if they had never seen or heard of razors or scissors, and most of them have developed a suntan to earn the envy of any Bondi bathing beauty. (*Northern Territory Times and Gazette,* September 10, 1948)

Most of the expedition members were taken to Darwin on September 9 for one week to secure their collections and restock their supplies (figure 5.3). In Darwin, expedition members were instructed not to comment on the work of the expedition to the media (*Daily Mirror,* August 21, 1948). Mammalogist David Johnson and cameraman Peter Bassett-Smith traveled on the Mission lugger *Victory* with the remaining equipment. David Johnson jumped ship at Cape Don and walked 160 miles overland apparently without a guide to Oenpelli (arriving October 19), in turn, acquiring a significant collection of mammals for the Smithsonian Institution. Expedition members finally arrived in Oenpelli on September 20, 1948, on board the government-owned launch *The Phantom* (Setzler, January 13, 1950: 28).

FIGURE 5.3
Our DC-3 transport RAAF moving us from Yirrikala to Darwin, September 1948. Collection of Frank Setzler, National Library of Australia, nla.pic-vn3723998.

6

Exploring the Great Unknown—Oenpelli

A big boomerang of blue water was shining in its verdant rim of rice-grass. Besides the billabong lagoon were a dozen tents, their canvas a sun-faded green. The Arnhem Land Expedition.

—*Simpson 1951: 5*

The final base camp for the Arnhem Land Expedition tested the nerves of even the most hardened team members. Charles Mountford had estimated that Oenpelli would be "the most spectacular, the most productive and, at the same time, the most uncomfortable of our research camps" and all these expectations were fulfilled (Mountford 1956: xxviii). As suggested in the above quotation from visiting ABC journalist Colin Simpson, the expedition camped at the side of the Oenpelli billabong, a site that is now home to the local community art center—Injalak Arts and Crafts Association. Most of the expedition members remained in or very near to Oenpelli throughout the three months, each conducting their independent research.

The township of Oenpelli sits in country belonging to the Mangerridji people who speak the Mangerr language. In 1948 Oenpelli was a Church Missionary Society settlement with a long and complex history. The township was originally established in the early 1900s by a Scotsman and buffalo shooter by the name of Patrick "Paddy" Cahill. Between 1824 and 1849, Timorese water buffalo were released from three failed British settlements on the Cobourg

Peninsula and Melville Island (Berndt and Berndt 1970: 5). The local mon-
soonal conditions suited them perfectly and they multiplied rapidly, spread-
ing down the peninsula and across Arnhem Land (Mulvaney 2004: 11). In
response to this boom in numbers, the Cobourg Cattle Company took out
leasehold for hunting in 1876. Along with this larger company, small semi-
mobile camps emerged predominantly in the river plains between the East Alligator River and what is now Darwin. These camps were usually made up of
one or two non-Aboriginal hunters along with varying numbers of Aboriginal assistants (Berndt and Berndt 1970: 5; Cole 1988; Cole 1975: 15–17).

John Mulvaney (2004: 12) suggests that Paddy Cahill realized the financial
rewards possible from buffalo shooting around 1891 while he was preparing
horses for the Palmerston Cup. By the end of the decade he was a renowned
shooter, particularly famous for his ability to shoot from his horse and kill
large numbers of buffalo in a single day. On the other hand, Keith Cole (1972:
49) suggests that around 1880, two buffalo shooters, Paddy Cahill
(1863–1923) and William Johnson (probably meant to be Johnstone) had a
camp somewhere on the western side of the East Alligator River (see also
Berndt and Berndt 1970: 5). This seems unlikely given evidence for his work
droving and racing horses in this period (Mulvaney 2004). Cahill did, however, usually work with hunting partners including Barney Flynn, an Irish-
man, William Johnstone, and E. O. Robinson (Mulvaney 2004: 13, 15).

How then did Cahill find himself settling at the East Alligator River region
and specifically the area known today as Oenpelli or Gunbalanya? The answer is
twofold: First, the government made it available for lease. Second, he knew the
terrain and had seen its great agricultural potential. Finally, he knew some of the
local Aboriginal people from having hired them to help with his buffalo-hunt-
ing enterprises. The Cahill family (Paddy, Maria, Tom, Ruby Mumford, and
friend William Johnstone) came to Oenpelli in February 1910 with approval for
his leasehold (in partnership with William Johnstone) being officially given in
April 1910. His lease included 640 acres of land, which was later reduced to 320
acres at Paddy's request, and he also held a pastoral permit (Mulvaney 2004: 35).
There is no evidence to suggest Cahill and Johnstone consulted with Aboriginal
owners of the land over their decision to settle in this region.

By the 1920s Paddy Cahill was considering retirement and there were two
possible paths for Oenpelli. The first was for the government to oversee the
settlement and provide the area with a caretaker. The second option was to

hand it over to a missionary society. Largely due to financial considerations, the government decided on the latter course and after considerable negotiations regarding which missionary society would control Oenpelli, the Anglican Church Missionary Society (CMS) took control in 1925 (Cole 1975: 17). Alf Dyer was immediately offered the position of superintendent of the new CMS mission, and he and his wife, Mary, readily accepted. They arrived in September 1925 (Cole 1972: 50–53).

The superintendent of the Oenpelli Mission at the time of the Arnhem Land Expedition was Ralph Barton (he remained in this position until 1951). Attitudes of the CMS toward local Aboriginal men and women changed throughout the mission era in Oenpelli, as demonstrated in the following passage from a CMS policy document "A Policy for Aboriginal and Half Caste Education":

> Native crafts and activities should be inculcated, so that the children may not be unnecessarily separated from the common life of the tribe. This will include the making of spears (and) for boys, dilly bags and other utensils for girls, skill in gaining a livelihood from the land, and all native lore which can help towards these ends. This part of the work can best be done by the elder natives themselves, not by the white teachers, and will not take place in school, but out of doors. (CMS 1946, cited in Cole 1975: 54)

Yet missionary historian Keith Cole (1975: 55) suggests a gap between mission policy and practice. Little was done to implement the new measures because of staff shortages and conservative teachers, and because Aboriginal people were not considered qualified to teach. Nevertheless, the policy of assimilation was impacting upon Oenpelli by the time the Arnhem Land Expedition arrived. Missions in the north of Australia were now encouraged to have a positive economic and welfare policy in addition to spiritual purposes or, in other words, missions were meant to prepare Aboriginal Australia for the "new era of civilisation" and stop them "living the life of parasites." Aboriginal people could, it was argued, be "turned into" gardeners, station hands, mechanics and even—artisans. "Every mission should be a community based on activity, based on training the natives for industry, the doing of things of value to themselves and to Australia" (from Mission Conference, February 17, 1947, cited in Cole 1975: 58). Meanwhile, the number of people living at Oenpelli had grown from approximately 190 in 1928 to 235 in 1947 (Cole 1975: 32, 59).

Artifact and art collecting and/or trading had not been a high priority for the mission staff based in Oenpelli and art production had, for some time, been actively discouraged. The only significant collection of bark paintings formed between Paddy Cahill's departure and the arrival of Ronald and Catherine Berndt in 1947 was missionary Alf Dyer's 1930 collection. Judith Ryan (1990: 10) has suggested that researchers or collectors wishing to work with the local Aboriginal people around Oenpelli were forced to enter through the mission staff and to cooperate with mission authorities. Yet, Ronald and Catherine Berndt[1] (1947 and 1949–1950) and the Arnhem Land Expedition (1948) had little to do with the mission and, in the case of Charles Mountford, his work was made difficult by antagonistic mission staff (May 2000). This is quite contrary to other mission stations in northern Australia where staff would often collect and despatch artworks and artifacts to museums and marketing depots throughout the world. Judith Ryan (1990: 10) agrees with Howard Morphy (1998: 27), stating that missionaries such as Theodore T. Webb, Wilbur Chaseling, and Edgar Wells saw the marketing of art as a way of making money for mission settlements and artists, but he goes further to suggest that they also viewed art as a means of asserting the value of Aboriginal culture. In short, expedition members faced mission staff at Oenpelli very different to the staff they had encountered at Groote Eylandt, Yirrkala, and Milingimbi Island. The Arnhem Land Expedition was unwanted and, once they arrived in Oenpelli, they were on their own.

Quite unusually for this time period, the same Aboriginal leader lived to oversee all of these changes—from the initial settlement by Paddy Cahill, to the coming of the CMS mission in 1925, and he was still living when the Arnhem Land Expedition visited in 1948. The life of the old man known as Kumutun and Marakara and Nipper is discussed in chapter 10, as he was a key artist for Mountford during the expedition. It is important to note that this traditional owner for Oenpelli is recorded by Aboriginal and non-Aboriginal people (including Paddy Cahill) as being a strong leader and, when necessary, he fought to retain Aboriginal rights in his country.

It is with this background in mind that we return to the work of the Arnhem Land Expedition at Oenpelli. Herbert Deignan, Robert Miller, and Raymond Specht were probably the researchers most excited about Oenpelli as there they found abundant birds, fish, and plants for their work and made some important discoveries and additions to their collections. Miller claimed that the waterways surrounding Oenpelli were the richest he had ever fished, and Specht discovered several new species of plants (Mountford 1975: 230). Raymond Specht's work included collecting specimens, covering them with newspaper and then transferring them to metal frames where they were placed in special drying ovens enclosed with water jackets that prevented scorching or burning (Setzler, January 13, 1950: 29; Thomas and May 2007). Specht (who would go on to become professor of botany at the University of Queensland) collected 13,500 plants, eight specimens from each species to be distributed to four museums in Australia, as well as the Smithsonian institution, Harvard University, Kew Gardens in England, and Leiden in Holland (Setzler, January 13, 1950: 29–30).

During his time at Oenpelli, Mountford continued to produce films with the assistance of Peter Bassett-Smith (see figure 6.1). In addition, he explored the many rock shelters around the community focusing mainly on "Gallery

FIGURE 6.1
Aborigines smear their bodies with lustrous clay to illustrate the life of bees. Aboriginal men from Oenpelli during filming for Charles Mountford in 1948. Photograph by Howell Walker, National Geographic Society (after Mountford 1949: 772). Courtesy National Geographic Society.

Hill" (Injalak Hill) and "Oenpelli Hill" (Arguluk Hill). Unable to take the rock art home, Mountford collected bark paintings with similar painted designs to the rock art using the same "shop" he used at the other base camps. He noted, however, that "many of the artists who produced bark paintings for me came from the Liverpool River country, the local mission station using most of the available aboriginal labour for the killing and skinning of water buffaloes" (Mountford 1956: 111). As discussed previously, the local mission staff did not support the work of the expedition and, as this quote suggests, did not encourage local Aboriginal people to collaborate with expedition members. To an even greater extent than at the other two base camps, Mountford failed to record interpretations or artist names for most of the ethnographic objects. In fact he names only Larida, Willirra, Kumutun, and Wulkini as painters despite collecting 159 paintings at Oenpelli, and each of these names is incorrectly recorded (e.g., Kumutun is Old Nipper Marakara).

Colin Simpson was a visiting ABC journalist who spent two weeks in Oenpelli with the expedition. He later produced a book, *Adam in Ochre* (1951), based on his experiences with the expedition. This book provides a different insight into the expedition members' activities at Oenpelli and, in particular, the work of Charles Mountford. Simpson recalls:

> The old men Mountford brought back to the tent had been hoeing the mission's melon patch. They looked unimpressive, they looked dreadful in cast-offs and shapeless relics of felt hats. They sat down on the grass, folding themselves down in that slow and diffident way they have with white men, one ringing his nose out with his fingers, another coughing. I thought to myself, "Nothing much can come of this." I was judging on appearances, presuming that the old men had shed their validity as aborigines and put off their old culture because they had put on rags of white-man clothing and were taking hand-outs from the mission. It was these old men and others they mustered who, transformed with paint and fervour, gave us the unforgettable performance of the . . . corroboree a few days later. (1951: 7)

On the same hills that Mountford was scouring for rock art, Frank Setzler and Fred McCarthy were scavenging for human remains. Setzler (January 13, 1950: 35) states, "Even though we could not obtain all of the skeleton material that I had located, that which we brought back constitutes the largest collection of Australian material in this country [USA]." Setzler and McCarthy conducted archaeological excavations on both Injalak and Arguluk Hill and removed many human bones in the process. Human skeletal remains were also removed from rock shelters where they had been interred for cultural purposes after death. Expedition members did not have permission from local Aboriginal people to remove these human remains. The collection of human remains will be discussed later in this book due to the present-day significance of this removal for local communities. Setzler and McCarthy's excavations also revealed collections of stone and some wooden artifacts. As Setzler states, he "spent the entire two months hiking with my boys into the hills and completely excavating twelve caves" (January 13, 1950: 35).

Setzler found the archaeological deposits to be fine and powdery with a great deal of ash. His method of excavation consisted of shoveling all of the deposit into sieves and bagging any stone, wood, or shell that remained (see figure 6.2). Little attention was paid to stratigraphic layering or standard

FIGURE 6.2
View of Fred McCarthy and FMS [Frank Setzler] shoveling and sifting cave deposits in front of a picture gallery, site #1, Oenpelli, October 1948. Collection of Frank Setzler, National Library of Australia, nla.pic-an24297484.

archaeological excavation procedures. Later in camp he would wash and classify the artifacts (Setzler, January 13, 1950: 35). On Injalak Hill Setzler excavated hundreds of stone scrapers and he was excited one day to find one of the scrapers still hafted to a wooden handle. He and McCarthy believed that this artifact answered the question of how these scrapers were used and they published an article on their find (Setzler and McCarthy 1950: 1–5).

During their time in Oenpelli the medical unit was housed in two large tents and conditions were not ideal for medical research (see figures 6.3 and 6.4). As Mountford (1975: 230) recalled, "The intense heat, and the dust, where cleanliness was so important, were a continuous trial." As well as working with Setzler on archaeological excavations, McCarthy traveled with Margaret McArthur and John Bray to Fish Creek where they undertook one of the most influential anthropological studies of their time (McCarthy and McArthur 1960). McArthur studied the diet and food habits of one Aboriginal group and McCarthy noted their methods of food gathering. Bray worked separately on his collection of entomological specimens (see figure 6.5).

Famous for his quirky and insightful poetry and songwriting, Bill Harney penned the following song based on the expedition's activities at Oenpelli.

"Oenpelli, 1948" by W. E. Harney
There was Frank amid the ashes a-digging up the bones,
    And Mac a-drawing pictures as he scrampled o'er the stones,
While Howell a-whirred his movie as the natives flashed the glare,
    And the Jackies all a-wondered why the hell the whites were there,
On the hot and flinty rocks of Oenpelli.

There was Monty after Mimis like a 'ound upon the trail,
    And Bert behind his whiskers after snipe and duck and quail,
There was Bob a-cursing leeches that were clinging to his knees,
    And Dave a-shooting dingbats as they flitted through the trees,
Mid the mozzies near the pool of Oenpelli.

There was Brian with his needle chasing natives through the scrub,
    And Kelvin getting breast-milk from the women—Ah! The rub,
It was only used for science or so they all declare,
    But the Jackies all are wondering why the hell the whites are there,
On the steamy humid plains of Oenpelli.

FIGURE 6.3
Dr. Brian Billington and Kelvin Hodges weigh an unidentified woman for medical re-
search at Oenpelli. Photograph by Howell Walker, National Geographic Society (after
Mountford 1949: 747). Courtesy National Geographic Society.

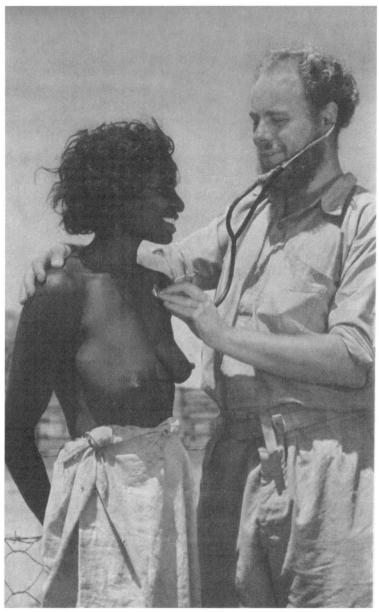

FIGURE 6.4
Dr. Brian Billington with an unidentified woman from Oenpelli. Photograph
by Howell Walker, National Geographic Society (after Mountford 1949: 767).
Courtesy National Geographic Society.

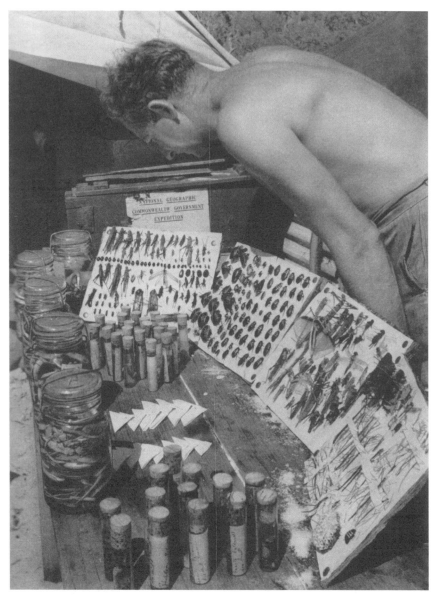

FIGURE 6.5
John Bray with his entomological collection during the Arnhem Land Expedition. Photograph by Howell Walker, National Geographic Society (after Mountford 1949: 751). Courtesy National Geographic Society.

There was Margaret out a-digging weighing tucker on the plain,
    And Mrs. Monty typing just like little drops of rain,
With John a-walking, walking, he is tramping all the while,
    And Reg amidst the good things greeting of us with a smile,
As we ate the tucker down at Oenpelli.

And Ray was after bushes with a ten-pound axe in hand,
    With Peter on his pictures tramping up and down the land,
While I'm a-writing, writing, they won't let me bash their ears,
    They tell me I'm a bludger, but by Christ they'll buy me beers,
When we leave the steamy plains of Oenpelli.

Colin Simpson described an everyday scene from the Oenpelli base camp:

> Down at the far end of the lagoon aboriginal women and boys would be catching fish in the scoop-nets they knot out of bark string, or diving after the bulbs of lily roots. They were a decent distance off and we always went in naked, all the men. The expedition's two women used to bathe further from the tents, right up at the other end from where the men stood out in the shallow water, copper-coloured down to the waist, then white-bottomed, then brown again, soaping themselves before they swam or just floated on the peace of the lagoon. (Simpson 1951: 10)

Rumors had leaked to the press that all was not well among the expedition members and as the expedition began to reach its conclusion Mountford realized that in order to protect the reputation of the expedition (and its stakeholders) he would need to ask his team to present a united front. He wrote to Alexander Wetmore at the Smithsonian Institution on November 5, 1948, stating that he was afraid his letters may have created a wrong impression and that the camp was actually a very harmonious one. He claimed that he had not heard of a single argument between any of the members (Mountford to Wetmore, November 5, 1948). At the same time, he requested that Frank Setzler not be allowed anywhere near the Australian ministerial or department heads for fear that he would not be discreet:

> Most of the trouble at Yirrkala was due to Mr. Setzler's inability to estimate the position, and his indiscreet chatter, though I am not suggesting the remarks were malicious, far from it. I am speaking plainly, so that you will know the reason for my request . . . I would deem it a favour if you did not file this letter. (Mountford to Wetmore, November 5, 1948)

Alexander Wetmore did file the letter and expedition members were asked to visit Adelaide together after the expedition so they could present a united front for the cameras. Herbert Deignan (to Wetmore August 26, 1948) states, "Mr. Mountford, for good and sufficient reasons resulting from the expeditions' recent troubles, wishes all of the party to arrive together in Adelaide at the end." Deignan (to Wetmore August 26, 1948) goes on to suggest that Mountford had been seriously injured in his civil-service career by the events during the expedition and expresses his surprise that nothing came out in the press despite gossip having reached as far as Canberra and Sydney.

The fieldwork component of the Arnhem Land Expedition officially came to a conclusion in early November 1948. The barge *Triumph* successfully transported the collections and the team members back to Darwin along the East Alligator River (Mountford 1956: xxix–xxx; see figure 6.6).

FIGURE 6.6
Lee's barge with our equipment going down the East Alligator River, November 1948. Collection of Frank Setzler, National Library of Australia, nla.pic-vn3723873.

SURVIVING THE ARNHEM LAND EXPEDITION

Throughout the last three chapters I have presented an overview of the field-work undertaken during the Arnhem Land Expedition. In particular, I have focused on the work relating to the ethnographic collection and the activities of Charles Mountford, Fred McCarthy, and Frank Setzler. This was clearly a politically complex and logistically daunting expedition and, in particular, Mountford's sacrifices to make it happen were extreme. On top of the pressure placed upon the leader from the government of Australia came the responsibility of satisfying museums in Australia and in the United States, as well as the National Geographic Society and individual members of the team. A private letter from secretary of the Smithsonian Institution Wetmore to Frank Setzler stated, "Mountford's difficulties are the ones usually found in a country where scientific research is not established as fully as it is with us. Under such circumstances there is usually more jealousy and contention than cooperation. We had plenty of it in the early days here in the United States" (August 10, 1948: 1). Mountford commented to Wetmore that "you will see my enemies, of whom you have already had some knowledge, are still active and powerful" (July 29, 1948: 2). Eventually these worries took their toll on Mountford's health and he suffered fainting spells, Setzler finally commenting, "our main hope now is to hold him down from worry and exhaustion, so that we can all safely return to Darwin" (October 6, 1948: 2).

The context of the Arnhem Land Expedition was highly political and Mountford was the go-between for the necessary institutions, having to please both governments and the scientists. Contrary to many of the scientists' beliefs the government motivations for the expedition were publicity, international relations, and increased understanding of the Aboriginal people of Arnhem Land for the purposes of administration. The delay of the expedition due to the Bikini Atoll atomic tests is a good example of this—without consultation with the expedition leader, the Australian government cancelled the expedition and revived it only when the appropriate American scientists were available for publicity.

The ethnographic collection acquired during the Arnhem Land Expedition was an offshoot and a bonus in terms of core aims; it must, therefore, be seen in the context of its acquisition. The distribution of this collection could assist in improving relations between the two countries by the government of Australia offering the United States representative samples.

Finally, there is as much to be read from the omissions from the official record of this expedition as from the words themselves. There was a clear lack of understanding relating to the impact of the expedition on the Aboriginal men and women who were considered the subjects of this research. There is no evidence to suggest that any consideration was given to the implications of the expedition for Aboriginal communities. In fact, there is little evidence to suggest much social interaction with Aboriginal people at all, aside from those expedition members who traveled away from the base camps with Aboriginal guides. I finish this chapter now with the revealing words of Frank Setzler who chose to conclude his 1950 lecture "Aboriginal Australia" to the National Geographic Society with the following words: "As the sun sinks in the Timor sea, we leave the aborigines, content with his mythological deities, yet conscious of the impact of our Atomic Age" (Setzler, January 13, 1950: 38). While the expedition may have been over, the politics and the lively negotiations for collections had just begun.

NOTE

1. The Berndts first visited Oenpelli in 1947 but their longest period of fieldwork took place from December 1949 to May 1950 (see Berndt and Berndt 1970).

7

Collecting Arnhem Land

Tom Griffiths (1996: 25) has argued that collections suppress their own historical, economic, and political processes of production. This is true of the Arnhem Land Expedition ethnographic collection, and it is one of the underlying aims of this book to address this issue. This chapter, therefore, reviews the processes involved in the shaping of the collection and the contemporary social attitudes that contributed to collection strategies. In other words, this is an exploration of mid-twentieth-century influences on the expeditions' field collecting. While it could be argued that individual collector preferences were the key factor in the types of objects collected, the influence of society and culture on the views of the collectors cannot be ignored. As stated previously, individual researchers were carrying mandates from their government and their cultural institutions and were, in essence, collecting for humanity.

In Australia, early researchers often collected ethnographic material culture from Aboriginal communities with what could be referred to as a Social Darwinian view. Many believed these Aboriginal cultures (or culture, as they believed at the time) represented an earlier form of Western culture. With a few notable exceptions, until the 1950s, researchers of Australian Aboriginal culture generally collected with the underlying assumption that their study group was an unchanging people with unchanging material culture (Trigger 1989: 141). As Murdoch stated in 1917, "The dark-skinned wandering tribes ... have nothing that can be called a history ... change and progress are the stuff of which history is made: these blacks knew no change and made no progress, as far as we can tell" (Attwood and Arnold 1992: x).

The result of this belief was that ethnographic collections were formed and used for studying what were assumed to be static, prehistoric cultures. Researchers saw this ethnographic material as providing them with the absent data in the archaeological record. It was believed that the gap resulting from perishable material not surviving in the archaeological record could be filled with modern ethnographic material (McBryde 1978). Though the question of Australia's static culture prior to European colonization was called into question by researchers such as Norman Tindale in southern Australia, interest in cultural change and regional variation did not mark Australian archaeology until the 1950s, particularly following the advent of radiocarbon dating (Trigger 1989: 143).

With colonization and the significant impact that this had upon Aboriginal cultures worldwide, people began to see Charles Darwin's predictions of Aboriginal cultures becoming extinct as becoming fact (Darwin 1871: 521). Though at first the devastation of other cultures was accepted as progress, eventually fear of losing something irreplaceable began to enter the minds of the colonizers.

Simpson described the "Australian Aboriginal" as "a patient who years ago was marked down as 'dying' and whose treatment since has consisted mainly of pillow-smoothing and doses of pity" (1951: 186). This fear led to urgency in recording and preserving and was the overwhelming motivating factor in the collection of Australian Aboriginal material culture in Australia during the early- to mid-twentieth century and possibly extending further (Clifford 1988: 231; Griffiths 1996: 26; Tuhiwai Smith 1999: 61). Not only was there a compelling need to collect and record material culture before cultures were lost but also before they changed through the influence of colonizing cultures. Many researchers and collectors in Australia, including Mountford, considered their work as salvage (Clifford 1988; Elkin 1964: 362; Griffiths 1996: 25).

Evidence of Mountford's anxiousness to collect and record is found in his funding applications during the 1930s and 1940s, including his 1945 application to the National Geographic Society. He speaks of his fear of the disappearance or change of aspects of Aboriginal culture caused by colonization, "This art is disappearing rapidly, thus the urgency to gather all details of the drawings, their significance and their relationship to the legendary stories" (Mountford, March 5, 1945: 3).

Mountford wanted to believe that the Aboriginal people he would meet during the Arnhem Land Expedition were somehow "authentic" in not having been in contact with other cultural groups. He stated, "Arnhem Land is an aboriginal reserve, and before the war, except for a few missions along the coast, was uninhabited by Europeans. The native culture was not, at that time, influenced by white civilisation; it is unlikely that the present military occupation has changed them" (Mountford, March 5, 1945: 3). As Anne Clarke (1998: 13) has argued, by 1948 Arnhem Land had become far less isolated, due to the large numbers of soldiers and airmen stationed in the region during World War II as well as the existence of missions located around the region. Dewar (1995: 22) has also emphasized contact in the 1920s with Japanese trepanging crews who would frequently trade with local Aboriginal people.

During the expedition Fred McCarthy at one point expressed concern at the situation in which he found himself. He stated, "I went to bed at 9pm but, though tired out, couldn't sleep because of our situation. Here we are, 16 of us, backed by the U.S. and Australian funds, but the natives are almost completely civilised, speaking English well and have dropped their ceremonial, hunting life" (McCarthy, April 14, 1948). He was also concerned about Mountford's choice of base camps and his own inability to work with Aboriginal groups living in their "normal" environment but, in response, he saw the opportunity for studying culture-contact. McCarthy felt that the choice of the large Arnhem Land townships (Umbakumba, Yirrkala, and Oenpelli) as base camps, instead of remote localities where Aboriginal people were living entirely by their individual efforts off the land, meant that valuable opportunities were lost to study their so-called primitive culture and to collect the objects in actual use (McCarthy n.d.a).

Even before reaching Arnhem Land, Setzler shared McCarthy's concerns that the Aboriginal cultures had already experienced the colonizing cultures and, therefore, would be of no use to the researchers. He lamented in a letter to Mountford (September 31, 1947), "In a recent article in Oceania I noticed that the natives around Army camps had taken to card playing. These natives may be so Europeanized that we would not be using them."

With this background, it is hoped that the act of collecting by expedition members, as outlined in previous chapters and to be expanded upon in this chapter, can be seen not only in the practical sense that it is applied but also in a wider sense of society, imperialism, and human nature.

It is a little surprising to find that no stated collection policy concerning ethnographic objects was established before expedition members left for Arnhem Land. Essentially, any decisions on what to collect were left to the individual members of the expedition. The majority of the collectors fell into discrete areas—the ichthyologist collected fish, the botanist collected plants; however, the nature of ethnographic collecting could not be so easily defined. As mentioned earlier, even in 1948 many people still believed that Aboriginal people were a stagnant race with an unchanging or barely changing material culture. Ethnographic objects, therefore, were thought to represent Aboriginal culture past and present. During the expedition, Mountford defined ethnographic material culture as nonexcavated objects. This is important—the only difference Mountford saw between ethnographic collection and archaeological collections was that one was excavated, the other was not. The result was overlapping research areas and academic arguments lasting decades.

McCarthy and Setzler held similar positions within their respective museums, the Australian Museum and Smithsonian Institution. Both worked within the archaeology-anthropology sections of their institutions and had extensive experience working with material culture, though Setzler had no experience with Australian Aboriginal material culture. Mountford, on the other hand, had ties to the South Australian Museum, as well as the government of Australia, which complicated the collection process for him.

Before beginning their expedition to Arnhem Land, very little correspondence was entered into between any of the participating institutions regarding the collection of ethnographic artifacts. As Mountford wrote to Dr. Arthur Bache Walkom of the Smithsonian Institution, "I did not mention anything about collections, because it might complicate matters, but you can take my personal assurance as leader that your museum will receive a representative series of all ethnological material collected" (December 31, 1947). The Smithsonian Institution's Alexander Wetmore actively encouraged Mountford to define the collection's distribution thoroughly prior to the start of the expedition. He writes:

Mr. Setzler will arrange with you in Australia some division of the anthropo-
logical material under which he will bring a part to this country for the National
Museum [of the United States], while the rest will remain with you in Australia.
This embodies the substance of memoranda that I have given you previously.
We are proceeding on the understanding that this is acceptable to you and to the
Australian authorities. As you and I have informed one another earlier these
matters should all be clarified in advance so that there will be no misunder-
standing at the end of the trip. (Wetmore to Mountford, January 15, 1948)

Mountford (December 31, 1947) gave vague promises to the authorities
that the material would be split among the primary institutions, yet, no questions were asked regarding exactly what the "material" would consist of. As a
result, little guidance meant the collectors went into the field with their own
ideas on what their institutions needed and what they would try to collect.

McCarthy came to Arnhem Land with the aim of filling gaps in the few existing collections of Australian Aboriginal material culture held by the Australian Museum, as well as to collect and document those objects that
expedition members observed were being made or used (Jones 1987: 12). Despite his intentions to fill gaps in the collections at the Australian Museum, he
soon came to realize many restricting factors on his work that became obvious in the field (Jones 1987: 12). He saw the presence of three anthropologists
on the expedition as limiting each other's scope even though it added to the
overall anthropological data (McCarthy n.d.b). To resolve this difficulty he
chose to specialize and selected those aspects of anthropological research and
collecting that offered the most productive results in the comparatively limited time spent in each of the three base camps (McCarthy n.d.a). His collection of approximately 193 string figures from Yirrkala is an example of these
actions.

Though we know that McCarthy intended to focus on acquiring specialist
collections, he does not give us any insights into what he intended these spe-
cializations to be. Mountford's vague promises before and during the expedition of a clean split of the ethnographic material meant that the Australian
Museum would receive artifacts collected by other researchers as well as Mc-
Carthy and, consequently, he had no reason to fear having only a limited representation of what he collected. As the anthropologist stated, "I want to work
on a set plan without interference so that I can complete some lines of work

and not get a confused picture of a tangled skin of work. . . . We have only a small time in each camp . . . and we have got to specialise to succeed" (McCarthy, March 18, 1948).

Setzler, too, had scant knowledge of the Aboriginal cultures of Arnhem Land. He stated, "Never having been in 'the land down under' I am indeed looking forward to this opportunity. My colleagues here in the museum are also anxious to start work in this relatively unknown section of Australia. As an anthropologist I have kept posted in a general way with the various Australian reports on the aborigines" (September 1, 1947).

Setzler (December 21, 1948) lamented that the Smithsonian Institution had never had a truly representative series of Australian anthropological specimens. This also meant that his experience of the material culture of Arnhem Land was limited. McCarthy's statement following the expedition would seem to support this fact. He states, "Arnhem Land was selected because the museums of Australia and America possess few specimens from this remote region" (McCarthy, January 16, 1949). It appears that Setzler had very little idea of what material to collect in Arnhem Land before his arrival, whereas McCarthy understood something of the material culture being used by the Aboriginal people in Arnhem Land and had a general idea of the type of material with which he would return.

On the other hand, Mountford knew what he wanted to obtain in Arnhem Land—art. The ethnologist had previously visited the Roper River area in the early 1940s and collected material culture, particularly bark paintings (Lamshed 1972: 107–8). McCarthy stated in his diary on one of the first days at Umbakumba that "Monty [Mountford] wants to do art and legends, and to get a collection" (McCarthy, March 18, 1948). Many months later McCarthy updated his view: "He [Mountford] is not really concerned whether we get a collection or not so long as he gets a private collection of bark paintings which, I believe, he wants for the purpose of exhibitions and lectures in the United States" (McCarthy, August 8, 1948).

The reasons for Mountford wanting this type of material require further elaboration. His intentions for the material would have influenced his collecting, yet these intentions are not entirely clear. For example, he told the chairman of the National Geographic Society Research Committee that he "would desire that the ethnological material collected on this expedition be lodged in the South Australian Museum, where it will be available for study" (Mountford, March 5, 1945: 6). In the field his intentions became a little clearer to other expedition members and became an ongoing area of disagreement. Mountford did intend for a large part of the ethnographic material collected to go to the South Australian Museum; however, McCarthy believed that he intended to *sell* it to them. The destination of the money realized from the proposed purchase is unknown (McCarthy, April 9, 1948). Early in the expedition, McCarthy recorded in his diary, "We had a talk about the ethno. [ethnographic] coll. [collection] Monty wants it split into three batches for Adelaide, Sydney and Washington, but this means that Australia gets 2/3 and the U.S. 1/3, Adelaide buys from Mountford his third altho [although] it contributes no funds or salary to the expedition, and there is some doubt about where the money Mountford receives goes" (McCarthy, March 18, 1948).

Though it would appear that Mountford's intention was always to collect ethnographic material, particularly bark paintings, his intentions for this material were not what contemporary researchers such as McCarthy would have considered appropriate. It would be difficult to dismiss the proposal that these intentions had a large influence on what he collected. Bark paintings, for example, would certainly sell for larger amounts of money than ethnographic material. Elliott (1992: 10) states that Mountford was also more willing to trade tobacco or money for bark paintings, carvings, painted paddles, bark coffins, spears, and ceremonial objects, and the artists must have been aware that these artifacts fetched higher prices than other material culture.

So, why did Mountford collect art? His collection strategies were certainly influenced by his belief that artistic expression could be studied independently of social organization, a view that would have been scorned by archaeologists such as McCarthy. Mountford once lamented:

> It was the scientist rather than the painter who studied "primitive art" and therefore approached the subject intellectually rather than emotionally. . . . The designs are analysed, compared, their sequences ascertained, and their ages estimated. But in such painstaking investigations one finds little appreciation of beauty, of balance in colour and form, or of appeal to the senses. (Mountford in Cant 1950: foreword)

This meant that he could collect art while ignoring the complex social structures surrounding it. In other words, Mountford could spend eight months collecting and then research his collection on return to the South Australian

Museum. In truth, Mountford collected Aboriginal paintings as *art* rather than *artifact* during a time when Aboriginal art was seen to reside more correctly within the precinct of orthodox anthropology. Mountford was ahead of his time with this attitude; ironically, his lack of contemporary training in archaeology and anthropology, his lack of skills in recording the social and cultural context for artifacts, and his lack of understanding relating to the role of "art" in Aboriginal societies led him to view paintings as largely aesthetic objects. In chapter 10 I explore the collection of paintings that Mountford formed during the Arnhem Land Expedition, a collection that was to become the core Aboriginal artwork for many Australian cultural institutions (see figure 7.1).

The collection strategies employed by expedition members tended to be determined by the individual and, once established, were employed at each base camp in very similar ways. Mountford's collection of paintings usually involved a discussion with the artist concerning the subject of the artwork, two days for the artist to complete his[1] work, another discussion between collector and artist regarding an interpretation of the design, and finally payment of approximately 10 shillings to 1 pound depending on the standard and size

FIGURE 7.1
Nanyin Maymuru, Mawalan Marika, and Wandjuk Marika at Yirrkala, August 11, 1948.
Photograph courtesy of Raymond Specht.

of the work. Setzler and McCarthy had few dealings with the artist before purchasing art works. They are not recorded as having paid cash for any items but, rather, traded tobacco, razor blades, and any other items they had lying around and could spare.

Other ethnographic material was likely collected by expedition members in a similar way. Fiber objects (baskets and bowls), for example, are shown being produced in photographs from the expedition and most show little evidence of wear. The collectors are unlikely, however, to have influenced the type of fiber art being produced. Instead, artists likely seized the opportunity to earn extra income from the sale of ethnographic items. It is unclear from historical records whether McCarthy paid for or traded materials for his collection of string figures. It is doubtful that he would not have compensated the artist after arguing with Setzler that they must be "given some reasonable value for the great amount of work involved" in producing other artifacts (McCarthy, August 8, 1948).

The question was posed earlier in this book as to what motivated these men and women to collect specimens of another culture? There are two separate issues that need to be dealt with when discussing the answer to this question. The first is the motivation of the sponsors, including the institutions, that sent their staff; and the second is the individual collector's role. As Pearce stated, "Museum objects are created by the act of collecting, usually twice over—firstly through the choices of the individual collector, and secondly, by the willingness of a museum to take the collected assemblage for reasons which have to do with its perceived aesthetic, historic or scientific value" (1992: 7).

The museums that sent their anthropological and archaeological staff to join the Arnhem Land Expedition did so because of their desire to gain a more extensive collection of Australian Aboriginal material culture. The expedition also offered the rare opportunity of field training for their staffs. The Smithsonian Institution was keen to improve relations between Australian and American scientists. For all these institutions there was also the appeal of gaining a collection, and this deserves some further discussion.

As Tom Griffiths states, "Anthropology in Australia was driven by the expectation of Aboriginal extinction and by the urgency of preserving the records of a dying race" (1996: 26). It is hard to understand that even as recently as 1948 people still believed Aboriginal Australians were a dying "race." Yet, it was not as simple as believing the people themselves were dying out. For researchers, such as anthropologists and archaeologists, it was the cultural death of Aboriginal Australia that they anticipated and feared—the polluting of cultural beliefs and practices by outside influences. The urgency to collect, therefore, was the same as if the people themselves were dying out. Cultural institutions desired to gain better, larger, and more representative collections of material from Arnhem Land because they feared the opportunity to collect authentic artifacts would soon be gone.

As mentioned earlier in this chapter, Mountford, McCarthy, and Setzler all spoke of their sadness at the perceived *cultural death* of the Aboriginal people of Arnhem Land. Setzler saw this as disappointing and unfortunate in terms of research, while McCarthy, though disappointed, expressed excitement at the possibility of studying culture contact.

Mountford's disappointment in the nontraditional lifestyle of his study group was less obvious than the other researchers, yet his belief in Aboriginal cultures as stagnant is constant in his publications. He stated as recently as 1961, "Surely the material culture of the aborigines is at no higher level, nor any more elaborate, than that of European Stone Age Man. Although we have no information about the philosophical and social life of Palaeolithic man, there does not seem to be any valid reason why it should have differed greatly from that of the primitive man of Australia" (1961: 2). Nevertheless, the contribution of Mountford as an individual to the formation of the Arnhem Land Expedition ethnographic collection needs to be remembered. Any collection is bound to reflect the collector in multiple ways. As Muensterberger states, "Obviously, his collection is bound to reflect certain aspects of his own personality, his taste, his sophistication or naiveté; his independence of choice or his reliance on the judgment of others" (1994: 4).

As discussed earlier, Mountford had other reasons for wanting to collect and particularly for wanting to collect bark paintings. Mountford desired a large collection of ethnographic material to assist in his personal research ventures (including display on lecture tours). It is also likely that he intended to sell and trade artifacts. Certainly, these ideas can be connected to the idea of preserving the records of a "dying race," but they also reflected his personal ambitions.

Though it may seem that the Arnhem Land Expedition ethnographic collection was manipulated into its resulting form by individual, independent researchers, it would be naive to think that the views of the cultures from which these collectors came did not influence their choices. Certainly, the needs of the individual and each individual's employer were determining factors, but the underlying beliefs relating to Aboriginal culture were also dominant. The result is an intriguing collection that can convey information about the collector, the collected, and the cross-cultural encounters that they shared.

NOTE

1. I have not yet found any records suggesting women painted for Mountford.

8

When We Have Put to Sea

My song is told but this I'll add, when we are gone some will be glad. The mission bell will peal with glee when we have put to sea.

—John E. Bray, October 27, 1948

The Arnhem Land Expedition resulted in vast and scientifically important collections ranging from entomology to botany to archaeology. Each of these collections has its own story to tell; however, in this chapter, my focus is on the ethnographic collection drawn together during the expedition's eight months in Arnhem Land. One of the most interesting aspects of the ethnographic collection is its complicated distribution to cultural institutions around the world following the expedition's return from Arnhem Land. This distribution itself can inform us about contemporary attitudes to collecting and material culture, as well as the politics of collecting in this time period. Charles Mountford claims that "the results of the expedition could hardly have been richer, both from the standpoint of human companionship and scientific results" (1956: xxx). While we may never know the exact number of ethnographic artifacts collected by this expedition, we do know that there are at least 2,144—making it one of the most significant collections of ethnographic material culture from a single time period.

The 1940s have been singled out as the high point in the collection of artifacts from Arnhem Land (Brittain 1990: 7) and the Arnhem Land Expedition collection was one of the largest dating from this period. Such a large number of artifacts stemming from a relatively short period would certainly be worthy of note, especially if kept as one collection. If this had occurred, however, this book would be significantly shorter. Like the story of the expedition itself, the distribution of the ethnographic collection is complex and surprising, and tracing this distribution has involved wide-ranging detective work. The result of this is an account of the movements of the ethnographic collection from 1948 to the present day including what could be termed the "second round" of collecting—the selective distribution of the artifacts.

The bulk of the ethnographic collection was 484 bark paintings making up 22.6 percent of the total known collection. Other key categories are 198 spears, 198 armlets, 193 string figures, 132 stone artifacts,[1] 118 baskets, 115 paintings on paper, and 99 figurines. Other artifact categories include spearthrowers, paddles, message sticks, dolls, shells, pipes, general containers, didgeridoos, and belts. While I focus on the distribution of this collection in this chapter, the nature of the collection will be explored further in chapter 9.

As already mentioned, no decision was made concerning the division of the ethnographic collection prior to the expedition leaving for Arnhem Land. This led to confusion, competition, and arguments in the field and also on the expedition's return. The distribution of the artifacts was influenced by all of these factors and others. Considering the number of researchers involved and the different institutions sponsoring the expedition, it is not surprising that the collections were broken up and distributed to different cultural institution's locations, not only around Australia, but the world.

Charles Mountford stated that he "would desire that the ethnological material collected on this expedition be lodged in the South Australian Museum, where it will be available for study when the monograph or scientific articles on the art and ethnology of this area is written" (March 5, 1945: 6). Initially he appears to have got his way and in late 1948, most of the ethnographic material belonging to the government of Australia was transported to Adelaide by road where the majority went into storage at the South Australian Museum (Elliott 1992: 10; Hipsley, June 28, 1954).

According to Fred McCarthy, a small amount of ethnographic material was also delivered directly to the Australian Museum and, subsequently, some of this material was forwarded to the Smithsonian Institution (today held in the National Museum of Natural History):

The following boxes have arrived in the first dispatch from Darwin: S1 to S43, and 63. Ethnological and archaeological collection, with personal scientific equipment of Setzler and myself. This collection will be . . . delivered to the Museum [Australian Museum]. The ethnological material for the U.S.N. Museum will have to be re-packed in the same boxes when the Australian Museum's collection has been taken out. The archaeological specimens will remain here, but the human skeletal collection will be sent to the U.S.N. Museum for study by one of its staff—portion of this collection will be returned to the Australian Museum. (February 10, 1949)

It appears from Fred McCarthy's letter that he had kept his ethnographic artifacts separate from those collected by Charles Mountford and had managed to avoid any of it going to Adelaide. Given the ever-worsening relationship between McCarthy and Mountford during the Arnhem Land Expedition, McCarthy must have fought hard to collect and keep an ethnographic collection for the Australian Museum, and he must have known that sending it first to the South Australian Museum may have resulted in his collection becoming assimilated. Nevertheless from 1949 to 1953, the majority of the ethnographic collection remained at the South Australian Museum while Charles Mountford, as honorary associate in ethnology, was said to be conducting research. It is important to note that Mountford never made an inventory of the Arnhem Land Expedition collections and subsequently they became confused with other artifacts he collected for the museum on different occasions, such as his visits to Oenpelli in 1949, Yirrkala in 1952, and Melville Island in 1954 (McCarthy, June 23, 1954).

Seven years after the Arnhem Land Expedition McCarthy took it upon himself to write to the director of the Australian Museum, Dr. J. W. Evans, encouraging him to alert the government of Australia to the whereabouts of the Arnhem Land Expedition collections they legally owned, stating, "I do not know what arrangements were made between the Commonwealth Government of Australia and the Smithsonian Institution in regard to the disposal of these collections, and it appears to me to be a matter for decision between them rather than for Mr. Mountford" (February 9, 1955). McCarthy outlined the current location of the ethnographic collections to Dr. Evans who, in turn, passed it on to staff at the Department of the Interior. After informing them that the main portion of the collection was still at the South Australian Museum, Evans went on to say, "In view of the fact that the Commonwealth

Government of Australia contributed substantially to the financing of this expedition, I consider it advisable to make . . . inquiries from your department, as the matter appears to me to be one for decision by your Government rather than personally by the leader of the Expedition" (February 11, 1955). McCarthy had deliberately and successfully started the process whereby the Arnhem Land Expedition ethnographic collection would be separated and distributed around the world. His motivation was almost certainly to upset Charles Mountford and his work at the South Australian Museum, perhaps revenge for some scathing comments by Mountford on McCarthy's research during the expedition (May 2000: 208–10). The deteriorating relationship between McCarthy and Mountford had a direct impact upon the distribution of the collection.

Earlier in this book I discussed the awkward relationship between Fred McCarthy and Charles Mountford during the expedition, but their relationship grew even more strained during the publication of the *Records of the American-Australian Scientific Expedition to Arnhem Land* throughout the 1950s. These arguments are best understood from their own words and the following quotes highlight the nature of, and some of the reasons for, this hostility. In a letter to Dr. Evans, McCarthy (October 1957) outlined some reasons for Mountford's hostility to him. He states:

There are several reasons for Mountford's hostility, as follow:

1. My refusal to grant him co-authorship of several papers . . . because I had done all of the work and he was not entitled in any way to joint authorship.
2. My analysis of Oenpelli cave painting sequences which he had failed to detect—he was extremely jealous of the work I did on cave paintings during the Expedition and has been critical of its results ever since.
3. The taking over from him of the Expedition's collection of bark paintings, after the late Professor Nadel had asked me for information about this collection and other material held by Mountford from the Expedition.

McCarthy made it clear that he had little respect for the quality of Mountford's research, stating, "The claims made by Mountford are completely unfounded and incorrect, they are in fact downright unscientific. They demonstrate either a lack of understanding of the true value of records of superimposition in cave paintings, or a deliberate refusal to do so" (January 18,

1956). In return, Mountford wrote letters to important people claiming that McCarthy's work was of a poor standard. For example, to the director of the United States National Museum[2] (Smithsonian Institution), he wrote, "I am sorry to say that, due to my refusal to accept some very poor work from Mc-Carthy . . . vol. II will follow Ray Specht's work Vol. III" (Mountford, March 16, 1957). The director immediately passed Mountford's letter to Frank Setzler who, in turn, passed the information back to McCarthy, along with the following comments:

> I'm sure we never realized the type of individual nor the uncanny methods such a person would use to promote his own ego. After all, you were the only one of the Australian group that he could not completely dominate. Unfortunately, he created a spell over Dr. Wetmore, who thinks he can do no wrong; moreover, N.G.S. [National Geographic Society] does not want to interfere in another country's affairs. (Setzler to McCarthy June 26, 1957)

McCarthy was outraged and produced a long and angry letter to Dr. Evans, the director of the Australian Museum, asking him to make an official complaint to the government of Australia. He stated:

> It is obvious that Mountford's statement to the US National Museum about my "very poor work" is for the purpose of discrediting me as his excuse for changing the order of publication of volumes II and III of the expedition reports. . . . In this correspondence he has consistently exceeded his editorial rights by using every possible opportunity to disparage my work. (McCarthy, July 10, 1957)

Dr. Evans supported McCarthy by writing to the Australian government including the statement, "The reasons for Mountford's disparaging remarks are well-known to me and do him no credit" (August 15, 1957).

Mountford must have been infuriated at McCarthy's attempts to have the Arnhem Land Expedition ethnographic collection removed from the South Australian Museum. Along with his letters to the Department of the Interior, McCarthy also wrote (via Australian Museum director Evans) to Dr. E. H. Hipsley, director of the Australian Institute of Anatomy, and Professor George H. Nadel of the Australian National University. He encouraged them to make enquiries and to try to add to their own collections from the 1948 collections (McCarthy, June 23, 1954). They seized the opportunity and began corresponding with the director of the South Australian Museum, Dr. Herbert Hale, asking for Arnhem Land Expedition artifacts to be sent (Hipsley, June 28, 1954).

No action was taken until Charles Mountford returned from fieldwork on Melville Island in 1954, but from October 1954 to March 1955, some of the Arnhem Land Expedition ethnographic collection was transferred to the Australian Institute of Anatomy (see table 8.1). Of the 676 ethnographic artifacts (the total collected minus the Australian Museum and the Smithsonian Institutions portion), 420 were transferred to the Australian Institute of Anatomy including 275 paintings (Meeting Minutes March 24, 1955). If these numbers do not seem to add up, you are correct. Fred McCarthy also wondered what happened to the rest of the ethnographic collection, stating to Dr. Evans, "There are several hundreds of wood carvings, sacred objects, etc., illustrated in vol. 1 of the Expedition Records by Charles Mountford that were concealed by him during the course of the expedition, and were not submitted for the sharing of the anthropological collection between the Australian Museum, U.S. National Museum, and the Commonwealth Government" (October 1957).

The artifacts held by the Australian Institute of Anatomy were transferred to the National Museum of Australia in 1984 where they remain today. The

Table 8.1. Ethnographic Artifacts Transferred from the South Australian Museum to the Australian Institute of Anatomy in December 1954 (based on information in "List Accompanying Notes of Meeting," March 24, 1955, in possession of the National Museum of Australia, Australian Institute of Anatomy File, Canberra)

Type of Artefact	Number	Type of Artefact	Number
Bark paintings	171	Bone knives	2
Paper paintings	104	Gum cement	2
Spears (or spear shafts, heads)	64	Model boats	2
Spear throwers	23	Shoulder bands	2
Arm bands	21	Woven bags (filled with fiber)	2
Woven baskets	10	Axes	1
Ceremonial posts	7	Bark amulets	1
Decorated paddles	7	Bark bundles	1
Carved figures	6	Bone containers	1
Decorated sticks	6	Bows	1
Sacred wooden objects	6	Conch trumpets	1
String bags	6	Decorated drum	1
Ceremonial boards	5	Decorated shells	1
Clubs	5	Decorated tablets	1
Ceremonial ornaments	4	Didgeridoos	1
String ornaments	4	Palm leaf baskets	1
Tobacco pipes	3	Shuttle	1
Bark baskets	2	Wire pins (set in wax)	1

409 ethnographic artifacts obtained by the United States National Museum are today stored at the National Museum of Natural History (Smithsonian Institution) in Washington, D.C. They also hold nearly all the human skeletal remains acquired during the Arnhem Land Expedition. As part of their large archaeological collection, the Australian Museum holds approximately 569 ethnographic objects and a collection of string figures, now mounted on cardboard, from the Arnhem Land Expedition. They also hold human skeletal remains and in 1975 repatriated an important ceremonial object back to Oenpelli (today also referred to as Gunbalanya, Kunbarlanja, or Kunbarllanjnja) in western Arnhem Land.

While for the majority of the ethnographic, archaeological, and physical anthropological collections, this marks the end of the story, the paintings on bark and paper are an exception. These artworks received special attention during the 1950s, were all but forgotten for decades, and have reemerged in recent years as items of pride and significance for their cultural institutions. Their stories need to be explored in further detail.

No inventory of the paintings or, as mentioned previously, any of the ethnographic materials was made by Charles Mountford during or after the Arnhem Land Expedition. My research has identified that at least 484 paintings on bark and 115 paintings on paper were collected, but others are certain to have made their way into private collections. Table 8.2 shows the distribution of the painting collection in 1955.

It was not clear to any of the collectors prior to the Arnhem Land Expedition how the paintings would be distributed. Promises had been made regarding representative samples being supplied to the major institutions (the Smithsonian Institution and the Australian Museum), yet no firm agreement existed.

Table 8.2. Arnhem Land Expedition Paintings on Bark and Paper Held by Different Institutions in 1955

Institution	Number of Paintings (Bark)	Number of Paintings) (Paper)
South Australian Museum	114*	11*
Australian Institute of Anatomy	171	104
Australian Museum	109	0
Smithsonian Institution	90	0
Total	**484**	**115**

*No institutional data available (compiled from external sources).

The paintings collected by Fred McCarthy, and those allocated to Frank Setzler, were delivered directly to the Australian Museum after the Arnhem Land Expedition and soon after forwarded to the Smithsonian Institution (see table 8.2). The remainder was stored at the South Australian Museum until 1955 when McCarthy reminded the Australian government that they owned them and should claim them back. In May 1955, the director of the Australian Institute of Anatomy wrote, "We have recently brought to Canberra from the South Australian Museum the Commonwealth's share of bark and paper paintings. These number 275, made up of 171 bark paintings and 104 paper paintings mounted on cardboard" (Murphy, May 23, 1955).

The most important factor in the distribution of the bark paintings as well as the paintings on paper was the outcome of a meeting held on March 24, 1955, at the office of Kevin Murphy, director of the News and Information Bureau. Charles Mountford and Dr. E. H. Hipsley of the Australian Institute of Anatomy were also in attendance at this meeting when it was decided that:

1. Each of the six Australian States would receive 12 bark paintings and 12 paper paintings.
2. The South Australian Museum would receive 20 bark paintings and 10 paper paintings.
3. The Commonwealth Government of Australia (to be held in Trust by the Australian Institute of Anatomy) would keep 79 bark paintings and 23 paper paintings. It was intended that 50 would be permanently held while 52 would be made available for gift or exchange to overseas countries and museums at the discretion of the Minister of the Interior (Meeting Minutes March 24, 1955).

In a letter to the director of the Australian Museum two months after this meeting, Kevin Murphy stated, "I have received strong representations from the Conference of Interstate Art Gallery Directors for a share of these paintings and have offered the conference 144 of them (72 bark and 72 paper) for distribution among the six capital city art galleries" (May 23, 1955).

In lieu of this decision, a meeting was held in August 1956 at the Queensland Art Gallery to decide which paintings each gallery would receive (Neale 1998: 210). The decision to give these paintings to art galleries in preference to museums was unusual for its time. In the case of the Queensland Art

Gallery, this was one of the first instances of Australian Aboriginal art being accepted for aesthetic rather than ethnographic qualities (Jones 1987; Morphy 1987, 1991; Neale 1998: 210; Taylor 1988). Before World War II, few Australian Aboriginal paintings were held in art galleries in Australia but rather were restricted to ethnographic collections of museums of natural history (Morphy 1991: 22).

Clearly the collection and distribution of paintings was different to other ethnographic objects acquired during the Arnhem Land Expedition. Today the following ten institutions hold and display paintings from this expedition and, yet, mystery still surrounds them:

1. The Art Gallery of New South Wales
2. The Art Gallery of South Australia
3. The Art Gallery of Western Australia
4. The Australian Museum
5. The National Gallery of Victoria
6. The National Museum of Australia
7. The National Museum of Natural History, Smithsonian Institution
8. The Queensland Art Gallery
9. The South Australian Museum
10. The Tasmanian Museum and Art Gallery

The lack of contextual information recorded by the collectors is the major source of this mystery and the term "bastard barks" was coined by Margo Neale (1998) to reflect this issue. In chapter 10 "A Series Most Promising," I delve into the nature of the painting collection and the significant role it played in the promotion of Aboriginal paintings as art rather than ethnographic object.

The ethnographic collection acquired during the Arnhem Land Expedition includes 2,144 known individual artifacts. There are some artifacts, however, that we know were collected but are no longer at their home institutions, as shown in table 8.3.

Officially, only one artifact was given to another institution following the official distribution of ethnographic material. The Australian Museum gave a basket (catalog number E52808) collected from Milingimbi Island to Dartmouth College (object number 51.8.12669). No artifacts were officially sold or

Table 8.3. Arnhem Land Expedition Artifacts Known to be Missing from Their Home Institution

Home Institution	Number	Type of Artifact	Notes	Origin
Australian Museum	E53175	Bark painting	Observed missing March 12, 1990	Oenpelli
South Australian Museum	A47646	Bark painting	Not located for this research	Yirrkala
South Australian Museum	A47702	Bark painting	Not located for this research	Yirrkala
South Australian Museum	A47753	Bark painting	Not located for this research	Oenpelli
South Australian Museum	A47775	Bark painting	Not located for this research	Oenpelli
South Australian Museum	A47686	Bark painting	Not located for this research	Yirrkala
South Australian Museum	A47619	Bark painting	Not received	Unknown
South Australian Museum	A47621	Bark painting	Not received	Unknown
South Australian Museum	A47625	Bark painting	Not received July 1, 1955	Unknown
South Australian Museum	A47645	Bark painting	Not received	Unknown
South Australian Museum	A47661	Bark painting	Not received	Unknown
South Australian Museum	A47682	Bark painting	Not received	Unknown
South Australian Museum	A47685	Bark painting	Not received	Unknown
South Australian Museum	A47703	Bark painting	Not received	Unknown
South Australian Museum	A47707	Bark painting	Not received	Unknown
South Australian Museum	A47709	Bark painting	Not received	Unknown
South Australian Museum	A47754	Bark painting	Lost or never received	Oenpelli
South Australian Museum	A47601	Carved wooden figure	Not received July 1, 1953	Yirrkala
South Australian Museum	A47606	Painted bark coffin	Not received July 1, 1955	Yirrkala
South Australian Museum	A47632	Painted wooden paddle	Not received July 1, 1955	Yirrkala
South Australian Museum	A47634	Carved and painted human figure	Not received July 1, 1955	Yirrkala
South Australian Museum	A47641	Wax figure	Not received July 1, 1955	Yirrkala
South Australian Museum	A47650	Carved and painted wooden figure	Not received July 1, 1955	Yirrkala
South Australian Museum	A47652	Carved and painted wooden figure	Not received July 1, 1955	Yirrkala
South Australian Museum	A47658	Carved and painted wooden paddle	Not received July 1, 1955	Yirrkala
South Australian Museum	A47659	Wooden message-stick	Not received July 1, 1955	Yirrkala
South Australian Museum	A47668	Carved and painted wooden paddle	Not received July 1, 1955	Yirrkala
South Australian Museum	A47669	Carved and painted wooden paddle	Not received July 1, 1955	Yirrkala
South Australian Museum	A47676	Decorated wooden pipe	Not received July 1, 1955	Yirrkala
South Australian Museum	A47677	Decorated wooden pipe	Not received July 1, 1955	Yirrkala
South Australian Museum	A47688	Painted wooden human figure	Not received July 1, 1955	Yirrkala
South Australian Museum	A47690	Painted wooden human figure	Not received July 1, 1955	Yirrkala
South Australian Museum	A47696	Painted wooden paddle	Not received July 1, 1955	Yirrkala

given to institutions not involved with the expedition. The obvious exception to this is the collection of bark and paper paintings that, as described above, was divided up among numerous art galleries around Australia as a gift from the government. Yet unofficially, Charles Mountford may have been selling and was most certainly giving away artifacts from the Arnhem Land Expedition ethnographic collection. There is no evidence to suggest that the ethnologist had permission from the Commonwealth of Australia to sell or give away the artifacts. Not having a catalog of the collection has made tracking unofficial movements of artifacts extremely difficult, and we will never know exactly how much of material was disposed of by Charles Mountford.

An entry in Fred McCarthy's field diary gives further insights into Charles Mountford's activities. McCarthy, referring to an earlier conversation with Mountford and Frank Setzler about the distribution of the collection, states that "Setzler is disappointed about it. The archaeological material goes to Sydney and Washington. The whole split should be Sydney and Washington. Selling of such a collection could have serious repercussions on Mountford and it is an unusual procedure" (McCarthy, March 18, 1948). There is evidence that Mountford was trading ethnographic artifacts to institutions or individuals overseas. This evidence comes in the form of a letter from Mountford to Rene d'Harnoncourt, director of the Museum of Modern Art in New York: "I am pleased to know that the bark painting has reached you at last. As you are probably aware, these things have to be sneaked out of Australia. It is hard to get official permission, but I had not forgotten my promise to you" (December 4, 1951: 135).

Further evidence of Mountford's unofficial and unorthodox distribution of the Arnhem Land Expedition artifacts can be found in the collection held by the Art Gallery of South Australia. There are sixty-two ethnographic artifacts from this expedition held in the gallery. The Australian government officially gave twelve bark and twelve paper paintings to this gallery in 1956, and today twenty-five bark paintings and twelve paintings on paper are recorded as being given to this gallery by the government. Ignoring the fact that thirteen more bark paintings were donated to this institution than were promised, there are still twenty-five ethnographic artifacts and one painted skull that made their way into the Art Gallery of South Australia as a result of Mountford's actions (see table 8.4). One important example is a bark painting (O.1913) by an artist recorded as "Mungaraui" and collected from Yirrkala in

Table 8.4. Arnhem Land Expedition Artifacts in the Art Gallery of South Australia that were not Part of the Official Gift from the Commonwealth Government in 1956

Donor	Number	Type of Artifact	Notes	Origin
Mountford	O.1913	Bark painting	Purchased for 11 pounds	Yirrkala
Mountford	O.1969	Bark painting	Gift of Charles Mountford	Unknown
Mountford	O.1914	Bark painting	Purchased for 11 pounds	Yirrkala
Mountford	O.1916	Bark painting	Gift of Charles Mountford	Groote Eylandt
Mountford	O.1917	Bark painting	Gift of Charles Mountford 1960	Groote Eylandt
Mountford	O.1918	Bark painting	Gift of Charles Mountford 1960	Groote Eylandt
Mountford	O.1919	Bark painting	Gift of Charles Mountford 1960	Yirrkala
Mountford	O.1855	Bark painting	Gift of Charles Mountford	Yirrkala
Mountford	O.1856	Bark painting	Gift of Charles Mountford	Yirrkala
Mountford	O.1857	Bark painting	Gift of Charles Mountford	Yirrkala
Mountford	O.1858	Bark painting	Gift of Charles Mountford, bark is of unknown origin	Unknown
Mountford	S.124	Carved wooden figure	Gift of Charles Mountford August 1957	Yirrkala
Mountford	S.125	Carved wooden figure	Gift of Charles Mountford August 1957	Yirrkala

Mountford	S.126	Carved wooden figure	Gift of Charles Mountford August 1957	Yirrkala
Mountford	A.642	Painted paddle	Gift of Charles Mountford August 1957	Yirrkala
Mountford	A.643	Carved wooden figure	Gift of Charles Mountford August 1957	Yirrkala
Mountford	A.644	Carved wooden pipe or musical instrument	Gift of Charles Mountford August 1957	Yirrkala
Mountford	S.119	Carved and painted wooden figure	Gift of Charles Mountford February 1955	Yirrkala
Mountford	S.120	Carved and painted wooden figure	Gift of Charles Mountford August 1957 or February 1955	Yirrkala
Mountford	S.123	Carved and painted wooden figure	Gift of Charles Mountford August 1957 or February 1955	Yirrkala
Mountford	O.1763	Bark painting	Gift of Charles Mountford	Oenpelli
Mountford	O.1764	Bark painting	Gift of Charles Mountford	Oenpelli
Mountford	O.1765	Bark painting	Gift of Charles Mountford	Yirrkala
Mountford	O.1760	Bark painting	Gift of Charles Mountford	Yirrkala
Mountford	O.1767	Bark painting	Gift of Charles Mountford	Yirrkala
Mountford	O.1768	Bark painting	Gift of Charles Mountford	Oenpelli

1948. This painting is recorded as being sold by Mountford to the Art Gallery of South Australia in 1960 for 11 pounds. Another painting in this collection (O.1762) by Groote Eylandt artist Minimini Numalkiyiya Mamarika is said to have been purchased with a grant from the South Australian government in 1957.

The only artifact recorded to have been stolen was a basket (catalog number E52802) that was on loan from the Australian Museum to the Commonwealth Department of Trade in 1966. Alongside of this, only one artifact is known to have been significantly damaged. A carved wooden pipe (catalog number A644) that was collected from Yirrkala in 1948 was being held by the Art Gallery of South Australia when it was damaged (possibly shown in Mountford 1956: 468, Pl. 65A, B).

Some of the ethnographic artifacts are today classified as secret or sacred. Currently fourteen bark paintings have been classified as not being suitable for public viewing by their Aboriginal traditional owners, and one aforementioned sacred artifact was returned to its Aboriginal traditional owners in 1975. Most of these measures have been undertaken by the Australian Museum; however, it is also known that the National Museum of Australia and the Art Gallery of New South Wales have investigated this aspect of their collections:

> Americans will see some of the results of the scientists' work exhibited in the U.S. National Museum at Washington next year. But members of the expedition know of no move to let the Australian public see Australia's share of the collection before it goes—piecemeal—to Australian museums. Why? Surely the Arnhem Land collection is of national interest and as many people as possible should have a chance to see all of it together. (*Daily Telegraph*, December 11, 1948: 13)

As illustrated by this *Daily Telegraph* newspaper article, the Australian public felt a sense of ownership over the Arnhem Land Expedition collections. The last time the ethnographic collection was together, it was boxed in a shed in Darwin awaiting transport to Adelaide and Sydney. There is, however, another side to this story. If the collection had not been distributed, far fewer people would have had the opportunity to view these artifacts and artworks. The unique nature of the expedition, with Commonwealth government backing, led to questions of ownership that continue through to today. However one looks at the collection, it has had wide-ranging impact from 1948 to the present. It is clear that the ethnographic collection, and even its distribution, encodes cultural and social information relating to the artists and their communities, the nature of museums and galleries, the personality and the desires of the collectors, the relationships that developed among the protagonists, and attitudes toward the producers of the objects.

NOTES

1. The archaeological collection also includes a number of stone artifacts; these are the nonexcavated stone artifacts.

2. The U.S. National Museum is now the National Museum of Natural History and both are part of the Smithsonian Institution. Throughout this chapter I will refer to them as the Smithsonian Institution.

9

Reflections on an Ethnographic Collection

The path taken by the Arnhem Land Expedition ethnographic artifacts has proven to be complex and, sometimes, difficult to trace. The reasons for these complexities are interwoven with human responses to other cultures and the institutions that have developed to preserve and present cultures. From an investigation into the historical events surrounding the Arnhem Land Expedition, two factors have appeared above all others in determining the nature of ethnographic collections. The first is the collectors, their selections and divisions of the artifacts and their links to different cultural institutions. The second is the nature of the cultural institution—art gallery or museum. These two factors, as well as the nature of the ethnographic collection itself, are central to the discussions in this chapter.

As Susan Pearce suggests, "Objects . . . have the power, in some sense, to carry the past into the present by virtue of their 'real' relationship to past events" (1992: 24). The ultimate aim of analyzing collections of material culture is to better understand human behavior that is both reflected by, and results in, the artifacts they contain (Fenton 1974). Most archaeologists today would not excavate a site without documenting their methodology. This may involve keeping a diary of why excavation took place in one area and not another, recording the levels excavated, from which levels the material derives, and so forth. All of these factors influence the nature of a collection and assist archaeologists in developing interpretations. It also allows other contemporary or future researchers to evaluate the methods used to reach these conclusions and judge whether the conclusions are valid. By better understanding processes involved in the acquiring of an ethnographic collection, researchers can make more reliable inferences about the cultures that produced them, the cultures that collected them, and interactions between the two parties.

Archaeologists often find themselves consulting institutional collections to make inferences about cultural groups. Two reasons for this may be that they offer the opportunity to analyze a large number of artifacts with definite connections to each other (provenance and so forth), and to view material that may not be produced in cultures today, or that may be produced differently or that may have different uses than those of the past. Archaeologists also study collections because they represent an easily accessible data store from which to obtain evidence for human behavior. While traditionally these collections may have been analyzed to make inferences about the producer's culture, more recently they have also been used for an insight into the collector's culture (Coates 1989). An analysis of an institutional collection, as well as highlighting the collector's society, can assist in better understanding the role of artifacts in the producers' culture prior to their collection and to understanding biases and the cross-cultural experiences taking place at the time and how these influenced the collecting process.

This book concentrates on the ethnographic collection formed during the Arnhem Land Expedition. The basic principles used by the expedition members to separate archaeological and ethnological artifacts are (1) collecting from archaeological deposits and (2) collecting artifacts made or used by people at the present time. It is important to note that very few objects from the ethnographic collection show any sign of use and, as such, this collection could be more accurately defined as objects or artifacts manufactured during the expedition for the purpose of trade. If ethnography is the study of contemporary cultures through firsthand observations, then ethnographic artifacts are those items collected from these people (Renfrew and Bahn 1996: 540). Here, I have deliberately retained the separations among archaeology, anthropology, and ethnography made by the collectors in the field. After all, even the simple decision to separate archaeological and ethnographic artifacts tells us something of the collector's culture.

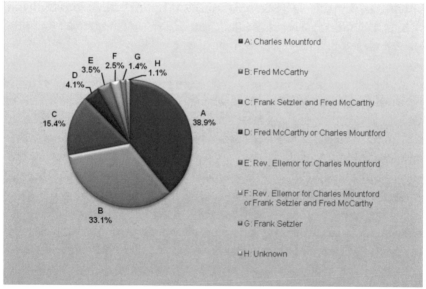

A: Charles Mountford

B: Fred McCarthy

C: Frank Setzler and Fred McCarthy

D: Fred McCarthy or Charles Mountford

E: Rev. Ellemor for Charles Mountford

F: Rev. Ellemor for Charles Mountford or Frank Setzler and Fred McCarthy

G: Frank Setzler

H: Unknown

FIGURE 9.1
Collectors of ethnographic artifacts during the Arnhem Land Expedition.

It is, of course, a given that whatever is collected is particularly significant to the individual collector. Obviously, his collection is bound to reflect certain aspects of his own personality, his taste, his sophistication or naiveté; his independence of choice or his reliance on the judgment of others. (Muensterberger 1994: 4)

Three men are known to be responsible for most of the 2,144 ethnographic artifacts collected during the Arnhem Land Expedition: Charles Mountford, Fred McCarthy, and Frank Setzler (see figure 9.1). The resulting collections were formed by their choices, their decision to divide collections, and their ties to particular cultural institutions. The questions to consider are what are the biases of the individual collectors in terms of type, number, and provenance of artifacts and how have these influenced the composition of the different institutional collections stemming from the Arnhem Land Expedition?

CHARLES MOUNTFORD

As leader of the Arnhem Land Expedition Charles Mountford had considerable responsibilities, yet, during the eight months in the field, he personally acquired nearly 1,000 ethnographic artifacts that today are an important part of museum and art gallery collections. But what exactly was it that Mountford wanted to, and did, collect? And what does this tell us about his attitude toward the Aboriginal cultures from which he was collecting?

Bark paintings, figurines, and paintings on paper represent 59.2 percent of all artifacts collected by Mountford during the Arnhem Land Expedition (see table 9.1).[1] The primary link between these three types is that they are "artistic." Sutton (1988: 3) has stated that some critics view the application of the term "art" to things made by Aboriginal people as an act of cultural colonialism. Morphy (1994: 655) generally agrees stating that the anthropology of art is not the study of objects of other cultures that Europeans have accepted as belonging to their category "art." Likewise, Taçon (1989: 236) acknowledges that various languages spoken across Arnhem Land have no separate term for "art" as most non-Aboriginal societies understand it. Morphy (1994: 655) goes on to state that if the anthropology of art is to make a useful contribu-

Table 9.1. Artifacts Collected by Charles Mountford during the Arnhem Land Expedition

Object Type	Number	Object Type	Number
Bark painting	341	Botanical specimen	3
Figurine	78	Net	3
Paper painting	75	Stick	3
Spear	68	Totem	3
Armlet	39	Necklace	3
Message stick	28	Harpoon	2
Basket	28	Axe	2
Paddle	27	Metal tool	2
Spear thrower	13	Fan	2
Pipe	12	Gum sample	2
Board	10	Worked stone	2
Cordage	8	Garment	2
Coffin	7	Tjuringa	1
Didjeridoo	7	Tassel	1
Plume	6	Sail	1
Bone Tool	6	Pole	1
Digging stick	6	Pigment	1
Belt	5	Painted stone	1
Boomerang	5	Bundle	1
Dancing stick	5	Drum	1
Clap stick	5	Head ring	1
Shell	4	Fire stick	1
Model canoe	4	Cylinder	1
Container	3	Mat	1
Club	3		

tion, then it must allow for the analysis of objects from other cultures on their own terms while also helping to identify categories of objects in other cultures that overlap with European categories of art objects. Morphy (1994: 655) does, however, offer the anthropological useful definition of art as "objects having semantic and/or aesthetic properties that are used for presentation or representational purposes." A great deal of the ethnographic objects collected by Charles Mountford fall into this category.

The idea that Mountford was primarily interested in the artistic pursuits of the Aboriginal communities he visited during his career has been discussed earlier in this book. It is important to know that the ethnologist's background was in the recording of art, including rock art, and not in anthropology. In contrast to the beliefs of many anthropologists in 1948, Mountford believed that artistic expression in Aboriginal cultures could be studied separately from social organization and, as Neale (1998: 210) has argued, Mountford was collecting bark paintings as art rather than artifact during a time when Aboriginal art was seen to fit more readily within anthropology. McCarthy's suggestion that Mountford "[was] not really concerned whether we [got] a collection or not so long as he [got] a private collection of bark paintings" (August 8, 1948) is evident in that this artifact type alone represents 40.9 percent of all the ethnographic material he collected. In short, Mountford was collecting in line with his own research interests (art) and plans.

From the first base camp (Groote Eylandt) Mountford collected 108 bark paintings and 47 spears plus other smaller groupings of ethnographic objects. At Yirrkala he collected 103 bark paintings and 74 figurines and, at the final base camp, he collected 117 bark paintings and 34 paintings on paper. Other artifacts were collected but in considerably smaller numbers than the aforementioned (see table 9.1). These figures suggest that Mountford, like McCarthy, was specializing with his collecting—focusing on acquiring a large number of a particular type of artifact from each base camp rather than a representative sample of the communities' material culture. The types of artifacts collected also suggest variations to his plan. One example of this is his collection of seventy-four figurines from Yirrkala. Only four more figurines were collected from other locations during the expedition. On Groote Eylandt his interest appears to have been in spears and, as with the figurines, a significantly smaller number were collected at the other locations. It could even be suggested that at Oenpelli his focus was on paintings on paper, but this was

Table 9.2.   Ethnographic Artifacts Collected from Groote Eylandt by Charles Mountford
during the Arnhem Land Expedition

Object Type	Number	Object Type	Number
Bark painting	108	Harpoon	2
Spear	47	Container	1
Armlet	16	Bundle	1
Spear thrower	11	Basket	1
Paddle	6	Club	1
Digging stick	6	Message stick	1
Dancing stick	5	Worked stone	1
Belt	5	Necklace	1
Board	5	Painted stone	1
Plume	4	Paper painting	1
Cordage	4	Pigment	1
Model canoe	3	Pipe	1
Figurine	3	Pole	1
Botanical specimen	3	Sail	1
Clap stick	3	Shell	1
Totem	3	Tassel	1
Garment	2	Head ring	1
Didjeridoo	2		

also because of a scarcity of local bark supplies. These artifacts were, of course, of secondary interest compared with bark paintings, which were collected from all camps and in very large numbers (see tables 9.2, 9.3, and 9.4). This implies that Mountford considered widespread Arnhem Land representation important for bark paintings. This differentiation in types of artifacts collected by location cannot, however, be assigned to collection strategies alone.

Table 9.3.   Ethnographic Artifacts Collected from Yirrkala by Charles Mountford during
the Arnhem Land Expedition

Object Type	Number	Object Type	Number
Bark painting	103	Clap stick	2
Figurine	74	Container	2
Paper Painting	26	Gum sample	2
Message stick	26	Metal tool	2
Paddle	21	Stick	2
Spear	15	Didjeridoo	1
Armlet	15	Cylinder	1
Pipe	11	Tjuringa	1
Coffin	7	Model canoe	1
Basket	5	Plume	1
Bone tool	5	Shell	1
Cordage	4	Spear thrower	1
Boomerang	2	Fire stick	1

Table 9.4.   Ethnographic Artifacts Collected from Oenpelli by Charles Mountford during the Arnhem Land Expedition

Object Type	Number	Object Type	Number
Bark painting	117	Didjeridoo	2
Paper painting	34	Club	2
Basket	22	Stick	1
Spear	6	Spear thrower	1
Board	5	Mat	1
Net	3	Drum	1
Necklace	2	Armlet	1
Fan	2		

The influence of local traditions in the production of artifacts was certainly an important aspect.

Mountford's overall contribution to institutional collections is featured in figure 9.2, which highlights the total number of Arnhem Land Expedition artifacts held by each institution and the percentage of these collected by Mountford. From this information, it can be interpreted that the biases behind the collecting of Charles Mountford influenced the composition of ten institutional collections, including both art galleries and museums. This influence is most obvious in the South Australian Museum where Mountford

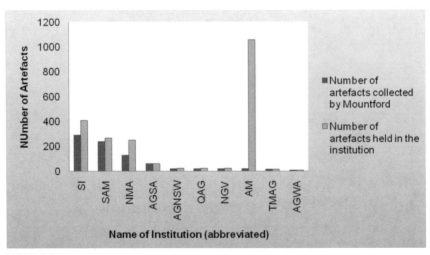

FIGURE 9.2
The distribution of artifacts collected by Charles Mountford during the Arnhem Land Expedition.

collected nearly 90 percent of the artifacts the museum received from the Arnhem Land Expedition. In turn, bark paintings comprise 38.4 percent of the
103 artifacts in this institution and another 62 artifacts (23.1 percent) are figurine, all reflecting the collector's interests. The majority of South Australian
Museum's artifacts from this expedition was collected from Yirrkala, and consists mainly of figurines. In contrast, the Oenpelli base camp is represented
primarily by bark paintings.

Groote Eylandt paintings are significantly underrepresented in the South
Australian Museum compared with material from the other base camps.
This is discussed in some depth in chapter 10, "A Series Most Promising" (see
also figure 9.3). The lack of artifacts from Groote Eylandt was the result of
decisions made by Mountford and it is possible that Groote Eylandt was not
an area of great research interest for him. Likewise, the museum may have
considered that its collection from this island (such as collections formed by
Norman Tindale) were large enough. Another possibility is that the decision
to pass on artifacts from Groote Eylandt was simply a practical matter as in
whether there was access to these artifacts when the material had to be
moved.

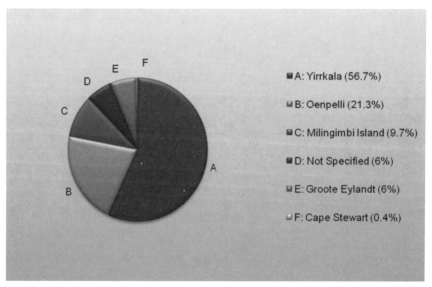

FIGURE 9.3
Origin of the of South Australian Museum's Arnhem Land Expedition artifacts.

Mountford collected over 70 percent of the Smithsonian Institution's Arnhem Land Expedition collection. Interestingly, most of his collection of spears from Groote Eylandt is held by this institution today. This is the only institution for which bark paintings are not the primary artifact, yet the difference in numbers between spears and bark paintings is only one (see table 9.5). The collection of spears may reflect Mountford's lack of personal interest in this type of artifact and may further reflect his desire to keep other artifacts (such as art) for research. Furthermore, as the decision regarding distribution was made in the field, some influence may lie with their representative (Frank Setzler) and the institution itself. This will be explored later in this chapter.

Mountford's influence is less obvious at the National Museum of Australia (the collection previously owned by the Australian Institute of Anatomy) where only 51.6 percent of their Arnhem Land Expedition artifacts are from Mountford's collection. Once again, bark paintings (82 specimens) predominate (for further information see table 9.6). Nearly half of these paintings were acquired from Groote Eylandt. As mentioned earlier, this bias toward Groote Eylandt was a direct result of Mountford's decision to not send these specimens to the South Australian Museum.

Table 9.5.   Arnhem Land Expedition Artifacts Held in the Smithsonian Institution

Object Type	Number	Object Type	Number
Spear	91	Necklace	4
Bark painting	90	Club	3
Armlet	43	Shell	3
Basket	31	Model canoe	2
Message stick	15	Stick	2
Cordage	14	Gum sample	2
Figurine	12	Harpoon	2
Worked stone	10	Pipe	2
Spear thrower	9	Net	2
Digging stick	7	Sail	1
Plume	7	Pigment	1
Paddle	6	Painted stone	1
Boomerang	5	Fire stick	1
Didjeridoo	5	Metal tool	1
Clap stick	5	Fan	1
Bone tool	5	Coffin	1
Container	4	Mat	1
Botanical specimen	4	Head ring	1
Garment	4	Cylinder	1
Belt	4	Drum	1
Totem	4	Bundle	1

Table 9.6.   Arnhem Land Expedition Artifacts Held in the National Museum of Australia

Object Type	Number	Object Type	Number
Bark painting	82	Pipe	4
Spear	30	Bone tool	2
Armlet	27	Message stick	2
Spear thrower	26	Container	1
Paper painting	18	Coffin	1
Basket	15	Club	1
Board	12	Worked stone	1
Paddle	8	Model canoe	1
Figurine	6	Shell	1
Pole	5	Totem	1
Dancing stick	5	Dijderidoo	1

Also worthy of note is Mountford's influence on the Art Gallery of South Australia's collection. Today the gallery houses sixty-two ethnographic artifacts from the Arnhem Land Expedition, 98.4 percent of them collected by Mountford. This number includes forty-one bark paintings (see figure 9.4). Over 50 percent of the artifacts from this expedition held in this institution were collected from Yirrkala. Mountford's influence on this

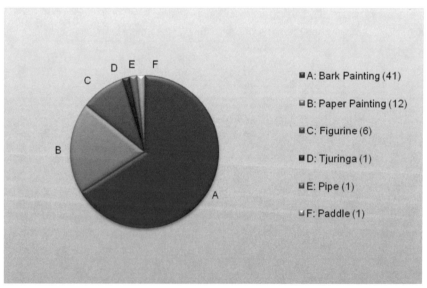

FIGURE 9.4
Arnhem Land Expedition artifacts held by the Art Gallery of South Australia.

gallery's collection is more obvious due to the unofficial transfer of Arnhem Land Expedition artifacts by Mountford, as discussed in the previous chapter.

Mountford's influence on the collections from the Arnhem Land Expedition is reflected in his biases and decisions that have informed ten institutional collections, museums and art galleries among them. The lack of artifacts collected by Mountford in the Australian Museum is worthy of note and will perhaps be more clearly understood following a discussion of McCarthy's collecting and distribution. Even though the Smithsonian Institution had a representative on the Arnhem Land Expedition, their collection is still primary the result of Charles Mountford's work. The result of this is a collection dominated by artifacts desired by the leader for his personal research interests with the dominance of spears being the only real exception.

FREDERICK "FRED" MCCARTHY

Fred McCarthy, the first museum curator in Australia to be trained in social anthropology, was the Australian Museum's representative on the Arnhem Land Expedition (Sutton 1988: 159). The collection strategies employed by Mountford and McCarthy during the expedition were significantly different and this is embodied in the resulting collections. First, Mountford came from a background outside of the anthropological establishment and appears not to have been interested in collecting a representative sample of Australian Aboriginal material culture. Instead he desired a collection of "artistic" artifacts. McCarthy, on the other hand, disagreed with Mountford's research aims and tried hard to keep well away from his focus areas (such as figurines). McCarthy's collection of "artistic" objects is limited and his range of material culture is much greater. While McCarthy came to Arnhem Land with the aim of filling gaps in the existing collections of material culture at the Australian Museum, he also desired to collect and record those objects that the expedition members observed being made and used (Jones 1987: 12).

So, what was McCarthy collecting? Table 9.7 shows that McCarthy's collection was smaller than Mountford's but represents a more diverse range of artifacts. It also represents less concern with what Mountford narrowly defines as art and more with other areas, such as children's toys. His two major collections were string figures (numbering 198) and armlets (numbering 107).

Table 9.7.   Artefacts Collected by Frederick McCarthy during the Arnhem Land Expedition[a]

Object Type	Number	Object Type	Number
String figure	193	Net	6
Armlet	107	Cordage	4
Bark painting	62	Club	4
Spear	56	Pipe	4
Doll	32	Stick	4
Spear thrower	21	Bone tool	3
Bow and/or arrow	16	Clap stick	3
Container	15	Basket	3
Shell	15	Bamboo	3
Pole	12	Gum sample	3
Figurine	11	Indeterminate	2
Digging stick	11	Coffin	2
Belt	10	Button	2
Paddle	10	Metal tool	2
Paint brush	9	Phallocrypt	2
Maraian	8	Worked stone	2
Fan	8	Harpoon	2
Didjeridoo	8	Head ring	1
Propeller	8	Model canoe	1
Board	7	Boomerang	1
Necklace	7	Model hut	1
Girdle	7	Ornament	1
Botanical specimen	6	Toy	1
Fire stick	6	Sail	1
Scraper	6		

[a]This list of artefacts today credited to McCarthy. Museum and art gallery records could be incorrect, and, as such, he may be responsible for other artefacts as well.

Apart from these two specialist collections, there is no obvious bias toward any aspect of the cultures he visited in collecting a range of weapons, tools, toys, musical instruments, containers, and so forth.

Despite his desire to avoid clashing with Mountford's research interest, McCarthy still collected sixty-two bark paintings. This is probably due to Mountford directing (and allowing) McCarthy to collect a limited number for the Australian Museum and, hence, reflects the aims discussed earlier to fill gaps in material culture at this museum. Bark paintings still make up only 8.75 percent of the ethnographic artifacts collected by McCarthy, which is significantly lower than Mountford's 40.2 percent.

Most of McCarthy's ethnographic artifacts come from the three base camps—Groote Eylandt, Yirrkala, and Oenpelli (see figure 9.5). This includes 364 artifacts from Yirrkala (primarily boosted by his collection of 193 string

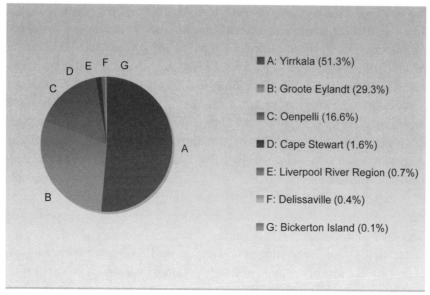

A: Yirrkala (51.3%)

B: Groote Eylandt (29.3%)

C: Oenpelli (16.6%)

D: Cape Stewart (1.6%)

E: Liverpool River Region (0.7%)

F: Delissaville (0.4%)

G: Bickerton Island (0.1%)

FIGURE 9.5
Provenance of artifacts collected by Fred McCarthy during the Arnhem Land Expedition.

figures from this camp). From Groote Eylandt, McCarthy collected 207 ethnographic artifacts including large numbers of spears and armlets. Likewise, this high percentage (as compared with the other base camps) may be the result of transportation or storage problems later in the expedition. Alternatively, the collectors may have simply considered the collection of spears from Groote Eylandt as sufficient for their research and found it unnecessary to collect large numbers from the other locations. From Oenpelli, McCarthy collected 118 ethnographic artifacts with bark paintings and spears dominating, and the number of armlets he collected significantly decreased at the final base camp: only five were acquired from this location, while forty-nine were collected from Groote Eylandt and fifty-two from Yirrkala.

The Australian Museum received most of the artifacts collected by their representative. Interestingly, Mountford collected only a tiny 1.9 percent of the artifacts held in the Australian Museum. This small number may be due to the poor relationship between the expedition leader and McCarthy. In other words, Mountford most likely refused to allocate many of his collected artifacts to the Australian Museum due to his dislike of their representative. Likewise, McCarthy may have been too proud to accept Mountford's artifacts.

The only other institution to have received artifacts collected individually by McCarthy is the National Museum of Australia (courtesy of the Australian Institute of Anatomy). Figure 9.6 shows that they hold spears, spear throwers, and worked stone collected by him. Considering the aforementioned statistics regarding the limited distribution of his material, the placement of these artifacts is noteworthy. During the original distribution of the artifacts between the Smithsonian Institution, the Australian Museum, and Charles Mountford, McCarthy may have traded a number of his spears, spear throwers, and pieces of worked stone in return for objects that Mountford had collected (such as bark paintings), thus ending up with the Australian Institute of Anatomy and later the National Museum of Australia.

McCarthy's influence, therefore, can be seen as less widespread than Mountford's considering most of his collection was deposited with the Australian Museum. McCarthy was in an awkward position during the Arnhem Land Expedition. On the one hand he was restricted in what he could collect by the presence of other anthropologists-ethnologists and was forced into specializing his collecting in areas Mountford was not interested in. On the

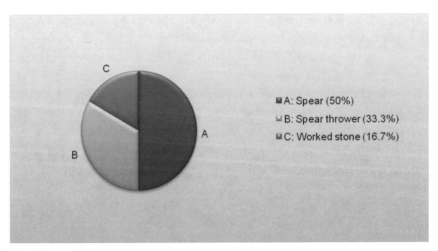

FIGURE 9.6
Artifacts collected by Frederick McCarthy and held in the National Museum of Australia.

other hand, as a trained social anthropologist and archaeologist, he desired a representative collection of material culture. His collection represents both of these areas.

FRANK SETZLER

Frank Setzler was not only the expedition archaeologist but he was also deputy leader of the Arnhem Land Expedition. His ethnographic collection is small in comparison with the archaeological materials he acquired. It is worth briefly discussing the nature of the archaeological collections as they relate to Setzler's ethnographic collecting.

In 1955 director of the Australian Museum Dr. J. W. Evans updated the director of the Department of Information on the location of the archaeological collection from the Arnhem Land Expedition. He stated, "The stone and bone implements collected by excavation and otherwise are in this Museum [Australian Museum], but [a] portion of this material has been selected as a representative series to be sent to the United States National Museum" (Evans, February 11, 1955). Some of the archaeological material was, in fact, delivered directly to the Australian Museum in 1948 and more in early 1949 (Hipsley to Hale, June 28, 1954). Mountford had no interest in the archaeological collection and the only division that was necessary was between the Smithsonian Institution and the Australian Museum. It was decided prior to the expedition that "every specimen of which no duplicate had been obtained would be returned to Australia. . . . All specimens of new species would also be returned, and a unique anthropological specimen would remain in Australia, only a cast being taken to the United States" (Setzler, December 21, 1948: 2).

Interestingly during the 1955 discussions relating to the whereabouts of the ethnographic artifacts, the archaeological material was also discussed. Kevin Murphy wrote to Evans stating that the archaeological collection should now be split three ways—the Australian Museum, United States National Museum (Smithsonian Institution), and the Department of Anthropology at the Australian National University (Murphy, May 23, 1955). The artifacts had been divided long before and this new third party seems to have been simply ignored. The Australian National University, having played no role in the expedition, would have been an unusual choice for the location of the material. The archaeological material is today still held in the Australian Museum with a representative sample in the National Museum of Natural History in Washington, D.C.

Table 9.8. Ethnographic Artifacts Collected by Frank Setzler during the Arnhem Land Expedition

Object Type	Number	Object Type	Number
Bark painting	11	Cordage	2
Spear	7	Boomerang	2
Armlet	3	Totem	1
Garment	2	Digging stick	1
Figurine	2		

Setzler's largest ethnographic collection included eleven bark paintings and seven spears (see table 9.8). Over 70 percent of these were collected while the group was camped on Groote Eylandt, and Oenpelli is not represented at all. Setzler did not collect a great deal of ethnographic material but, when he did, it was primarily bark paintings or spears. These two artifact types are the largest collections held in the Smithsonian Institution from the Arnhem Land Expedition. The small numbers presented make it impossible to reach many conclusions regarding Setzler's biases and general collection strategies. Setzler's ethnographic artifacts may reflect the casual way in which collection was taking place during the expedition or perhaps they represent lulls in archaeological fieldwork and opportunistic moments for collecting.

FREDERICK "FRED" McCARTHY AND FRANK SETZLER

Aside from their independent collecting, Fred McCarthy and Frank Setzler together made a significant contribution to the Arnhem Land Expedition ethnographic collection. They joined forces for a number of archaeological excavations during the expedition. This included excavations at Winchelsea Island, Port Langdon, Port Bradshaw, Milingimbi Island, Melville Bay, and at sites near Oenpelli such as Injalak Hill. Thus, the two expedition members were often working away from the base camps for archaeological purposes when they had the opportunity to collect ethnographic material (Mountford 1956: 267). Table 9.9 illustrates that together these men collected 330 ethnographic artifacts. Worked stone (stone artifacts) was the largest artifact type collected by these two men with 126 pieces. It is likely that they were interested in the present-day uses of many of the stone artifacts they were excavating. Other collectors from the expedition largely ig-

Table 9.9. Ethnographic Artifacts Collected Jointly by Frank Setzler and Frederick McCarthy during the Arnhem Land Expedition

Object Type	Number	Object Type	Number
Worked stone	126	Clap stick	2
Basket	54	Fire stick	2
Pigment	39	Pole	2
Spear	25	Figurine	1
Armlet	17	Feather	1
Spear thrower	11	Paper painting	1
Paint brush	7	Cordage	1
Message stick	6	Container	1
Belt	5	Coffin	1
Shell	4	Bull thrower	1
Ornament	4	Botanical specimen	1
Paddle	4	Bone tool	1
Pipe	3	Sail	1
Didjeridoo	2	Stick	1
Bees wax	2	Glass	1
Bark painting	2	Indeterminate	1

nored this artifact type. Fiber objects (baskets) also represent a considerable percentage of their collection, including fifty-four individual pieces (16.4 percent of their collection) (see figures 9.7 and 9.8). Mountford was not collecting baskets from any location in large numbers. The occurrence of this artifact type in the collection of McCarthy and Setzler may be evidence that these researchers were trying to avoid Mountford's areas of research and perhaps identifying a significant artifact type that was being overlooked by others.

McCarthy and Setzler's joint collection could be seen as representing the combined efforts of the researchers to collect specimens of interest to themselves and their institutions. It is notable that only two bark paintings are known to have been collected by the men as a team (though some bark paintings do not have a collector recorded). This may have been the reason Mountford asked Reverend Arthur Ellemor to send paintings to him after Setzler and McCarthy returned to the base camp from Milingimbi Island (Mountford 1956: 267). The largest number of artifacts from their collection came from Milingimbi Island and represent 57.9 percent of their entire combined collection (see figure 9.9). Table 9.10 expands on this by illustrating the artifact types the pair acquired while visiting Milingimbi Island. While the high number of baskets collected may be representative of

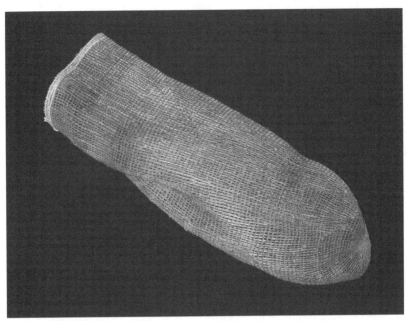

FIGURE 9.7
Dilly bag (basket) collected by Frederick McCarthy and Frank Setzler during the
Arnhem Land Expedition and now in possession of the National Museum of Nat-
ural History, Smithsonian Institution. Catalog number E387540.

strong local traditions, it is also likely that it reflects the bias of the collectors. Yet, Setzler and McCarthy are not recorded as having requested any
particular artifacts during their stay on this island. Instead the men collected the material brought to their tent by local (and visiting) people. Certainly this does not mean it is more representative of the material culture
of the societies, but it does mean the collection may be less representative
of collector's bias.

Is it possible that the Milingimbi Island collection reflects that Aboriginal
communities were producing these artifacts solely for trade with collectors?
As Judith Ryan has stated, "Throughout the 1930s and 1940s Aboriginal bark
painters learned to anticipate the requirements of particular collectors and to
produce works which would guarantee payment in tobacco currency" (1990:
16). Though she is referring to the production of one artifact type, it is reasonable that this could apply to a greater number of artifacts produced for the
Arnhem Land Expedition, and in particular, for the impromptu collecting of

FIGURE 9.8
Dilly bags (basket) collected by Frederick McCarthy and Frank Setzler during the Arnhem Land Expedition and now in possession of the National Museum of Natural History, Smithsonian Institution. Catalog numbers E387539A and E387540F.

Setzler and McCarthy on Milingimbi Island. Morphy has also stated that "the Methodist missions established at Milingimbi Island and Yirrkala in the 1920s and 1930s encouraged the production of craft, including bark paintings, for sale to a wide market and provided major collections for museums" (1989: 27). The large collection of baskets and spears in McCarthy and Setzler's Milingimbi Island collection could be a result of the Aboriginal communities having the experience to predict a desire for such artifacts on the part of the researchers.

The collection that McCarthy and Setzler formed was distributed to four museums and one art gallery in Australia and the United States.[2] Over 80 percent went to the Australian Museum where it represents 26.3 percent of the museum's Arnhem Land Expedition collection. Interestingly, the South Australian Museum received a small percentage of McCarthy and Setzler's collection including thirteen baskets from Milingimbi Island.

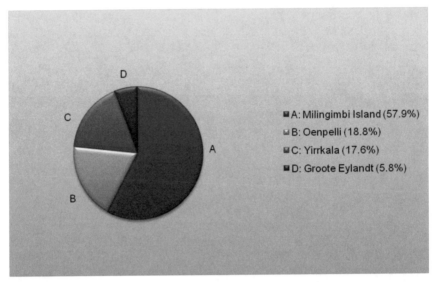

FIGURE 9.9
Provenance of ethnographic artifacts collected by Frank Setzler and Frederick Mc-
Carthy during the Arnhem Land Expedition.

Table 9.10. Ethnographic Artifacts Collected from Milingimbi Island by Frank Setzler and Frederick McCarthy during the Arnhem Land Expedition

Object Type	Number	Object Type	Number
Basket	53	Pole	2
Worked stone	37	Paper painting	1
Spear	24	Figurine	1
Armlet	17	Feather	1
Spear thrower	11	Cordage	1
Paint brush	7	Coffin	1
Message stick	6	Bull thrower	1
Belt	5	Botanical specimen	1
Paddle	4	Bone tool	1
Ornament	4	Shell	1
Pipe	3	Stick	1
Bark painting	2	Bees wax	1
Didjeridoo	2	Indeterminate	1
Fire stick	2		

CULTURAL INSTITUTIONS

Clearly the collectors had a significant impact on the institutional collections that were formed, but what role did the nature of the cultural institution and its underlying aims and beliefs have in forming the collection? Mountford has been labeled one of the first collectors of Aboriginal art as *art* rather than artifact (Morphy 1998: 29; Neale 1998: 212; Ryan 1990: 17). This idea and the influence of Mountford on all institutional collections deriving from the Arnhem Land Expedition is reflected in the distribution of the collections to museums, where artistic artifacts of Aboriginal cultures were traditionally kept, and in art galleries, where Aboriginal art had not been acquired in great numbers by most.

The Museums

There are several trends that appear when looking at the Arnhem Land Expedition ethnographic collections held by museums today. First, bark paintings are found in large numbers in all museums, yet they are not always the primary artifacts held. The National Museum of Australia and the South Australian Museum were both greatly influenced by Mountford's choices and, in turn, artworks are dominant. At the Smithsonian Institution, spears and bark paintings are almost even in number whereas at the Australian Museum, string figures, worked stone, armlets, and bark paintings are relatively evenly represented. These paintings were being acquired, stored, and curated as artifact rather than art. It is interesting that the only museum to have sent a representative trained in social anthropology (the Australian Museum) received the most diverse collection from Arnhem Land (see table 9.7).

Ryan (1990: 14) states that before the 1950s the major collectors of Aboriginal art were anthropologists with interests in mythology, ritual, and kinship systems. These anthropologists were primarily interested in the relationship of art to ceremony and what it revealed about the culture. Morphy (1998: 29) states that anthropological interest in Aboriginal Australian art increased around the time of World War II when it began to be viewed as an expression of religious values rather than an indicator of evolution. The distribution of Arnhem Land Expedition artistic artifacts to both museums and art galleries occurred during this crossover period. From these findings it appears that museums were not yet ready to give up their reign over Aboriginal art to art galleries despite a push from the latter institutions.

The lack of paintings on paper in museums further suggests that the medium played a role in artifact selection. As Peter Sutton (1988) has argued, Westerners often discouraged Aboriginal art because of its so-called crudeness. The art was crude not only because of "the slight degree of finesse" but also because of its media (Sutton 1988: 37). Ironically, where Aboriginal artists have used smoother and more "acceptable" media, they have been criticized by those who consider such innovations inauthentic (Sutton 1988: 38). It is possible that those selecting the paintings to be held by museums held this view of paintings on paper as not being traditional enough to be housed in a museum.

The Art Galleries

As stated earlier, the Commonwealth of Australia offered twelve bark paintings and twelve paintings on paper to each of the state art galleries of Australia (including the Tasmanian Museum and Art Gallery). The figures discussed in this chapter, and the previous one, suggest that these conditions were not met and instead a great many variations emerged. The most obvious is with the Art Gallery of South Australia, which received a total of fifty-three paintings, rather than the twenty-four they were promised. The Art Gallery of New South Wales received two more paintings than promised, while the Queensland Art Gallery and the National Gallery of Victoria each received one more. The Tasmanian Museum and Art Gallery and the Art Gallery of Western Australia received fewer than they were promised. Along with the differences in numbers gained by each art gallery, a difference in the types of paintings received appears. For example, rather than the promised twelve bark and twelve paper paintings, the National Gallery of Victoria received sixteen bark paintings and seven paintings on paper. On the other hand, the Art Gallery of New South Wales received sixteen paintings on paper and only eight bark paintings. So what does this all mean? It could be assumed, considering the difference in number is evident in all the collections, that some selection was involved on behalf of the art galleries.

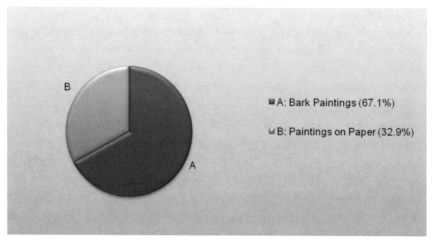

A: Bark Paintings (67.1%)

B: Paintings on Paper (32.9%)

FIGURE 9.10
Percentage of bark versus paper paintings from the Arnhem Land Expedition in art galleries.

Figure 9.10 shows the percentage of paintings on paper held in art galleries in contrast to the percentage of bark paintings held. Art galleries appear to have been unfazed about choosing paintings on a bark medium rather than a less so-called crude medium such as paper (Sutton 1988: 37). Their push for a share of the Arnhem Land Expedition artifacts and, in turn, their deliberate selection in many cases of paintings on bark in preference to those on paper would seem to suggest that they were eager to absorb Aboriginal art into the art gallery experience and to accept these materials as art rather than artifact.

Despite this interest in artworks, those paintings in galleries such as the Queensland Art Gallery were not accessioned until much later (Neale 1998: 210). To consider these bark paintings as equal partners in the fine arts was premature for these institutions. Morphy may have been underestimating the impact of these accessions when he stated, "A few paintings collected by Mountford . . . had been distributed by the Australian Government to the main state art galleries, but it was the collections . . . made by Stuart Scougall and Tony Tuckson for the Art Gallery of New South Wales in 1958 and 1959, that had the more significant impact" (1998: 29). The wheels of change were without doubt set in motion by the 1948 acquisitions.

DISCUSSION

A question was posed at the beginning of this book regarding the influences on institutional collections that derived from the Arnhem Land Expedition ethnographic artifacts. This has been explored through two main avenues: first, the collectors, their selection, and division of the artifacts and their ties to particular institutions; second, the nature of the institution, art gallery, or museum. This research has shown the collection strategies to be complex; however, particular trends have appeared in many areas. Naturally, the overwhelming answer to this initial query is that the collectors chose and distributed the artifacts, thereby influencing in a great many ways the collections that resulted. The collectors did not go into these communities and collect random artifacts but rather selected those that best suited their needs. Mountford had an overwhelming influence on many institutions while the other two collectors influenced primarily their home institutions.

The collections held in all art galleries, the National Museum of Australia, and the South Australian Museum have largely resulted from decisions made by Charles Mountford. Placing aside questions of regional variations and the individual abilities of the artists or manufacturers within Aboriginal communities, Mountford was responsible for the selection and distribution of a great deal of the Arnhem Land Expedition material. This analysis has shown a bias toward art objects at all locations visited by the leader, in particular, a bias toward bark paintings. These facts concur with the evidence suggested for Mountford's aims and intentions in chapter 5. In terms of distribution, his decision to hold very few paintings from Groote Eylandt in the South Australian Museum but rather to pass them on to art galleries and, eventually, the National Museum of Australia, has meant distinct biases in these collections in terms of provenance. Naturally, it has also meant a lack of representation from Groote Eylandt in the South Australian Museum. Mountford and his decision to allocate particular artifacts he did not require or desire to museums have, for example, helped form the collection in the Smithsonian Institution, particularly in reference to spears.

Fred McCarthy appears to have been interested in representation and specialization which, though appearing contradictory, actually succeeded in the field. His collection of worked stone being used in the communities, children's toys, as well as both men's and women's artifacts are just a few examples of his wider-reaching collection strategies. It is likely that his training as a social anthropologist influenced his collection strategies and, unlike with Mountford, there is no evidence that McCarthy desired personal gain (other than training and publications) from his collections. His commitment to gaining a significant collection for the Australian Museum is evident in his arrangements for the material to come directly to this institution rather than via Adelaide with everything else. It could be argued that the Australian Museum benefited from the Arnhem Land Expedition more than any other institution with not only a large collection but also the most representative of artifacts from the Arnhem Land Aboriginal cultures.

The second part of this chapter was concerned with the nature of the institution receiving artifacts from the Arnhem Land Expedition and how this impacted their selection. It appears that this expedition occurred in a transition period for art galleries and museums in terms of art objects. This research has shown that art galleries wanted these paintings in their institutions and often selected those on bark over those on paper when the opportunity arose. Museums, on the other hand, were also keen to acquire Aboriginal art and, as was traditional, keep art as artifacts. The lack of paintings on paper in museums may further suggest that it was thought to be the medium that made paintings "ethnographic" for these institutions. Ironically, the primary collector for many museums appears to have been unconcerned with the medium, instead concentrating on the imagery. Ryan stated in reference to Aboriginal art before the 1950s, "Its aesthetic power had not been unlocked" (1990: 17). The Arnhem Land ethnographic collection may reflect the start of the unlocking process.

In the following chapter I will delve deeper into the significance of collecting paintings during the Arnhem Land Expedition. As can be clearly seen throughout this chapter, the paintings on bark and paper that were collected as part of the ethnographic collection were given special consideration at the time. While the exact number will probably never be known, today 484 bark paintings and 115 paintings on paper are identified as having been collected during the Arnhem Land Expedition, and their story deserves a more detailed telling.

NOTES

1. I have not attempted to change or update the names that Mountford gave to the artifact types he collected; for the sake of continuity I have left them as recorded.

2. National Museum of Australia, Australian Museum, Smithsonian Institution, South Australian Museum, and the Queensland Art Gallery.

10

A Series Most Promising

On May 17, 1948, Fred McCarthy retreated to his tent to write the latest entry in his comprehensive field journal, just as he did religiously each day. On this particular day he wrote a sentence that grabbed my attention upon reading. He stated, "The artists continue to produce up to five bark paintings a day and my series is looking very promising" (McCarthy May 17, 1948). The notion that McCarthy (and, of course, Mountford) were attempting to acquire a series of paintings is interesting and inspired the title to this chapter. A series invokes ideas of interconnectedness among the paintings and, while important individually, together these paintings tell larger stories. In this chapter, I explore some of these larger stories; for example, what does the collection as a whole tell us about the cross-cultural interactions that took place in 1948, and what can the painting collection reliably convey about the people and the cultures on both sides of the exchange—the producers and the collectors.

The paintings on bark and paper that were collected as part of the ethnographic fieldwork were given special consideration by the collectors at the time and make up over 20 percent of all the ethnographic material collected. While the exact number will probably never be known, today 484 bark paintings and 115 paintings on paper are identified as having been collected during the Arnhem Land Expedition. Reasons for this painting bias have been hinted at throughout this book and in this chapter I delve further into the intricacies of collector and producer. Today these paintings remain the most

FIGURE 10.1
Painting on bark collected from Oenpelli during the Arnhem Land Expedition, artist un-
known, in possession of the Art Gallery of South Australia, O.1740. This bark painting was
exhibited widely (e.g., Worcestor Art Museum, USA, Feb 17–April 3 1966, Allentown Art
Museum, United States, April 14–May 12 1966, Adelaide Festival of Arts 1960, Australian
Aboriginal Art State Art Galleries exhibition 1960–1, UNESCO World Art Series 1954: Pl..
xxix) before finding a permanent home at the Art Gallery of South Australia. Charles
Mountford states, "This bark painting . . . shows two spirit men, *Eradbatli* and *Kumail-Kumail* ready to take part in a ceremony. *Eradbatli*, on the right, is wearing a headdress
made of twigs and decorated with feathers. The cross-hatching on his chest indicates his
stomach. The artist has also painted the upper and lower intestines, the spinal column
and the bones of the arms and legs. The cross-hatching on *Kumail-Kumail* indicates only
his body decorations" (1966: 36).

exhibited and publicized aspect of the expedition ethnographic collections
and are items of pride for the institutions holding them and the descendents
of the artists who produced them. This latter relationship is complex but it is
relevant to remember that, as Howard Morphy explains, "To Aboriginal people art is linked to land, history and identity, and in journeying to other places
it carries those connotations with it" (1998: 37). The descendents of the artists

who produced the paintings in 1948 retain cultural connections with these paintings, despite the separation of time and place.

COLLECTING ARNHEM LAND ART

In 1948 the Arnhem Land Expedition visited some regions that are home to what are arguably the world's longest continuing artistic traditions. It is important to understand something of these traditions in order to understand the paintings collected in 1948. Archaeologists have identified sequences of rock art in and around Arnhem Land dating back tens of thousands of years and it is likely that the first people to arrive on the north coast of Australia brought artistic skills and styles with them. For example, at one archaeological site (Nauwalabila I) in Kakadu National Park a large piece of high-quality ochre was found and had been used as a source of red pigment. This ochre was found in a layer of the site that dated between 53,000 and 60,000 before present (Flood 1997: 9; Roberts, Jones, and Smith 1993: 58–59). Many researchers have discussed the rock art traditions specific to Arnhem Land (see Brandl 1973; Chaloupka 1984, 1993; Lewis 1988; Taçon 1989; Taçon and Chippendale 1993), and today Aboriginal people in some parts of Arnhem Land continue to produce rock art just as their ancestors did before them (e.g., Lofty Bardayal Nadjamerrek and Thompson Yulidjirri in western Arnhem Land).

Portable art did not replace rock art but, rather, was contemporaneous with it and closely related. It is said by Aboriginal elders that the bark-painting medium owes its origins to sketches on the inside of bark wet-season shelters where paintings would be used to assist in telling stories relating to local Aboriginal culture (personal communication Yulidjirri October 12, 2002). As such, this art may have served similar purposes to that in rock shelters—education and decoration. While artistic traditions vary dramatically across Arnhem Land, Luke Taylor (1996: 15) and Jon Altman (1982: 15) suggest that, specifically at Oenpelli, artists associate the public nature of their bark paintings produced for sale with realms of "public" art, that is, rock and bark shelter art, and that it provided a means by which an artist could gain access to secret knowledge and, in turn, ritual status.

As early as 1807, in a sketch of a burial place on Maria Island, Tasmania, painted sheets of bark are illustrated in the background (Ryan 1990: 1). Later in the nineteenth century, Bunce (1857: 49–50), Curr (1886: 273), and Smyth (1878: 292) discussed and illustrated paintings produced on bark and developed

FIGURE 10.2
Painting on paper collected from Yirrkala during the Arnhem Land Expedition, artist unknown, in possession of the National Museum of Australia. Mountford (1956: pl.155B, p. 493–94) titled this painting *The Moon-man, Alinda,* and he recorded the story as follows: In creation times the moon-man, *Alinda,* and the parrot-fish man, *Dirima,* were always disagreeing over some trivial matter. During one unusually violent quarrel, each picked up his clubs and belaboured the other so badly that both died. Then the spirit of the moon-man, *Alinda,* said to the spirit of the parrot-man, *Dirima:* "You are to become a parrot-fish and live in the sea, and when you die, you'll never come to life again, but I am going to be the moon in the sky, and although I'll die like the rest of you, I'll only be dead for three days, then I'll live again." So, from that time onwards, the parrot-fish and the whole of creation, once dead, never came to life. But although, each month, the moon becomes thinner and thinner until he finally dies, after three days he again shows as a silver streak which grows progressively larger until it reaches its full size. Describing this particular painting, Mountford writes, "In the centre are the two opponents belabouring each other with clubs, on the lower left is the dead parrot-fish with his weapon lying beside him, and on the lower right, the dead moon." (1956: 495)

theories relating to their uses within their Aboriginal cultural groups. In western Arnhem Land elders remember sleeping in bark shelters covered with paintings of animals and humanlike figures (personal communication Yulidjirri, October 12, 2002, see figure 10.3). From these accounts and other historical sources, it is today accepted that painting on bark had a role in Aboriginal cultures of Arnhem Land prior to the emergence of a non-Aboriginal market

FIGURE 10.3
Photograph by Captain Sir G. H. Wilkins titled Drawings Done by the Natives on the Bark of their Dwellings at Island Camp near Goyder River, Northern Territory (after Wilkins 1929: 177).

for them. Some scholars have argued this role included occasional ceremonial use as well as the painting of the bark walls of temporary dwellings (Berndt and Berndt 1988: 422–23; Groger-Wurm 1973: 8–10; Mountford 1956: 8; Ryan 1990: 1; Taylor 1982: 25).

Bark painting is executed under traditional constraints associated with rights of inheritance, age, and sex. Howard Morphy (1987: 18), Fred McCarthy (1974: 39), and Lloyd Warner (1937: 136) are three researchers who have argued that these constraints are consistent with those relating to other media. Morphy (1987: 18) has stated that Australian Aboriginal designs are owned and that this ownership is related to social structure that can be expected to vary throughout the continent in correlation to changes in societies. He argues that within a wide repertoire of designs each artist will have a number that are exclusively their own. Cooke (1982: 27) and Taylor (1982: 25) have contended that today artists are usually senior men who have a prominent role in ritual. Yet, contrary to this, Mountford noted in 1948 that he "did not meet an aboriginal who could not, or did not want to paint. There is certainly no special artist class" (1956: 15) and he observed no women painting, thus, assuming it was a man's role in society.

With the intrusion of collectors into Arnhem Land, the notion of bark paintings as permanent and saleable objects emerged (Crocker 1987: 26; Ryan 1990: 1; Smith 1988: 295). The earliest collections of paintings on bark were formed by explorers who simply removed sheets of bark from unused wet-season shelters (Brody 1985: 14; Carrington 1890: 73; Carroll 1983: 44; Taylor 1996: 17; Worsnop 1897: 37). This includes the earliest collection of western Arnhem Land bark paintings (Iwaidja language group) acquired by Foelsche from the Port Essington region for the Macleay Museum in 1878 (Taçon and Davies 2004). Likewise, Carrington formed another important early collection in this way during his visit to Field Island in 1887 (Carrington 1890: 73; Carroll 1983: 44; Brody 1985: 14).

Judith Ryan (1990: 14) stated that none of these and other nineteenth-century collections are said to have been commissioned. Baldwin Spencer is often credited with being the first patron of Aboriginal art, when in 1912 he commissioned (and traded tobacco for) a series of bark paintings from Oenpelli representing the rock art that he had observed (Mulvaney 2008: 148–49). Spencer (1928: 793–94) states that he found the paintings "so interesting that, after collecting some from their studios, which meant taking down the slabs on which they were drawn, that formed, incidentally, the walls of their Mia-mias [bark shelters], I commissioned two or three of the best artists to paint me a series of canvases, or rather 'barks.'" The artists were paid according to the size of their "canvas"; one stick of tobacco for a two feet by one foot and up to three sticks of tobacco for those measuring three feet by six feet and upward (Spencer 1928: 793–94; Mulvaney 2008: 148–49).

Another anthropological collector of influence in Arnhem Land was Lloyd Warner who, between 1926 and 1929, collected a number of paintings from Yolngu at Milingimbi Island. Donald Thomson also compiled an extensive collection of ethnographic artifacts including bark paintings primarily from Yirrkala and Milingimbi Island in the 1930s and 1940s (Ryan 1990: 14). At the same time, Reverends Theodore Webb (Milingimbi Island) and Wilbur Chaseling (Yirrkala) were also promoting the production of art and forming important collections prior to the 1948 Arnhem Land Expedition and may have had a role in establishing the nature of artefacts desired by visiting researchers, as well as price scales (Morphy 1991). As Howard Morphy states, "Thus artwork and handicrafts became commodities sold by Yolngu to obtain tobacco and resold by the mission as a small but necessary part of its overall economic strategy" (1991: 14).

In the late 1940s, Ronald and Catherine Berndt collected bark paintings from around Arnhem Land and began an important change in the detail recorded about the artists and interpretations (Stanton 2008). Other important collectors included Reverend Alfred John Dyer between 1920 and 1930 from Groote Eylandt and Oenpelli; Norman Tindale from Groote Eylandt in 1922; Miss M. Mathews from Goulburn Island in the 1930s; and Frederick Harold "Fred" Gray and Frederick Rose from Groote Eylandt between 1938 and 1945. In the 1940s Leonard Adam collected from Groote Eylandt and Milingimbi Island.

Many of the reasons why Aboriginal artists from the Arnhem Land region traded bark paintings have been documented elsewhere (see, in particular, Taylor 1996). One major reason appears to be their desire for Western goods, especially tobacco. The desire for tobacco at this time was unquestionably great; Spencer himself even says that "any child of four or five years and upwards smokes whenever he or she gets the chance" (1928: 827). Alongside of this, tobacco became a valuable exchange good within Aboriginal cultural groups and their ceremonial exchange cycles. Judith Ryan (1990: 10) has even credited Spencer with being the first to introduce the trade of tobacco for artworks. Whatever its origins, tobacco has been an almost constant alternative currency in Arnhem Land art trading since 1912.

Another well-documented reason for the trading of bark paintings may have been their ability to serve as a unique tool for artists to explain their culture to foreign visitors. As Ronald Berndt recounts, "I was learning about the country and its religious associations as manifested through myth, ritual and song. On their own initiative, the men who were explaining such matters to me undertook the task of representing what they were telling me in another dimension—by painting on bark" (1983: 29). The anthropologist suggests the artists depicted what they were talking about as a way of "underlining its veracity" (Berndt 1983: 30).

ABORIGINAL PAINTING AS FINE ART

The idea of Aboriginal art as "fine art" arose largely following World War II (Morphy 1987, 1991; Taylor 1988). Before this, few Aboriginal paintings were held in art galleries in Australia. Instead they were restricted to ethnographic

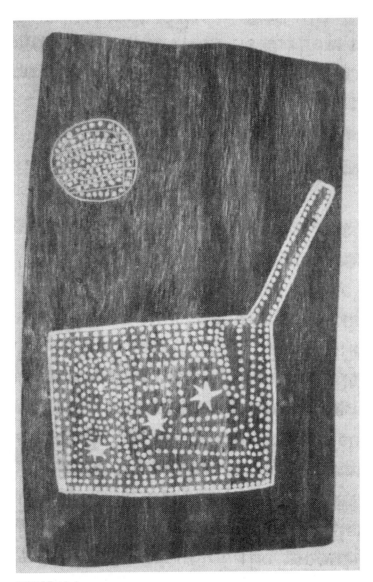

FIGURE 10.4

Painting on bark collected from Groote Eylandt during the Arnhem Land Expedition, artist unknown, in possession of the National Museum of Australia, 1985.67.41. Mountford (1956: pl.151E, p.482) titled this painting *The Constellation of Orion and the Pleiades* and he describes the painting as "the fishermen, *Burum-burum-runja*, are the three stars (Orion's belt) in the rectangle, and the smaller dots, their children. The extension (Orion's sword) in the lower left-hand corner symbolizes the line of fish the celestial fishermen caught in the creek, *ataluma* (Milky Way). The dots within the circle on the lower right are the wives, *Wutarinja* (the Pleiades)."

collections of museums of natural history (Morphy 1991: 22). As detailed in chapter 8 "When We Have Put to Sea," the allocation of paintings from the Arnhem Land Expedition to art galleries as well as museums was an important turning point in this movement. Margo Neale has argued that this early enthusiasm from the galleries was reluctance to "look a gift horse in the mouth" (1998: 210) and states that the galleries were flattered to have been treated to such a gift. It is important to remember, however, that it was the art galleries who made the initial move and requested a selection of paintings from this expedition (Murphy, May 23, 1955). As the director of the Australian Museum, Kevin Murphy stated, "I have received strong representations from the Conference of Interstate Art Gallery Directors for a share of these paintings and have offered the conference 144 of them" (May 23, 1955).

A meeting was held in August 1956 at the Queensland Art Gallery to decide which paintings from the Arnhem Land Expedition each state gallery would receive (Neale 1998: 210). The decision to give these paintings to art galleries in preference to museums was unusual for its time, as this was one of the first instances of Australian Aboriginal art being accepted for aesthetic rather than ethnographic qualities (Morphy 1987, 1991; Neale 1998: 210). Yet, despite this initial enthusiasm, the paintings in many of the galleries, such as Queensland Art Gallery, were not accessioned until much later (Neale 1998: 210).

For art galleries this was a gift they were not sure how to manage and to consider these paintings as equal partners in the fine arts was premature. As mentioned earlier, Morphy states that it was collections "made by Stuart Scougall and Tony Tuckson for the Art Gallery of New South Wales in 1958 and 1959, that had the more significant impact" (1998: 29). In many ways this is true as the Arnhem Land Expedition paintings languished in art gallery storage areas for decades before being appreciated and displayed. The key findings from this allocation of painting is that it was the art galleries who requested bark paintings for their institutions, and it was the Arnhem Land Expedition paintings that brought six state art galleries together to discuss bark paintings and their future role in art galleries rather than museums—this meeting was one of the first of its kind in Australia.

THE PROVENANCE OF THE ARNHEM LAND EXPEDITION PAINTINGS

Not surprisingly, the paintings collected during the Arnhem Land Expedition mostly came from the three base camps visited for three months each—Groote

FIGURE 10.5
Painting on bark collected from Oenpelli during the Arnhem Land Expedition, artist unknown, in possession of the Art Gallery of South Australia, O.1768. Mountford (1956: 187–88, pl. 51F) titled this painting, *The Man, Noulabil* and he describes it as such, "*Noulabil*, with his wife and family, lives in a large hollow tree at the base of the Arnhem Land plateau. Although normally a quiet and peaceful fellow, he has been known to attack and even kill Aborigines who tried to cut down his tree. *Noulabil* is particularly afraid of the lightning-man, *Mamaragan* . . . who travels in the thunderstorms. When a thunderstorm approaches, *Noulabil* comes out of his hollow tree and, wiping the perspiration from beneath his arms, orders the lightning-man to pass on one side. Sometimes *Mamaragan* obeys, but if he does not, *Noulabil* and his family flee to the caves of the plateau, because *Mamaragan* once shattered *Noulabil's* tree with the stone axes which have grown on his knees and hands."

Eylandt, Yirrkala, and Oenpelli (see figure 10.6). Considerably less time was spent, and less material was collected, at Milingimbi Island. The so-called Liverpool River Region paintings were actually collected in Oenpelli. Artists from the Liverpool River Region are known to have visited Oenpelli during the Arnhem Land Expedition and, as such, the paintings were produced and collected in Oenpelli (Mountford 1956: 111). As Mountford recalled, "On my first visit to Oenpelli in 1948 many of the artists who produced bark paintings for me came from the Liverpool River country, the local mission station using most of the available aboriginal labour for the killing and skinning of water buffaloes" (Mountford 1956: 111).

All of the base camps for the Arnhem Land Expedition yielded roughly the same numbers of bark paintings and it is possible that Mountford planned to collect similar numbers of paintings from each of the base camps (see figures 10.7 and 10.8). Likewise, it is possible that Mountford's experience of collecting at the first base camp may have influenced collection strategies employed at the other locations. The collection of bark paintings was not significantly

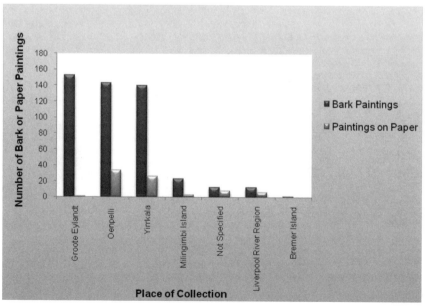

FIGURE 10.6
Provenance of bark and paper paintings collected during the Arnhem Land Expedition.

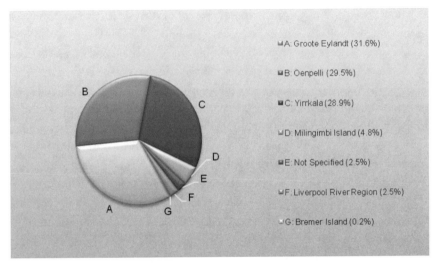

FIGURE 10.7
Provenance of bark paintings collected during the Arnhem Land Expedition.

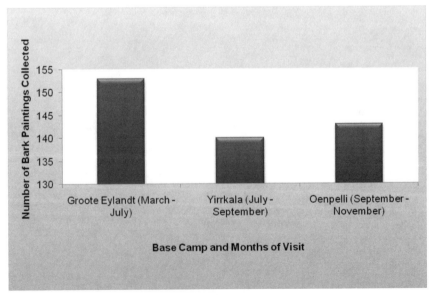

FIGURE 10.8
Number of bark paintings collected from the base camps during the Arnhem Land Expedition.

increasing or decreasing as the expedition progressed. This is perhaps surprising, as it would be expected that factors such as transportation and storage would have meant a decrease in collecting as the expedition progresses. One way of exploring this is by looking at the relationship between paintings produced on bark and those on paper. The following discussion aims to explore the reasons for, and the impact of, the introduction of paper as a medium for painting.

EXPLORING THE MEDIUM—FROM BARK TO PAPER

While paintings on paper were collected from five different locations during the Arnhem Land Expedition, there are some trends in their collection worthy of note (see figure 10.6). The first is that only one was collected from the first base camp, Groote Eylandt.[1] It is only on arriving at their second base camp that Mountford began acquiring larger numbers of paintings on paper. One reason for this difference may be that Mountford had not foreseen at the first camp the problems with transportation that would occur from collecting a large number of bark paintings. Neale has argued that the use of paper was "a pragmatic decision based on the scarcity of bark during the dry season and the inconvenience of transporting such large numbers of works" (1998: 212). If transportation was a major consideration then the sharp jump in collection of paintings on paper at Yirrkala and Oenpelli should have coincided with a significant decrease in the collection of bark paintings in these centers, which is not the case. Interestingly, Mountford records that "as the supply of prepared sheets of bark at Yirrkala and Oenpelli became exhausted, I provided the artists with sheets of rough-surfaced dark grey and green paper" (1956: 13). This movement toward paintings on paper, therefore, may reflect a more abundant supply of bark on Groote Eylandt.

It is important to remember, however, that Mountford brought this paper with him with the intention of giving it to artists, just as he had on expeditions earlier in his career. He always intended to gain examples of art on paper during the Arnhem Land Expedition, just as he had done earlier in Central Australia. Mountford had little experience collecting bark paintings in Arnhem Land prior to this 1948 expedition, yet he may have known enough to predict a shortage of bark. If not, we can only assume that he intended to gain examples of art on this medium and that it was not an emergency backup as most people assume. It is clear from historical records that it was the imagery that motivated Mountford's collecting rather than the medium. Indeed, in *Records of the American-Australian Scientific Expedition to Arnhem Land Vol. 1*, the only acknowledgement that some of the paintings illustrated are actually on paper and not bark is in a small footnote that states, "The paintings on these sheets of paper can be distinguished in the illustrations by the smooth ground" (Mountford 1956: 13). The phenomenon of painting on paper and, in turn, the transferring of cultural norms across media also indicates the adaptable and dynamic cultures from whom they were collecting.

WHO COLLECTED THE ARNHEM LAND EXPEDITION PAINTINGS?

Charles Mountford is credited with collecting over 70 percent of all the bark paintings from the Arnhem Land Expedition (see figure 10.9). This explains why many of the institutions holding Arnhem Land Expedition paintings, such as the National Gallery of Victoria and the Queensland Art Gallery, have labeled it the "Mountford Collection" (Neale 1998: 216; Ryan 2000: 1). Fred McCarthy was the only other main contributor to the collection, being credited with sixty-two bark paintings plus involvement in the collection of forty-seven others. Though originally permitted to collect only fifteen bark

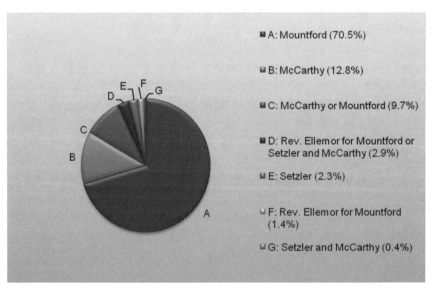

A: Mountford (70.5%)

B: McCarthy (12.8%)

C: McCarthy or Mountford (9.7%)

D: Rev. Ellem or for Mountford or Setzler and McCarthy (2.9%)

E: Setzler (2.3%)

F: Rev. Ellem or for Mountford (1.4%)

G: Setzler and McCarthy (0.4%)

FIGURE 10.9
Collectors of bark paintings during the Arnhem Land Expedition.

paintings for the Australian Museum, McCarthy was granted leave to collect more after forcing the issue with Mountford (McCarthy, May 19, 1948).

At Milingimbi, the local Reverend assisted expedition members by obtaining what Setzler and McCarthy did not have time to collect or record during their visit. Reverend Ellemor also later collected interpretations of designs and carved pipes (Ellemor, June 21, 1949). At the same time as Setzler and McCarthy were visiting Milingimbi, Mountford arranged for the local Reverend to collect other bark paintings with interpretations and send them to him (Mountford 1956: 267). This was an interesting arrangement, considering men from his own expedition were on the island collecting. It may reflect that individuals were collecting, at that stage, for their own institutions and, hence, there was competition for paintings.

Finally, Frank Setzler is recorded as having collected eleven bark paintings and may have been involved in collecting two others. This data is based on museum and art gallery records and, in this case, I believe that the allocation of these barks paintings to Setzler is an administrative mistake by the Smithsonian Institution. They were probably collected by either Fred McCarthy or Charles Mountford and were given to Frank Setzler for the Smithsonian Institution at the end of the expedition. As discussed earlier, each of these men had different methods for collecting and recording interpretations for paintings. This can be seen in the records held by the different institutions today.

WHERE ARE THE ARTISTS?

> Some writers suggest that only a limited number of aboriginal men are employed as artists. This is not so. All men were willing to and could paint, although, naturally, some are more skilled than others. (Mountford 1956: 13)

One of the most disappointing aspects of the Arnhem Land Expedition paintings is the lack of contextual information recorded by Charles Mountford at the time of their collection. Because of the issues discussed in this chapter and earlier, Mountford recorded less and less information as the expedition progressed. By the time he reached Oenpelli, only four artist names were recorded for 177 paintings collected. So, what do we know about the artists from the documentation surrounding the expedition? Table 10.1 is a list of all the people named in literature relating to the Arnhem Land Expedition as having contributed to the ethnographic collection and some produced a number of

Table 10.1. Some of the Artists Who Produced Works for the Arnhem Land Expedition in 1948

Name	Location	Name	Location
Banjo Tatalara	Groote Eylandt	Nambinara	Groote Eylandt
Burawanda	Groote Eylandt	Namingarukara	Groote Eylandt
Charlie	Groote Eylandt	Nangapiana	Groote Eylandt
Korpitja (Kulpidja)	Groote Eylandt	Neningirukwa Jaragba	Groote Eylandt
Macagana (Makogina, Machogana)	Groote Eylandt	Numayaga Wurramurra	Groote Eylandt
Minimini Mamarika	Groote Eylandt	Turunga	Groote Eylandt
Kumutun	Oenpelli	Unawanda	Groote Eylandt
Wulkini Kunwinjku	Oenpelli (Liverpool River)	Wurramara, Mangganga	Groote Eylandt
Mawalan (Moalun) Marika	Yirrkala	Yalioura	Groote Eylandt
Wandjuk Marika	Yirrkala	Bininuewuy	Milingimbi Island
Nanjin (Nangjin, Nanyin)	Yirrkala	Johnny	Milingimbi Island
Barumba Wurramara	Groote Eylandt	Larida	Oenpelli
Dakilarra Wurramara	Groote Eylandt	Willirra	Oenpelli
Gulbidja Bara	Groote Eylandt	Bananga	Yirrkala
Gulpitja	Groote Eylandt	Birrikitji Gumarna	Yirrkala
Mamria	Groote Eylandt	Brother of Mawalan	Yirrkala
Gumuk Dhalwangu	Groote Eylandt	Bunungu	Yirrkala
Janminara	Groote Eylandt	Kamberai	Yirrkala
Jindia	Groote Eylandt	Matarman	Yirrkala
Kneepad Bara Bara	Groote Eylandt	Mowara	Yirrkala
Kulprati	Groote Eylandt	Mungaraui	Yirrkala
Kumbiala	Groote Eylandt	Wakuthi Marrawili	Yirrkala
Manguguna	Groote Eylandt	Naradjen (Narritjin Maymuru)	Yirrkala
Manuwunda	Groote Eylandt	Yama	Yirrkala
Mouta	Groote Eylandt	Yirrwala	Yirrkala
Nambaduba Maminyaman	Groote Eylandt		

This is not a complete list of artist names but rather just some names mentioned by the expedition members in their diaries and other correspondence. The spelling of names has been deliberately left as recorded by Mountford.

paintings for Mountford, Setzler, and McCarthy. I have retained the spelling recorded by Mountford in 1948 and added some known alternative spellings. It is important to note that this is far from a complete list and much more research is needed to accurately credit those responsible for producing many of the ethnographic items collected in 1948. Even so, many of the paintings will remain labeled with "unknown artist." This work is ongoing.

Mountford did acknowledge four men as the main artists that worked with him—Mauwalan (Yirrkala), Nangapiana (Groote Eylandt), Kumutun (Oenpelli), and Wulkini (Liverpool River).[2] Expedition botanist Raymond Specht also reiterated their importance in his 2006 recollections of the expedition stating, "The main artists—Nangapiana on Groote Eylandt, Mauwulan at Yirrkala, Kumutun at Oenpelli—were very tolerant and pleased to explain their art" (2006a).

Little is known of *Wulkini* or *Wulkini Kunwinjku* (figure 10.10) from the Liverpool River Region and Mountford recorded no information on his history or cultural affiliations. His last name, Kunwinjku, is the name of a dominant language group in the region today and is probably a mistake by Mountford. At least it provides an insight into his language group. Mountford did not record the names of artists for the paintings he collected from Oenpelli in 1948 and, as such, it is difficult to know which paintings are the works of Wulkini.

Twelve bark paintings and six paintings on paper are recorded as being collected from the Liverpool River Region. As we already know, Liverpool River artists such as Wulkini came to Oenpelli to produce paintings for the researchers because the local Aboriginal artists were required for work, killing and skinning water buffalo (Mountford 1956: 111). Sadly, despite extensive consultation with west Arnhem Land Aboriginal people, none of the Liverpool River paintings could be linked to a named individual.

On Groote Eylandt Nangapiana (figure 10.11) is credited with being the main artist and one of his known works is shown in figure 10.12. This painting is described by Mountford as follows: "The fishermen have speared both a dugong and a green turtle. The two oarsmen at the stern keep the canoe straight as the creatures, in their efforts to escape, pull it through the water. The man in the bow handles the lines to prevent them from becoming tangled. . . . This design resembles a cave painting which I found at Chasm Island" (1956: 97).

FIGURE 10.10
Wulkini from the Liverpool River Region, a prominent artist for the Arnhem Land
Expedition (after Mountford 1956: 14).

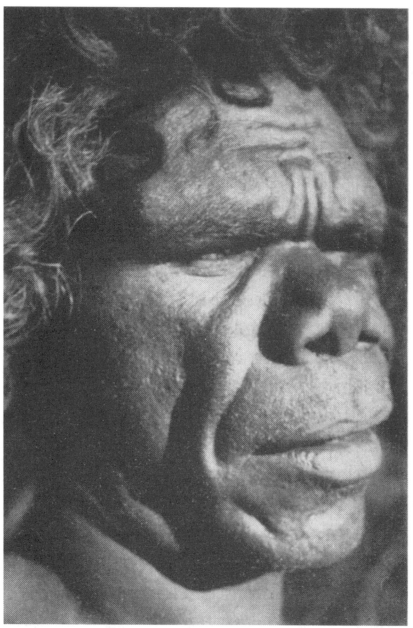

FIGURE 10.11
Nangapiana from Groote Eylandt, a prominent artist for the Arnhem Land Expedition.

FIGURE 10.12
Painting by Nangapiana (Groote Eylandt) titled A Fishing Scene (after Mountford 1956: pl.32c).

Born in 1908 and dying in 1967, Mawalan (also spelled Mauwalun or Moalun by expedition members) Marika was a highly regarded leader of the Rirratjingu people of northeast Arnhem Land and a contributor to the famous Bark Petitions presented to the federal government in the 1960s (see figure 10.13). As a significant bark painter, his work was commissioned by the Art Gallery of New South Wales in their first expedition to the area in the late 1950s. Figure 10.14 shows Mawalan with one of his wooden sculptures at Yirrkala in August 1948. Many of Mawalan's family members are also represented in the Arnhem Land Expedition collection, including his eldest son Wandjuk Marika.

In Oenpelli, Mountford named Kumutun as the main artist he worked with, yet I know of only one of the paintings he collected listing this senior man as the artist (see figure 10.15). Kumutun should not feel too offended. Only two other Oenpelli artists are officially recorded as artists in Oenpelli, *Larida* and *Willirra*. What makes this even sadder is the fact that for many of the paintings from Oenpelli we will never know the artists. With the move-

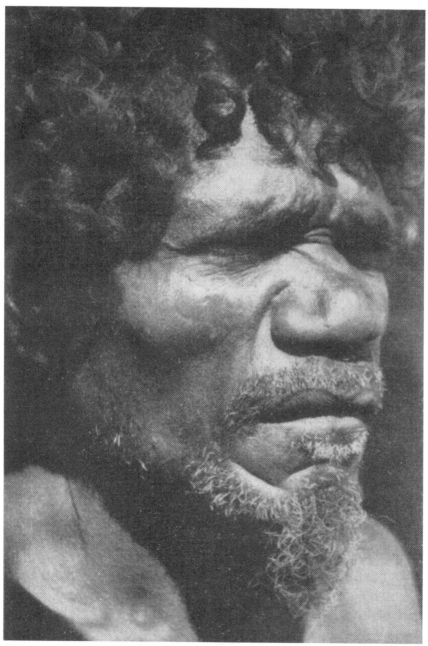

FIGURE 10.13
Mauwulan (Mawalan Marika), a prominent artist for the Arnhem Land Expedition.

FIGURE 10.14
Photograph of Mauwulan (Mawalan Marika) by Frank Setzler titled Carving and Painting of Wooden Figurine at Yirrkala, August 1948. National Library of Australia, nla.pic-
vn3724155.

ment of people in western Arnhem Land during the 1940s and 1950s and earlier, many of the artists may have been simply visitors to this community.

Who then are the artists for the 159 paintings collected from Oenpelli in
1948? Kumutun is certainly one of them (see figures 10.15 and 10.16). He has
been referred to by many names over the course of his life including Nipper
Murrakara, Marakara, Old Nipper Maragar, Marrakarra, and Kumutun. "Kumutun" may be a variation on "Gumurdul," the surname of the current traditional owners in Oenpelli and the children of Kumutun. The adventures and
the challenges of Nipper's life could fill the pages of a novel and, as for the
other artists I have mentioned, I cannot do justice to him in this chapter. Kumutun was a prolific artist and is also represented in early collections from
Oenpelli including the 1912–1913 Spencer and Cahill collection and later collections formed by Ronald and Catherine Berndt.

Nipper is remembered as a strong leader for Oenpelli and this is highlighted in one dramatic and well-recorded incident from 1917. In February
1910 a buffalo shooter who had been working in the region for some time

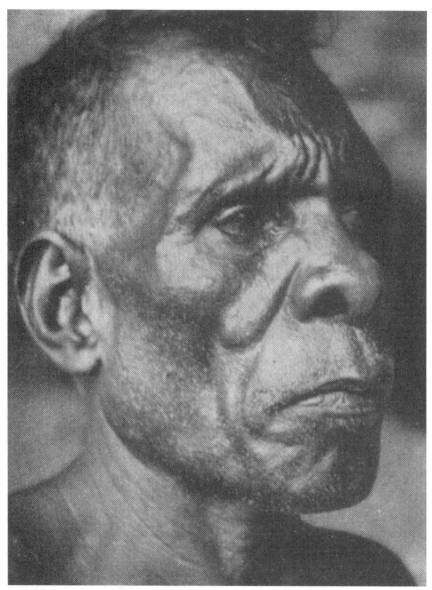

FIGURE 10.15
Kumutun (Nipper) from Oenpelli (after Mountford 1956: 14).

FIGURE 10.16
Kumutun (Nipper) from Oenpelli standing behind seated man (after Cole 1975: iii).

moved permanently to Oenpelli with his family (Maria, Tom, and Ruby Mudford) and friend William Johnstone. They were granted leasehold in April 1910.[3] There is no evidence to suggest Cahill and Johnstone consulted with Aboriginal owners of the land over their decision to settle in this region. The land they were assuming control of belonged to Nipper (Kumutun) and his family.

In 1917 Paddy Cahill and his family (along with a non-Aboriginal assistant O'Brien, two Aboriginal housemaids Marealmark and Topsy, and the Cahill's dog) were poisoned with Strychnine, placed in their butter. Though none except the dog were killed, all were seriously ill and were lucky to survive. Cahill blamed Aboriginal men by the names of Romula, Nulwoyo, Billy Munnierlorka and Nipper Murrakara (Kumutun). On October 10, 1917, Paddy Cahill wrote of these events to his friend Baldwin Spencer: "You can imagine my feelings and the frame of mind that I was in. Mrs Cahill vomiting, O'Brien almost dead, the two lubras rolling on the ground vomiting and likely to die at any moment . . . when I got things fixed up, Romula said 'you look out boss 'nother one boy put poison in the water bag.'"

In his October 10 letter Cahill accuses Nipper (Kumutun) as being the ringleader and states that he was told Nipper ordered the men to poison him after a group meeting where other men had expressed concern at Cahill's rules. Mulvaney (2004: 62) sums it up when he argues that as the owner of the land on which Cahill worked and lived, Nipper may have suffered many discourtesies, prompting his reactions in 1917.

In fact, it is through Paddy Cahill's arguments with Nipper (Kumutun) that we know so much about this Aboriginal artist. Nipper is said to have worked for a Mr. F. A. Smith as a buffalo shooter for many years and is known to have been a skilled shooter. At one stage he speared and nearly killed an Aboriginal man who also worked with Smith, yet Nipper was so profitable he was allowed to get away with things that other Aboriginal people would have been punished for. As Cahill wrote to Spencer, October 10, 1917: "Nipper done as he liked among the other natives, armed with a rifle there was no disputing his authority," and in the same letter he continues, "I blame this man for all the trouble." Soon after this event, Nipper was imprisoned for killing one of Paddy Cahill's cows.

Nipper was clearly an Oenpelli community leader and was respected and feared by both Aboriginal and non-Aboriginal people in the region. In his life he saw changes that most people cannot even imagine, from first encounters with white explorers, to buffalo shooters, and then missionaries, and many of these incidents are evidence of his resistance to people who were threatening his community—culturally, socially, and economically. At the same time, he was a skilled artist who features in a number of important collections from this region, across a vast period of time. One example of his work is shown in figure 10.17 and is described by Mountford (1956: 242) as depicting a kangaroo hunt.

These highlighted artists are just a fraction of those who produced works for the Arnhem Land Expedition, and research to revisit the painting collection and fill gaps in the information relating to artists is ongoing.

FIGURE 10.17
Painting by Kumutun (Nipper) collected during the Arnhem Land Expedition and titled The Kangaroo-Man, Kurabara, and the Dog-Man, Buruk (after Mountford 1956: pl.66a).

SEPARATING THE PAINTING COLLECTION

Very often when visiting museums or galleries to discuss their Arnhem Land Expedition paintings, I am asked about two issues. The first is the cultural meanings and significance of the paintings and the artists, and the second is how representative their own institution's set of paintings is of the overall Arnhem Land Expedition collection. The first question is significantly harder to answer and will continue to be an ongoing issue for institutions who care about contextualizing their collections and take the time to consult members of the Arnhem Land Aboriginal communities from which the paintings arise. It is clear, however, that the interpretations recorded by Charles Mountford in 1948 do no justice to the deep and interconnected cultural meanings embedded in the paintings. The second question of representation is easier to answer.

First, the Australian Museum received 109 bark paintings and no paintings on paper from the Arnhem Land Expedition (see figure 10.18). These paintings were collected by both Fred McCarthy and Charles Mountford and were part of the three-way allocation (South Australian Museum, Australian Museum, Smithsonian Institution) that occurred in the field at the end of the expedition. McCarthy had a major say in the nature of the Australian Museum's collection, yet, in the field he does not seem to have influenced the artist's choice of topic, as Mountford was known to have done. In terms of the regions from which the bark paintings emerge, the Australian Museum has a remarkably representative set with thirty-eight from Oenpelli, thirty-six from Yirrkala, and thirty-four from Groote Eylandt. It is surprising, however, that McCarthy only acquired one painting from Milingimbi Island for the Australian Museum, given that he spent a considerable amount of time on the island.

Like the Australian Museum, the Smithsonian Institution has a collection representative of the three base camps. In total, they possess thirty-four paintings from Oenpelli, thirty-three from Yirrkala, and twenty-three from Groote Eylandt. They did not receive any of the paintings produced on paper. Both the Australian Museum and the Smithsonian Institution collections are clear evidence that regional representation was the key issue at the meeting between Mountford, Setzler, and McCarthy that that took place at the end of the expedition to distribute the paintings between their three institutions.

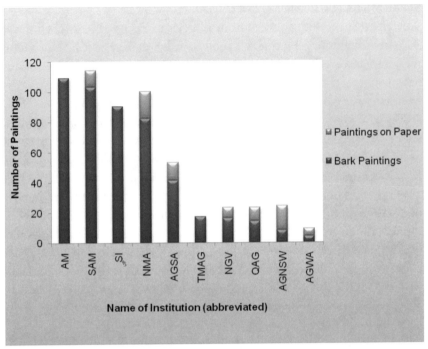

FIGURE 10.18
Number of bark and paper paintings from the Arnhem Land Expedition in different institutional collections.

The South Australian Museum is perhaps the most interesting in terms of regional representation. If we consider just the bark paintings, the largest percentage comes from the last base camp, Oenpelli (forty-nine paintings). The only other significant group are thirty-seven bark paintings collected from Yirrkala, and only eleven Groote Eylandt bark paintings were kept for the South Australian Museum. Given that it was Mountford who decided which paintings were kept by this institution and which were transferred to the Australian Institute of Anatomy in 1955, this is a deliberate bias.

So, why did Mountford choose to give away the Groote Eylandt bark paintings when the Australian government came calling in 1955? Some reasons for his disinterest may be that he did not intend to undertake ongoing research on Groote Eylandt or, more likely, he believed that the South Australian Museum already had a sizable collection of Groote Eylandt paintings, thanks to collectors such as Norman Tindale.

Whatever his reason for not including a representative collection of Groote Eylandt paintings in the South Australian Museum collection, the impact was more significant than one might think. His decision influenced the representation of Aboriginal art in art galleries throughout Australia. The Australian Institute of Anatomy was left with an abundance of paintings from Groote Eylandt and, as a result, art galleries were choosing their paintings from a Groote Eylandt–biased collection. All of the art galleries took possession of significantly more paintings from Groote Eylandt than any other location. For example, the Queensland Art Gallery holds twelve from Groote Eylandt, one from Milingimbi Island, and one from Yirrkala, and the Art Gallery of New South Wales holds seven from Groote Eylandt and one from Oenpelli (see May 2000 for a more detailed breakdown of the individual collections). The National Museum of Australia's collection also illustrates these actions with more than twice the number of bark paintings from Groote Eylandt than any other location visited (see figure 10.19). Mountford's selection of particular paintings to send to the Australian Institute of Anatomy in 1955 was the primary influence on the nature of art gallery collections from this expedition— some of the earliest and most influential Aboriginal paintings these institutions possess.

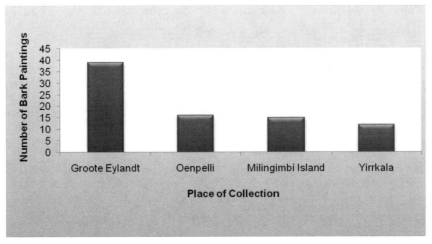

FIGURE 10.19
Provenance of bark paintings from the Arnhem Land Expedition held in the National Museum of Australia.

There is another clear dividing line between the paintings received by museums and art galleries from the Arnhem Land Expedition—the medium. The South Australian Museum today holds only 11 paintings on paper from a total of 115 collected in 1948. Even more obvious is the fact that the Australian Museum and the Smithsonian Institution received no paintings on paper (as opposed to 109 and 90 bark paintings). The question is, then, who made this decision? It would appear that it was a decision made by the three main collectors—Mountford, McCarthy, and Setzler—at the time they were dividing the collection in Darwin. Later, Mountford continued this trend by choosing to retain only eleven paintings on paper for the South Australian Museum. Museums were clearly keen to retain bark paintings, a more traditional medium on which to produce Aboriginal art.

In summary, there are two key biases in the institutional collections formed from the Arnhem Land Expedition paintings—media and place of collection. Nearly 63 percent of the paintings on paper collected are today held in art galleries while they retain 21 percent of the bark paintings collected. Art galleries

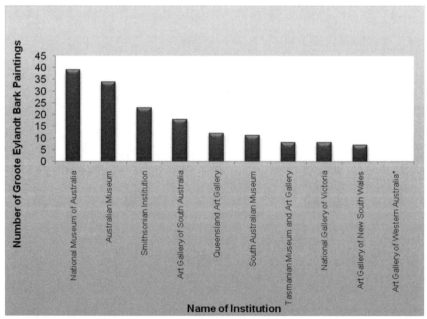

FIGURE 10.20
Number of Groote Eylandt bark paintings in institutional collections.

also took possession of 53 Groote Eylandt bark paintings, out of a total 154 collected (see figure 10.20).

The skewed percentage of paintings on paper in art galleries was clearly not of their choosing. Rather, it was forced upon them by having to select from the paintings not kept by museums. Margo Neale (1998: 210) quotes director of the National Gallery of South Australia Robert Campbell in 1955 stating that he was keen to select paintings before the anthropological people picked and he got the leftovers. In fact, the anthropologists had already made their choices twice (once at the distribution meeting during the expedition and once at the South Australian Museum) and had predetermined the nature of the collections the art galleries would acquire.

DISCUSSION

The Arnhem Land Expedition resulted in a diverse collection of paintings from three significant areas within Arnhem Land that today provide a remarkable resource. It would appear that the cultural and disciplinary biases of the collectors influenced the forms that institutional collections of paintings from the Arnhem Land Expedition take today. There is little doubt that the large number of bark paintings collected during the expedition was due to Mountford's eagerness to obtain such a collection. There is also little doubt that he had a significant influence over the dispersal of the paintings and, therefore, the art gallery collections that exist today. Mountford's choice, however, to collect bark paintings would appear to have been based on the desire to obtain the imagery rather than the actual art form. His collection of paintings on paper reflects this idea, as does his description of paper as bark in the publications resulting from the expedition (Mountford 1956).

Mountford's interest in Aboriginal culture was largely based around art but he did not consider himself an anthropologist as much as a recorder of culture (Lamshed 1972: 159). It is important to realize that the ethnologist believed artistic expression could be studied independently of social organization, a view scorned by his colleagues (Elliott 1992: 7). This may be reflected in his eagerness to collect artistic forms of expression and his lack of concern at artists using paper or bark to produce this art. Mountford believed that someone could better interpret this art in the future and his concern was in preservation so that future research could be conducted (Lamshed 1972: 188). The 1948

Arnhem Land Expedition collections are some of the worst documented collections from this time period in Australia.

While this chapter has been largely concerned with the non-Aboriginal collection and treatment of these paintings, it is important to consider the significance of these collections for Aboriginal people. Tuhiwai Smith has asserted, "It is through these disciplines that the Aboriginal world has been *re*presented to the West and it is through these disciplines that Aboriginal peoples often *re*-search for the fragments of ourselves which were taken, catalogued, studied and stored" (1999: 58–59). She is here referring to disciplines such as anthropology and archaeology and her words have significance for the Arnhem Land Expedition and its collections. It is clear that in 1948 Aboriginal Australians were "recorded" alongside the flora and the fauna of Arnhem Land. Their photographs were taken, their movements recorded, their body parts measured, their implements and artistic creations collected and the findings published. What impact did this have on the communities visited? And what is the legacy of the Arnhem Land Expedition collections for Aboriginal communities today? In the following and final chapter I explore these issues and the importance of the collected materials that provide a tangible link between past and present.

NOTES

1. This is not to say that more were not collected and will be documented in the future.

2. I have deliberately left the spelling of names the same as Mountford recorded in 1948, as the spelling itself is an important historical record.

3. John Mulvaney (2004) provides a detailed history of the life and work of Paddy Cahill at Oenpelli.

11

The Ongoing Impact

A fish that looks exactly like a leaf, a multi-coloured praying mantis, intricate string games the aborigines play, a fungus used to cure wounds, a stone axe that answered a long-asked question—these are a few of the discoveries of Australian and American scientists of the Arnhem Land expedition.

—ABC Weekly, *November 27, 1948: 13*

To explore the history and analyze an ethnographic collection formed only sixty years ago, when some of the participants are still living, seems premature and may be frightening for those who expected to be dead before becoming part of the archaeological or historical record. Despite these fears, this book is far from an ad hominem criticism of those who came before but rather emphasizes some of the changes that have, and have not, occurred in the disciplines of archaeology, anthropology, museology, and others areas concerned with such expeditions and their collections. I spoke in the opening to this book about the confronting nature of many cross-cultural interactions and the significance of such events in individuals' lives. Alongside of providing some final thoughts and facts about the Arnhem Land Expedition, this final chapter explores the significance of the expedition for people today.

The Arnhem Land Expedition is a well-documented, cross-cultural encounter but the diaries and the films tell only one part of the story. Exploring the history and the nature of the collections as I have done in this book can potentially help to bridge this gulf. Throughout this book I have tried to take you on a journey from the preparation for the expedition, into the field, and across Australia and the world as the ethnographic objects found their way to new homes. These stories bring us closer to the people involved and tell us more about their beliefs, practices, and influences on contemporary society. Yet, this is not a story with an end. Today most institutions grapple with poorly contextualized collections and the nature of their acquisition. At the same time the Aboriginal communities visited in 1948 deal in part with a legacy of loss created by the collectors. Most of the objects collected in 1948 were produced for trade and are, therefore, symbols of empowered communities seizing the opportunity to exchange with the visitors. Other items have different stories to tell. In line with this, I begin this chapter with a case study from the expedition and ask how it affects lives today. How has the expedition influenced our view of the people (Aboriginal and non-Aboriginal) involved and how has it continued to impact upon the lives of indigenous Australians?

In 2007 representatives of indigenous groups from around the world addressed a United Nations meeting in New York and declared, "Indigenous peoples must participate as equal partners in all stages of data collection, including planning, implementation, analysis and dissemination" (May 22, 2007). This is a feeling that resonates through the work of most of those associated with professional institutions and involved in the collection of cultural items or properties today but which would seem astonishing to the 1948 collectors. Clearly, attitudes toward the collection and ownership of cultural properties have changed (see, e.g., McBryde 1985; Messenger 1989; Smith 2005; Tuhiwai Smith 1999).

As discussed in chapters 4, 5, and 6, the collectors of ethnographic artifacts during the Arnhem Land Expedition came with preexisting attitudes toward Australian Aboriginal people and to the acquisition of their material culture. So, could we call the acquisition of the ethnographic collection ethical for its time? The answer to this is far from straightforward. The Aboriginal people were not victims but were largely active participants in these exchanges, especially in relation to ethnographic artifacts. Individuals were paid for their artifacts or were traded tobacco or items such as razor blades. For its time, the payment scale used by Charles Mountford and the other collectors appears to have been quite fair. McCarthy's diaries tell us that 10 shillings to 1 pound was paid for each bark painting, 4 shillings to 10 shillings for spears, 5 shillings to 10 shillings for baskets, 10 shillings to 15 shillings for mats and so forth (Mc-Carthy August 8, 1948).

It also appears that few of the collected ethnographic artifacts existed prior to the expedition members arriving or, in other words, *most ethnographic artifacts collected during the Arnhem Land Expedition were made for sale* and the majority of others were artifacts that could easily be spared (such as children's toys). Aboriginal people in these regions had experience with collectors. They understood the process of exchange, they understood that the objects would be taken away, and some would have understood they would be displayed. As Luke Taylor argues for western Arnhem Land, "Kunwinjku artists have struck an excellent balance between their requirements for art and the opportunities provided through the market to obtain income and extend their social and communicative horizons" (1996: 3).

In other words, these collections illustrate an important period in the developing market for Aboriginal art and artifacts—a time when Aboriginal groups were reaching compromises between the protection of certain knowledge from uninitiated people and the need or desire for trade items and cash (Taylor 1996: 24). In western Arnhem Land, such issues had been arising since 1912 when Baldwin Spencer began commissioning bark paintings (Spencer 1928: 793–94; May 2006: 76–77). Charles Mountford's decision to establish a tent as a shop for people to bring items they wanted to sell inadvertently played into the hands of the Aboriginal communities trying to establish boundaries for items to trade. Local people were empowered to decide what to trade.

Unlike many earlier collections from Australia, this ethnographic collection contains very few artifacts that should not have been removed from their communities. The result is that Aboriginal communities embrace these ethnographic collections as an important part of their heritage rather than a legacy of loss. However, other collections from the Arnhem Land Expedition have a different legacy. One example of this is the collection of human skeletal remains (the physical anthropological collection) formed by Frank Setzler and Fred McCarthy. It is important to briefly explore this controversial collection, in order to have a more thorough understanding of the positive and negative collection strategies employed—and their differing legacies.

The acquisition of the ethnographic collection was significantly different to the physical anthropological collections formed during the Arnhem Land

Expedition. There was little exchange involved in the collection of human remains and little, if any, consultation. The ongoing impact of this collection, therefore, is very different to the largely positive legacy of the ethnographic collection.

Human skeletal remains are known to have been taken from the following eight locations during the Arnhem Land Expedition:

1. Chasm Island
2. Winchelsea Island
3. Bartalombo Bay (Groote Eylandt)
4. Port Bradshaw
5. Milingimbi Island
6. Gallery Hill (Oenpelli)
7. Oenpelli Hill (Oenpelli)
8. Red Lilly Lagoon (near Oenpelli)

The significance of this collection and the struggle for their return will be explored throughout this chapter as one example of the impact that such collecting expeditions have had.

As I was finishing this book in Oenpelli I received an e-mail from a colleague in Canberra telling me that many of the human remains taken during the Arnhem Land Expedition were to be returned in 2008. The Aboriginal and Torres Strait Islander Commission (ATSIC) had been developing a case for their return since 2001 when I brought the matter to their attention. As a result of my research for this book, I became aware of the human remains from this expedition in early 2000 when I visited the Smithsonian to view and photograph the bark-painting collection. I was shown the remains by staff at the National Museum of Natural History and allowed to produce a list of the collection. The Arnhem Land Expedition human remains made up the majority of their Australian collection and, despite little research ever having been undertaken, was a collection of significance to them.

From this point on, as an aside to historical research relating to the ethnographic collection, I collected literature relating to the human remains and some of this is documented in May 2001 and May and colleagues 2005. The

most significant of these findings was an agreement between Charles Mountford and Secretary of the Smithsonian Institution Alexander Wetmore. On
April 23, 1951, Mountford wrote to Wetmore suggesting the skeletal material
from the Arnhem Land Expedition remain at the Smithsonian, "until we are
ready to put them in the Museum in Canberra." Mountford's estimate was
that a national museum would be built in four to five years and that it was unnecessary to transport the material twice. Wetmore, in response to Mountford
later in 1951, agreed to his suggestion, stating the Smithsonian Institution
would hold the material "until your authorities are ready to receive them." The
skeletal material was then forgotten for decades.

The return of the Arnhem Land Expedition skeletal material is particularly
significant as only one item collected during the Arnhem Land Expedition has
ever been returned to its Aboriginal community. This was a ceremonial object
acquired from Oenpelli in 1948 and repatriated by the Australian Museum in
1975. The significance of this impending 2008 return, therefore, inspires me
to tell a longer story about their collection and distribution as an example of
the ongoing impact of this sixty-year-old expedition.

> The term "trade" assumes at the very least a two-way transaction between those
> who sold and those who bought. It further assumes that human beings and
> other cultural items were commodities or goods and were actually available "for
> sale." For indigenous peoples those assumptions are not held. From indigenous
> perspectives territories, peoples and their possessions were stolen, not traded.
> (Tuhiwai Smith 1999: 89)

During the 1948 Arnhem Land Expedition more than 241 individual human bones were excavated or removed from their place of internment by
Fred McCarthy and Frank Setzler. The story of their collection and distribution is not a usual one for Aboriginal groups around the world, nor is the
delay in bringing them home again. Today the removal of human remains
in the name of science and their return to communities is an issue being
negotiated and debated around the world. Some would suggest that the
preservation and appreciation of cultures through the collection of any
material items or human remains is fundamental to the preservation of the
past (see, e.g., Ortiz 2003: 15). As Frank Setzler stated, "These specimens

are most important to our science of anthropology. . . . This skull will not only be well preserved in our museum but will contribute much to the study of these primitive aborigines" (January 13, 1950: 34). Others would question the ownership of these materials by anyone.

REMOVING THE ANCESTORS

In the old days, before I was born, they use to put them [the bodies] on a platform and leave them there until the flesh is gone. Then the elders, the old men, would collect the bones and take them up the hill. They would colour them with red ochre. Red is an important colour for the spirit. Then they would leave them there forever. Other Bininj [local Aboriginal] people would come and see them or show them to young people. They would tell them stories about how they had been put up here and painted and so on. When we look at the bones it reminds us of the people who've been living here.

—*Gabriel Maralngurra, Oenpelli 2002*

Most of the sites from which the human remains were removed are of the utmost significance as cultural or spiritual sites today as they were sixty years ago when the Arnhem Land Expedition visited. Did the collectors know this? It is likely they did. Cressida Fforde points out, "Settlers were aware of the sanctity of Aboriginal graves. While some collectors appeared unconcerned at the prospect of removing human remains and grave goods, others did so with trepidation" (2002: 27). Likewise, it is clear that for the collectors who worried their actions were wrong the belief that their work was for the good of science maintained them. If Basedow in 1904 was aware of Aboriginal concerns with the removal of human remains, then McCarthy and Setzler must have also been aware of the issues more than forty years later (Fforde 2002: 27).

While Mountford claims that throughout the expedition Aboriginal people cooperated with team members and happily assisted with their research, expedition botanist Raymond Specht has, for example, recently suggested that there was less cross-cultural interaction at the final base camp, Oenpelli, than in other places visited. This was largely due to the local Anglican mission's lack of enthusiasm for the Arnhem Land Expedition (Specht 2002) or, as Mountford recalls "the local mission station using most of the available aboriginal labor for the killing and skinning of water buffaloes" (1956: 111). So why did the mission not cooperate? They had negative experiences with earlier researchers and they knew the impact such visitors could have. At Oenpelli, Dick Harris had hosted anthropologist Donald Thomson who arrived on July 1, 1936, and stayed for a few days before walking overland toward Goulburn Island (Cole 1975: 36–37; Cole 1980: 26). Thomson reported to the Australian government following this visit and criticized the work of the mission stations in Arnhem Land. In particular he was concerned that:

> The collecting of natives, not detribalised into compounds or institutions, should be prohibited. If it is desired to teach Christianity to these people, it should be insisted that the Christian teacher or missionary be prepared to visit the people in their own country, and not to gather them about a station or mission school. (Thomson 1935–1936: 45)

This negative report made the anthropologist an enemy of the Church Missionary Society, including their official historian, Keith Cole, who many years later labeled Thomson's suggestions for change as "simplistic and naïve" (Cole 1975: 37).

As a result, interaction between local Aboriginal people and expedition members at Oenpelli was limited and there is little information available within Oenpelli today relating to the removal of the human remains from this region. Senior Aboriginal community member Jacob Nayinggul (2002) suggests that people may have assumed the collectors were interested only in "baskets and paintings" and may have been unaware they were "picking up bones."

The human remains from the Arnhem Land Expedition were collected as part of the archaeological research program and Fred McCarthy and Frank Setzler declared that they "took advantage of every opportunity to examine and if possible excavate carefully as many sites as possible" (McCarthy and Setzler, in Mountford 1960: 216). These excavations emerged with hundreds of artifacts as well as human remains. Other artifacts and human remains were simply removed from rock ledges or surface scatters. Oenpelli community member Wilfred Nawirridj (2002) explains the significance of these rock ledge burials in western Arnhem Land:

> Well, the oldest people they use to do this. They didn't go and just bury it in the ground area. They use to put it inside the cave or the hollow log and all that. So

that's our culture. Our old traditional way. That's our culture, no one use to go and see those bones especially all that balanda [non-Aboriginal people]. Only the Aboriginal people use to go and show all the young people. Only the Traditional Owners can say something to the bones.

Frank Setzler's records state that the human remains from Gallery Hill (known locally as Injalak Hill) were collected from narrow rock crevices. He suggests that they found few remains in the archaeological excavations they undertook on this hill. He also states, "The bones were disarticulated; they may have been originally placed in the crevices in the customary paper bark wrappings, all of which had disintegrated. Some of the bones had fallen out of the narrow crevices and were found on the ground" (Setzler 1948a). The remains represent both sexes and range from adults to infants and one skull from this site has European fabric attached to it, suggesting it was a recent burial (Setzler 1948b). Frank Setzler's photographs back up these statements.

Setzler states the following in regard to another burial site: "The skeletons from Oenpelli Hill [known locally as Arguluk Hill] were found in a small rock crevice on the north side of cave site nos. 1 and 2, on the highest point of Oenpelli Hill. These skeletons were disarticulated and indicated the effect of weathering" (Setzler 1948a). The significance of this site (Arguluk Hill) is best described by Oenpelli community member Gabriel Maralngurra (2002):

> Right at the top of Arguluk Hill is a cave with a few paintings. There use to be burials in this cave. Arguluk is *Manimunak Djang* or Magpie Goose Dreaming. The hill is a *wirllarrk* or egg from a *manimunak.* It is a sacred place for men's business and it is an important place for initiation ceremonies.

Alongside of the human remains removed from rock ledges, the archaeologists obtained remains during the excavation of site #2 on Oenpelli Hill (Arguluk Hill) (Setzler 1948a). The remains, once again, represent both sexes but the ages of the individuals are not estimated by the collectors (Setzler 1948b). Finally, the archaeologists took a single adult female skull from a site near Red Lily Lagoon, which is around 10 kilometers from Oenpelli. As traditional owner of Oenpelli, Donald Gumurdul explains, "Well I think the material that

they took out we want it back, it's very special, because it must be our ancestors before when I was born. Some of them are my great, great grandfathers.
We will rebury them up there in that cave, I know where it is. It's important to
us especially me and Jacob [Nayinggul] and all them Mengerrdji tribe" (Gumurdul 2002).

Not all of the skeletal material collected from Arnhem Land was solely
Aboriginal Australian in origin. One Aboriginal man who assisted the Arnhem Land Expedition on Groote Eylandt, Gerry Blitner, recalls that "Frank
Setzler, he wanted all the bones that he could find and all the Macassan heads
that he could see" (Thomas 2007a). For example, during excavations at Port
Bradshaw Setzler and McCarthy came across and collected two individuals
who were thought to be of "Malay" origin. The archaeologists excavated a rec-
tangular rock formation measuring eight feet by four feet and soon came
across the two burials just two feet, nine inches down. Both were evidently
buried at the same time. After perplexing at the unusual burial style they approached expedition guide Bill Harney for assistance. He reported the following story to them:

> In 1916 Captain Luff from Thursday Island, with five trepang or lugger boats,
> had a camp along the shores of Port Bradshaw. During one of his return trips
> to Thursday Island he left a half-caste from the latter island and a Malay in
> charge of his trepang camp on this peninsula. They were assisted by three na-
> tive families from Borroloola. One day in April the half-caste was sitting on
> a log near the beach while the Malay was swimming near by. Two natives
> from the Port Bradshaw region sat on either side of the half-caste. At a pre-
> arranged signal another Port Bradshaw native came from behind and threw
> a spear into the back of the half-caste. Seeing the commotion the Malay
> started swimming towards a small cutter, but the Port Bradshaw natives
> harpooned him as they would a dugong or turtle. The Borroloola natives
> were able to escape in a small cutter to Borroloola, where they reported the
> murder to the police. A month later the police came to Port Bradshaw, dis-
> covered the bodies and buried them along the beach. (McCarthy and Setzler
> 1960: 230)

While Oenpelli and Port Bradshaw have been a focus here, human remains
were also collected from the locations shown in table 11.1.

Table 11.1.   Locations from which Human Remains were Collected during the Arnhem Land Expedition

Location	Location
Chasm Island	Milingimbi Island
Winchelsea Island	Gallery Hill (Injalak Hill), Oenpelli
Bartalombo Bay, Groote Eylandt	Oenpelli Hill (Arguluk Hill), Oenpelli
Port Bradshaw	Red Lily Lagoon, near Oenpelli

TRACING ANCESTORS

The fieldwork component of the Arnhem Land Expedition officially came to a conclusion in early November 1948. So, what happened to the human remains once they were removed from Arnhem Land? They were packed into crates and delivered to the Australian Museum and, from there, forwarded directly to the Smithsonian Institution in Washington, D.C. The Smithsonian Institution received this collection because their staff intended to undertake extensive research and publish the results in the official records of the expedition (Mountford 1956, 1960; Mountford and Specht 1958; Specht 1964). It was decided in the field that following this research, the human remains (often referred to as the "biological specimens") were to be returned to the Australian Museum in Sydney. Fred McCarthy sheds more light on the long-term plans for the human remains:

> On August 16, 1954, I received a confidential letter, which must not be quoted, from the Head Curator of Anthropology at the United States National Museum, which quotes the following statement from a letter written by Mountford to the Secretary of the Smithsonian Institution, on April 23, 1951: "There is a move to establish a Museum at our National capital, and I am making a now official inquiry as to whether it would be possible for you to store in Washington the biological specimens belonging to Australia until we are ready to put them in the museum at Canberra, which may be in four or five years time. That would save a double transfer and a risk of damage to the specimens." Setzler comments "that is why they are still here and evidently—C.P.M. [Charles Pearcy Mountford]—never had any intention that these specimens were to go to your Museum." (February 9, 1955)

As discussed earlier, Mountford did, in fact, write the letter to Wetmore, from which McCarthy quotes, suggesting the remains from the Arnhem Land Expedition be kept at his institution "until we are ready to put them in the

Museum in Canberra" (Mountford, April 23, 1951). Wetmore also agreed stating the Smithsonian Institution would hold the material "until your authorities are ready to receive them" (Wetmore 1951). The National Museum of Australia was established in 1980 but its current premises did not open until March 11, 2001, decades later than Mountford had predicted.

In 1955, when assessments were being made on the other collections of material from the 1948 expedition, the skeletal material again came into question. Apparently forgetting his correspondence with Wetmore, or realizing that no national museum was to be built in the near future, Mountford met with Kevin Murphy (Department of Information) and J. W. Evans (director of the Australian Museum) to decide upon the distribution. In reference to the skeletal material it was stated that "these are at present at the Smithsonian Institute, which is being asked to return two-thirds to Canberra to be kept here" (Meeting Minutes, March 24, 1955). If this request was made, it was not followed through and considering all of the other suggestions regarding the collections were followed up after the meeting, it seems unusual that this one alone was ignored (May 2000: 227; May et al. 2005).

Perhaps remembering that the skeletal material was initially to be returned to the Australian Museum (and almost certainly prompted by McCarthy), Murphy wrote to Evans two months after the meeting stating "that Dr. Kellogg's museum [Smithsonian Institution] should retain one-third of this material and return the remaining two-thirds to me in Canberra for subsequent distribution as determined" (May 23, 1955). Today, sixty years later, around a third of the skeletal material known to have been acquired during the Arnhem Land Expedition is still held at the National Museum of Natural History (Smithsonian Institution) in Washington, D.C. In 2008 representatives from Groote Eylandt (Thomas Amagula and Joaz Wurramurra) and Oenpelli (Donald Gumurdul and Alfred Nayinggul) flew to Washington D.C. to take home some of the remains after the Smithsonian agreed to abide by the original agreement and return two-thirds of the collection. In early 2009 these remains were returned to country after an absence of 60 years. Negotiations for the return of the remaining third of the collection continue.

COMPLETING THE JIGSAW

Even though we have discussed the situation in which the Aboriginal groups of Arnhem Land find themselves, this story must resonate across Australia and around the world—indigenous groups searching for the fragments of their culture that have been removed in the name of scientific research.

This case study is just one example of the impact that the Arnhem Land Expedition had, and continues to have, on the Aboriginal communities they visited. So, when assessing the significance of the findings from this study, the question must first be asked—significance for whom?

It is clear that the people in the Aboriginal communities visited during the Arnhem Land Expedition were recorded alongside the flora and fauna of the Arnhem Land region. Their photographs were taken, their movements recorded, their implements and artistic creations collected, and the findings published—primarily for the benefit of non-Aboriginal people. To a large extent Aboriginal people were pawns in a game being played by the Commonwealth of Australia. Aboriginal people were used to further political and social goals, such as publicity, while the impact this would have upon the communities was ignored. Alongside of this are Mountford, McCarthy, and Setzler who made a living from Aboriginal knowledge and material culture. These researchers gained kudos and promotion within their institutions as well as outside recognition.

It is hoped that Aboriginal communities will find this book useful. For example, it provides important information on the present distribution of the collections and an understanding of the role it played and continues to play in non-Aboriginal culture. Alongside of this, the findings presented in this book, such as aspects of representation of Aboriginal cultures in museums and art galleries, the changing role of Aboriginal artifacts in Western culture and, specifically, museums and art galleries, may assist in the understanding of the significance of this expedition and the collections.

Despite the obvious negative aspects that plague the Arnhem Land Expedition, it should also be declared that this expedition provided a unique opportunity for Aboriginal communities who were, by 1948, well aware of the desires of researchers. The wish for an ethnographic collection placed these communities in a situation of power in a variety of ways and, in turn, they made the most of these opportunities, gaining money, food, and goods (albeit in small amounts) in return for a number of services.

It is important to understand that this encounter was part of a wider movement influenced by contemporary beliefs relating to the nature of so-called Western and Aboriginal cultures. Why, in 1948, was collecting from Aboriginal Australians such an important endeavor for governments and cultural institutions? Much of this book has been concerned with an understanding of the phenomenon of collecting and as Foucault has stated, "The idea of accumulating everything, of establishing a sort of general archive, the will to enclose in one place at all times, all epochs, all forms, all tastes, the idea of constituting a place of all times that is itself outside of time and inaccessible to its ravages, the project of organising in this a sort of perpetual and indefinite accumulation of time in an immobile place, this whole idea belongs to our modernity" (1986: 26).

In the context of this book the key issues are notions of collecting or salvaging specimens of cultures and the impact of Social Darwinism on collecting in Australia. While the desire to collect could initially be seen as straightforward, on closer examination they are often found to have aspects that have ingress to other, nonmuseological aspects of life. The influence of Social Darwinism and the "evolutionary ladder" placed Australian indigenous people on rungs lower than most other cultures and meant that the Arnhem Land Expedition members came to Arnhem Land with certain beliefs influencing their work. A belief that the cultures they were studying were soon to be lost, primarily through outside influences, meant a sense of urgency underlined the collection of material culture. Though all of these theoretical influences had come into question through other investigations, this has still proven to be the primary cultural understanding surrounding the Arnhem Land Expedition ethnographic collection. The most obvious evidence of this is in the disappointment felt by members of the Arnhem Land Expedition on discovering their "stone-age men" wearing jeans, playing cards, and using American slang on Groote Eylandt.

Also significant is the fact that museums and art galleries desired certain objects and certain types of art from this expedition—and not always what they had traditionally collected. Morphy (1998: 29) has suggested that interest in Australian Aboriginal art increased and shifted following World War II. He stated that researchers became interested in art as an expression of religious values rather than an indicator of evolutionary progress. This, in turn, contributed to changing views from one of Aboriginal art as primitive to works by these artists being seen and admired for their aesthetic value (Morphy 1998: 26). The paintings collected during the Arnhem Land Expedition found homes across Australia and the world and were integral to shifting societies' views of Aboriginal art as fine art rather than artifact. At the same time, this research has shown that even in 1948, museums and art galleries were not yet willing to comply with this new phenomenon.

CONTEMPLATING COLLECTING

There is much work still to be done relating to the Arnhem Land Expedition and its collections and I hope that this book will assist in bringing the collections to the attention of the people who have the skills and the time to conduct this work. It is essential that museums and art galleries consult with the communities visited by the Arnhem Land Expedition to contextualize their artifacts. The lack of Aboriginal voices in the records and documentation of this expedition must be addressed by museums and art galleries that today house the collections. This consultation will assist in determining the identity of the manufacturers of many of the artifacts collected and provide a further opportunity for communities to reengage with the collections and associated film, sound, and photographs (see, e.g., Thomas 2007a). In keeping these artifacts, museums and galleries enter into a contract of engagement with Arnhem Land communities—for the benefit of all.

> What it accomplished is said to have been scientifically considerable, but is not measurable now, and perhaps never will be. Such findings take years to write and codify and publish and disseminate. When that is completed, the use of them is only at the beginning. (Simpson 1951: 40)

References

Aagaard-Mogensen, L. (Ed.). 1988. *Problems in contemporary philosophy: Vol. 6. The Idea of the museum: Philosophical, artistic, and political questions.* Lewiston, NY: Edwin Mellen Press.

Advertiser, Adelaide (1948, February 28). *Arnhem Land is far from unknown.*

Altman, J. (1982). Artists and artisans in Gunwinggu society. In P. Cooke and J. Altman (Eds.), *Aboriginal art at the top* (pp. 12–16). Maningrida, Northern Territory: Maningrida Arts and Crafts.

Anonymous. (1957, March). Review of art, myth and symbolism. *Walkabout*, 45.

Attenbrow, V., and Khan, K. (1994). FD McCarthy: His work and legacy at the Australian Museum. In Sullivan, M, Brockwell, S, and Webb, A. (Eds.), *Archaeology in the north, proceedings of the 1993 Australian Archaeological Association Conference.* Darwin: North Australia Research Unit.

Attwood, B. and Arnold, J. (Eds.) (1992). *Power, knowledge and the aborigines.* Melbourne: La Trobe University Press.

Australasian Post. (1951, July 5). *Calwell: Deputy.*

Barton, H. (2007). Starch residues on museum artefacts: implications for determining tool use. *Journal of Archaeological Science, 34*(10), 1752–62.

Bennett, T. (1995). *The birth of the museum.* London: Routledge.

Berndt, R. (1958). The Mountford volume on Arnhem Land art, myth and symbolism: A critical review. *Mankind, 5/6*, 249–61.

Berndt, R., and Berndt, C. (1954). *Arnhem Land: Its history and people.* Melbourne: *FW Cheshire.*

Berndt, R., and Berndt, C. (1970). *Man, Land and Myth in North Australia: the Gunwinggu people.* Sydney: Ure Smith.

Berndt, R., and Berndt, C. (1988). *The world of the first Australians, Aboriginal traditional life: past and present.* Canberra: Australian Institute of Aboriginal Studies.

Berndt, R.M. (1983). 'A living Aboriginal art: the changing inside and outside contexts'. In P. Cook and P. Loveday (eds.) *Aboriginal arts and crafts and the market.* Darwin, Australian National University Northern Australia Research Unit Monograph. pp. 29–36.

Block, E. (1987). *Possum Skin Rugs.* Unpublished Honors BA Dissertation, Australian National University, Canberra.

Bouteiller, M. (1957). Review of *Records Of American/Australian Scientific Expedition to Arnhem Land, Vol. 1: Art, Myth and Symbolism. L'Anthropologie, 61*(1–2), 148–49.

Brandl, E. (1973). *Australian Aboriginal Paintings in Western and Central Arnhem Land: temporal sequences and elements of style in Cadell River and Deaf Adder Creek art.* Canberra: Australian Institute Of Aboriginal Studies.

Briggs, L. J. (1945, April 20). Letter to G. Grosvenor, in possession of the Smithsonian Institution Archives, Accession file 178294, Washington, DC.

Brittain, N. (1990). *The South Australian Museum collection of Aboriginal bark paintings from Northern Australia.* Unpublished Honours BA Thesis, Flinders University of South Australia, Adelaide.

Brody, A. (1985). *Kunwinjku Bim: Western Arnhem Land Paintings from the collection of the Aboriginal Arts Board.* Melbourne: National Gallery of Victoria.

Brown, P. (1995). Cannery days: Museum exhibits and Heiltsuk perspectives. *Northern review, 14*, 48–57.

Buhmann, J., Robins, R., and Cause, M. (1976). Wood identification of spearthrowers in the Queensland Museum, *A.I.A.S. newsletter, 5*, 43–44.

Bunce, D. (1857). *Australasiatic reminiscences*. Melbourne: Government Printer.

Calwell, A. (1947, February 28). Letter to J. J. Dedman, in possession of the National Archives of Australia, Series A 9816/4, 1947/89, Part One NADC, Arnhem Land Expedition, Canberra.

Calwell, A. (1978). *Be just and fear not*. Adelaide: Rigby Limited.

Cant, J. (1950). *Australian aboriginal art paintings*. London: Berkeley Galleries.

Carrington, F. (1890). *The Rivers of the Northern Territory of South Australia*. Royal Geographic Society of Australasia (S.A. Branch) Proceedings 2: 56–76.

Carroll, P. (1983). 'Aboriginal Art from Western Arnhem Land'. In P. Loveday and P. Cooke (Eds.), *Aboriginal Arts and Crafts and the Market*. Darwin: The Australian National University North Australia Research Unit, pp. 44–49.

Chaloupka, G. (1984). *From Palaeoart to Casual Paintings*. Darwin: Northern Territory Museums and Art Galleries.

Chaloupka, G. (1993). *Journey in Time: the world's longest continuing art tradition: the 50,000-year story of the Australian Aboriginal rock art of Arnhem Land*. Chatswood, N.S.W.: Reed.

Chapman, W. R. (1985). Arranging ethnology: A. H. L. F. Pitt Rivers and the typological tradition. *History of anthropology, 3*, 15–48.

Clarke, A. (1998). Engendered fields: The language of the 1948 American-Australian expedition to Arnhem Land. In *Redefining Archaeology, Feminist Perspectives*. Canberra: North Australia Research Unit.

Clifford, J. (1988). *The predicament of culture: Twentieth century ethnography, literature and art*. Cambridge, MA: Harvard University Press.

Clifford, J. (1997). Museums as contact zones. In *Routes: Travel and translation in the late twentieth century* (pp. 186–219). Cambridge, MA: Harvard University Press.

Clunas, G. (1991). *Superfluous things: Material culture and social status in early modern china*. Cambridge, MA: Polity Press.

Coates, I. (1989). *The social construction of the John Forrest Australian Aboriginal ethnographic collection: Past and present*. Unpublished Honours BA Thesis, Australian National University, Canberra.

Coen, L. H. (1983). *Register to the papers of Otis Tufton Mason.* National Anthropological Archives, Smithsonian Institution.

Cole, K. (1972). *Oenpelli Pioneer: A biography of the Rev. Alfred John Dyer, pioneer missionary among the Aborigines in Arnhem Land and founder of the Oenpelli Mission.* Melbourne: Church Missionary Historical Publishing.

Cole, K. (1975). *A history of Oenpelli.* Darwin: Nungalinya Publications.

Cole, K. (1980). *Dick Harris, missionary to the Aborigines: A biography of the Reverend Canon George Richmond Harris, M.B.E., pioneer missionary to the Aborigines of Arnhem Land.* Melbourne: Bendigo, Keith Cole Publications.

Cole, T. (1988). *Hell west and crooked.* Sydney: Collins Publishers.

Cooke, P. (1982). Towards a balance. In Cooke, P., and Altmann, J. (Eds.), *Aboriginal art at the top* (pp. 26–28). Maningrida: Maningrida Arts and Crafts.

Cooper, C. (1975). *The Beechworth collection of Aboriginal artefacts.* Unpublished Honors BA Thesis, Australian National University, Canberra.

Crimp, D. (1987, March–May). The postmodern museum. *Parachute, 46,* 65–67.

Crocker, A. (1987). *Charlie Tjaruru Tjungurranyi: A retrospective 1970–1986.* Orange: Orange City Council.

Curr, E. (Ed.). (1886). *The Australian race: Its origin, languages, customs, place of landing in Australia, and the routes by which it spread itself over that continent,* 4 vols. Melbourne: Government Printer.

Daily Mirror. (1948, August 21).

Daily Telegraph. (1948, December 11). *Man About Town.*

Daniels, G. (1975). *A hundred and fifty years of archaeology,* 2nd ed. London: Duckworth.

Darwin, C. (1859). *The origin of species.* London: Murray.

Darwin, C. (1871). *Descent of man.* New York: Modern Library.

Deignan, H. (1948, August 26). Letter to A. Wetmore, in possession of the Smithsonian Institution Archives, Accession File 178294, Washington, DC.

Dewar, M. (1995). *The 'Black War' in Arnhem Land: Missionaries and the Yolngu 1908–1940.* Canberra: North Australia Research Unit.

Dominguez, V. (1987). Of other peoples: Beyond the salvage paradigm. In Foster, H. (Ed.), *Discussions in contemporary culture* (pp. 131–37). Seattle: Bay Press.

Duncan, C. (1995). Civilizing Rituals: Inside public art museums. New York: Routledge.

Elkin, A. P. (1945, May 30). Letter to the Secretary of the National Geographic Society, in possession of the Smithsonian Institution Archives, Accession file 178294, Washington, DC.

Elkin, A. P. (1961). Review of art, myth and symbolism. *Oceania, 32*(1), 54–58.

Elkin, A. P. (1964). *The Australian Aborigine*, 4th ed. Sydney: Angus and Robertson.

Ellemor, A. (1949, June 21). Letter to Mountford, in possession of the State Library of South Australia, Mortlock Library, Mountford-Sheard Collection, Publication Correspondence 1949–1951, V.525.

Elliott, C. (1992). *American Australian scientific expedition to Arnhem Land.* Unpublished Cataloging Consultancy Report, National Museum of Australia, Canberra.

Elsner, J., and Cardinal, R. (Eds.). (1994). *The cultures of collecting.* Melbourne: Melbourne University Press.

Evans, J. W. (1955, February 11). Letter to the Director of the News and Information Bureau, in possession of the Australian Museum Archives, Series 235 G70/513, Sydney.

Evans, J. W. (1957, August 15). Letter to Kellogg, in possession of the Australian Museum Archives, series 235, Central Correspondence Files 1949–1969; G70/513, Arnhem Land Expedition, Sydney.

Evening Star. (1948, July 19). Smithsonian scientists move into new camp in Australian Jungle.

Fagan, B. (1998). *Clash of cultures.* Lanham, MD: AltaMira Press.

Fenton, W. (1974). The advancement of culture studies in modern anthropological research. In Richardson, M. (Ed.), *The human mirror: Material and spatial images of man* (pp.15–36). Baton Rouge: Louisiana State University Press.

Fforde, C. (2002). *Collecting the dead: Archaeology and the reburial issue.* London: Duckworth.

Fforde, C., Hubert, J., and Turnbull, P. (Eds.). (2004). *The dead and their possessions.* New York and London: Routledge.

Flood, J. (1997). *Rock Art of the Dreamtime: Images of Ancient Australia.* Pymble, N.S.W.: Angus & Robertson, and New York: HarperCollins Publishers.

Florek, S. (1993). F. D. McCarthy's string figures from Yirrkala: A museum perspective. *Records of the Australian Museum,* Supplement 17, pp. 117–24.

Foucault, M. (1970). *The order of things.* London: Tavistock Publications.

Foucault, M. (1977). *Discipline and punish: The birth of the prison.* Harmondsworth: Penguin.

Foucault, M. (1986). Of other spaces. *Diacritics, 16*(1), 22–27.

Giddens, A. and Pierson, C. (1998), *Conversations With Anthony Giddens: Making Sense of Modernity,* Palo Alto: Stanford University Press.

Glassow, M. A. (1980). Recent developments in the archaeology of the Channel Islands. *The California Islands: Proceedings of an interdisciplinary symposium* (pp. 79–99). Santa Barbara: Santa Barbara Museum of Natural History.

Goswamy, B. (1991). Another past, another context: Exhibiting Indian art abroad. In Karp, I., and Lavine, S. (Eds.), *Exhibiting cultures: The poetics and politics of museum display* (pp. 68–78). Washington, DC: Smithsonian Institution Press.

Griffiths, T. (1996). *Hunters and collectors: The antiquarian imagination in Australia.* Cambridge: Cambridge University Press.

Groger-Wurm, H. (1973). *Australian Aboriginal bark paintings and their mythological interpretation, Vol. 1: Eastern Arnhem Land.* Canberra: Australian Institute of Aboriginal Studies.

Gruber, J. W. (1962). Review of AASEAL Records Vol. 2 Anthropology and Nutrition. *Archaeology,* Autumn.

Gumurdul, D. (2002). Personal correspondence to Sally K. May. Senior Traditional Owner, West Arnhem Land.

Haagen, C. (1994). Bush toys: Aboriginal children at play. Canberra: Aboriginal Studies Press.

Hamby, L. (Ed.). (2005). *Twined together: Kunmadj Njalehnjaleken.* Gunbalanya: Injalak Arts and Crafts.

Harrison, R. (2004). Kimberley Points and colonial preference: New insights into the chronology of pressure flaked point forms from Southeast Kimberley, Western Australia. *Archaeology in Oceania, 39*(1), 1–11.

Herald (Melbourne). (1945, July 20). *Mystery land will be revealed to all.*

Hipsley, E. H. (1954, June 28). Letter to Hale, in possession of the National Museum of Australia, Arnhem Land Expedition file, Canberra.

Hodder, I. (1999). *The archaeological process: An introduction.* Oxford: Blackwell Publishers.

Hofstadter, R. (1944). *Social Darwinism in American thought.* Cambridge, MA: Harvard University Press.

Hooper-Greenhill, E. (ed.). (1989). *Initiatives in museum education.* Leicester: Department of Museum Studies, University of Leicester.

Hudson, K. (1987). *Museums of influence.* Cambridge: Cambridge University Press.

Hunter, A., and Donovan, S. (2005). Field sampling bias, museum collections and completeness of the fossil record. *Lethaia, 38*(4), 305–14.

Hurst, Thomas, D. (2000). *Skull wars: Kennewick man, archaeology and the battle for Native American identity.* New York: Basic Books.

Johnson, D. H. (1955). The incredible kangaroo. *National geographic, 108*(4), 487–500.

Jones, C. (1987). *The toys of the American Australian Scientific Expedition to Arnhem Land ethnographic collection.* Unpublished Diploma Thesis, University of Sydney, Sydney.

Kaberry, P. M. (1962). *Records of the American-Australian Scientific Expedition to Arnhem Land Records: II. Anthropology and Nutrition. Geographical Journal, 128*(2), 229.

Kabo, V. R. (1958). Review of American Australian Scientific Expedition to Arnhem Land Vol. 1: Art, Myth and Symbolism. *Journal of the Institute of Ethnography of the Academy of Sciences,* v.1., p.5.

Karp, I., and Levine, S. (ed.). (1991). *Exhibiting cultures.* Washington, DC: Smithsonian Institution Press.

Katz, J. (2003). *Japanese paintings in the Ashmolean Museum, Oxford.* Oxford: Ashmolean Museum.

Kaye, H. L. (1986). *The social meaning of modern biology: From Social Darwinism to sociobiology.* New Brunswick and London: Transaction Publishers.

Kealhofer, L., Torrence, R., and Fullagar, R. (1999). Integrating Phytoliths within use-wear/residue studies of stone tools. *Journal of archaeological science, 26*(5), 527–46.

Knell, S. (ed.). (2004). *Museums and the future of collecting.* Aldershot: Ashgate Publishing.

Kunz, E. F. (1988). *Displaced persons: Calwell's new Australians.* Sydney: Australian National University Press.

Lamshed, M. (1972). *Monty: A biography of CP. Mountford.* Adelaide: Rigby.

Layton, R. (1997). *An introduction to theory in anthropology.* Cambridge: Cambridge University Press.

Lovejoy, O. (1964). *The great chain of being.* Cambridge, MA: Harvard University Press.

Lumley, R. (ed.). (1988). *The museum time machine: Putting cultures on display.* London: Routledge/Comedia.

Lyotard, J. F. (1984). *The post modern condition: A report on the condition of knowledge.* Manchester: Manchester University Press.

Macdonald, S., and Fife, G. (ed.). (1996). *Theorizing museums: Representing identity and diversity in a changing world.* Cambridge, MA: Blackwell.

MacGregor, A. (1997). *Summary catalogue of the continental archaeological collections in the Ashmolean Museum.* Oxford: Ashmolean Museum.

Mail (Adelaide). (1948, March 13). *What secrets will they find in Arnhem Land?*

Mail (Adelaide). (1948, July 17). *Scientists camping amid jungle, swamp.*

Maralngurra, G. (2002). Personal correspondence to Sally K. May. Artist, West Arnhem Land.

May, S. K. (2000). *The last frontier? Acquiring the American-Australian Scientific Expedition ethnographic collection 1948.* Unpublished Honours BA Thesis, Flinders University of South Australia, Adelaide.

May, S. K. (2001). *Report on the American-Australian scientific expedition to Arnhem Land physical anthropological collection 1948.* Unpublished report, Department of Archaeology, Flinders University of South Australia.

May, S. K. (2003). Colonial collections of portable art and intercultural encounters in Aboriginal Australia. In Faulstich, P., Ouzman, S., and Taçon, P. S. C. (Eds.), *Before farming: The archaeology and anthropology of hunter-gatherers* (pp. 1–17). Oakland, CA: AltaMira. v.1, 8, pp. 1–17.

May, S. K. (2005). Collecting the "Last Frontier." In Hamby, L. (Ed.), *Twined together* Melbourne: Museum Victoria, pp. 77–81.

May, S. K. (2006). *Karrikadjurren—Creating community with an art centre in indigenous Australia.* Unpublished PhD Dissertation, Centre for Cross-Cultural Research, Australian National University, Canberra.

May, S. K. (2007). Gerald Blitner interviewed by Sally K. May [digital film recording]. Research School of Humanities, Australian National University.

May, S. K., Gumurdul, D., Manakgu, J., Maralngurra, G., and Nawirridj, W. (2005). "You Write it Down and Bring it Back . . . That's What We Want."—Revisiting the 1948 Removal of Human Remains from Gunbalanya (Oenpelli), Australia. In Smith, C., and Wobst, H. M. (Eds.), *Indigenous peoples and archaeology.* London: Routledge.

McArthur, M., Billington, B. P., and Hodges, K. J. (2000). Nutrition and health (1948) of Aborigines in settlements in Arnhem Land, northern Australia. *Asia Pacific Journal of Clinical Nutrition, 9*(3), 164–213.

McArthur, M., McCarthy, F., and Specht, R. (2000). Nutrition studies (1948) of nomadic Aborigines in Arnhem Land, northern Australia. *Asia Pacific Journal of Clinical Nutrition, 9*(3), 215–23.

McBryde, I. (Ed.). (1978). *Records of times past: Ethnohistorical essays on the culture and ecology of the New England tribes.* Canberra: A.I.A.S.

McBryde, I. (Ed.). (1985). *Who owns the past?* Oxford: Oxford University Press.

McCarthy, E. D. (1984). Towards a sociology of the physical world: George Herbert Mead on physical objects. *Studies in symbolic interaction, 5,* 105–21.

McCarthy, F. (n.d.a). Report on scientific work, in possession of the Australian Museum Archives, Series 10 1927–1956, 22/1948, Sydney.

McCarthy, F. (n.d.b). Entry in Diary Six, in possession of the AIATSIS Library, MS3513 Box 22 Item 269, Canberra.

McCarthy, F. (1948, March 18). Entry in Diary One, in possession of the AIATSIS Library, MS3513 Box 22 Item 269, Canberra.

McCarthy, F. (1948, April 9). Entry in Diary Four, in possession of the AIATSIS Library, MS3513 Box 22 Item 269, Canberra.

McCarthy, F. (1948, April 11). Entry in Diary One, in possession of the AIATSIS Library, MS3513 Box 22 Item 269, Canberra.

McCarthy, F. (1948, April 14). Entry in Diary One, in possession of the AIATSIS Library, MS3513 Box 22 Item 269, Canberra.

McCarthy, F. (1948, May 17). Entry in Diary One, in possession of the AIATSIS Library, MS3513 Box 22 Item 269, Canberra.

McCarthy, F. (1948, May 19). Entry in Diary Two, in possession of the AIATSIS Library, MS3513 Box 22 Item 269, Canberra.

McCarthy, F. (1948, July 18). Entry in Diary Four, in possession of the AIATSIS Library, MS3513 Box 22 Item 269, Canberra.

McCarthy, F. (1948, July 19). Entry in Diary Four, in possession of the AIATSIS Library, MS3513 Box 22 Item 269, Canberra.

McCarthy, F. (1948, August 8). Entry in Diary Four, in possession of the AIATSIS Library, MS3513 Box 22 Item 269, Canberra.

McCarthy, F. (1948, August 26). Entry in Diary Four, in possession of the AIATSIS Library, MS3513 Box 22 Item 269, Canberra.

McCarthy, F. (1949, January 16). Radio interview with 7HT. Hobart, transcript in possession of MS3513 Box 22, Item 265, AIATSIS, Canberra.

McCarthy, F. (1949, February 10). Letter to the Director of Australian Museum, in possession of the Australian Museum Archives, Series 10 22/1948, Sydney.

McCarthy, F. (1952). Aboriginal rain-makers and their ways. *Australian museum, 10*, 302–5.

McCarthy, F. (1953). Purse-net fishing in Arnhem Land. *Australian museum, 11*(1), 21–23.

McCarthy, F. (1954, June 23). Letter to Professor Nadel, in possession of the National Museum of Australia, Arnhem Land Expedition file, Canberra.

McCarthy, F. (1955). Arnhem Land baskets. *Australian museum, 11*(9), 283–88.

McCarthy, F. (1955, February 9). Letter to J. W. Evans, in possession of the Australian Museum Archives, Series 235, Central Correspondence Files 1949–1969; G70/513, Arnhem Land Expedition, Sydney.

McCarthy, F. (1956, January 18). Internal Australian Museum memo to J. W. Evans, in possession of the Australian Museum Archives, Series 235, Central Correspondence Files 1949–1969; G70/513, Arnhem Land Expedition, Sydney.

McCarthy, F. (1957, July 10). Memo to J. W. Evans, in possession of the Australian Museum Archives, Series 235, Central Correspondence Files 1949–1969; G70/513, Arnhem Land Expedition, Sydney.

McCarthy, F. (1957, October). Letter to J. W. Evans, in possession of the Australian Museum Archives, Series 235, Central Correspondence Files 1949–1969; G70/513, Arnhem Land Expedition, Sydney.

McCarthy, F. (1974). *Australian Aboriginal decorative art.* Sydney: Australian Museum.

McCarthy, F., and Setzler, F. (1960). The archaeology of Arnhem Land. In Mountford, C. P (Ed.), *Records of the American-Australian Scientific Expedition to Arnhem Land, Vol. 2: Anthropology and Nutrition* (pp. 215–95). Melbourne: Melbourne University Press.

McCarthy, F. D., and McArthur, M. (1960). The food quest and the time factor in Aboriginal economic life. In Mountford, C. P. (Ed.), *Records of the American-Australian Scientific Expedition to Arnhem Land: Vol. 2, Anthropology and Nutrition* (pp. 145–94). Melbourne: Melbourne University Press.

Meeting Minutes. (1955, March 24). In possession of the National Museum of Australia, Australian Institute of Anatomy File, Canberra.

Messenger, P. M. (Ed.) (1989) *The Ethics of Collecting Cultural Property: Whose Culture? Whose Property?* Albuquerque: University of New Mexico Press.

Morphy, H. (1987). The Art of Northern Australia. In Edwards, W. (Ed.), *Traditional Aboriginal society: A reader* (pp. 10–33). Melbourne: Macmillan.

Morphy, H. (1991). *Ancestral connections.* Chicago and London: University of Chicago Press.

Morphy, H. (1994). The Anthropology of Art. In Ingold, T. (Ed.), *Encyclopaedia of anthropology* (pp. 648–85). London: Routledge.

Morphy, H. (1998). *Aboriginal art*. London: Phaidon Press.

Morris, A. G. (1987). *The reflection of the collector: San and Khoi skeletons in museum collections*. South African archaeological bulletin, *42*(145), 12–22.

Mountford, C. P. (n.d.a). Letter, in possession of the State Library of South Australia, Mortlock Library, Mountford-Sheard Collection, V.76, p. 17.

Mountford, C. P. (n.d.b) Letter, in possession of the State Library of South Australia, Mortlock Library, Mountford-Sheard Collection, V.76, p. 12.

Mountford, C. P. (n.d.c). Letter, in possession of the State Library of South Australia, Mortlock Library, Mountford-Sheard Collection, V.77, p. 387.

Mountford, C. P. (n.d.d). Letter, in possession of the State Library of South Australia, Mortlock Library, Mountford-Sheard Collection, V.76, p. 176.

Mountford, C. P. (n.d.e). Letter, in possession of the State Library of South Australia, Mortlock Library, Mountford-Sheard Collection, V.76, p. 274.

Mountford, C. P. (n.d.f). Letter, in possession of the State Library of South Australia, Mortlock Library, Mountford-Sheard Collection, V.76, p. 19.

Mountford, C. P. (1945, March 5). Letter to the Chairman of the National Geographic Society Research Committee, in possession of the Smithsonian Institution Archives, Accession File 178294, Washington, DC.

Mountford, C. P. (1947, January 23). Letter to A. Wetmore, in possession of the Smithsonian Institution Archives, Accession File 178294, Washington, DC.

Mountford, C. P. (1947, January 28). Letter to Gilbert Grosvenor, in possession of the National Anthropological Archives, Setzler files, Box 7, Folder 4, Arnhem Land Correspondence 1948–1949, Folder 1 of 2, Washington, DC.

Mountford, C. P. (1947, October 20). Letter to Frank Setzler, in possession of the National Anthropological Archives, Setzler files, Box 7, Folder 4, Arnhem Land Correspondence 1948–1949, Folder 1 of 2, Washington, DC.

Mountford, C. P. (1947, December 28). Letter to Frank Setzler, in possession of the Australian Museum Archives, Series 10 Correspondence 1927–1956, 22/1948, Sydney.

Mountford, C. P. (1947, December 31). Letter to Dr. Walkom, in possession of the Australian Museum Archives, Series 10 Correspondence 1927–1956, 22/1948, Sydney.

Mountford, C. P. (1948, July 29). Letter to A. Wetmore, in possession of the Smithsonian Institution Archives, Accession File 178294, Washington, DC.

Mountford, C. P. (1948, November 5). Letter to A. Wetmore, in possession of the Smithsonian Institution Archives, Accession File 178294, Washington, DC.

Mountford, C. P. (1949). Exploring Stone Age Arnhem Land. *National geographic, 96*(6), 745–82.

Mountford, C. P. (1951, April 23). Letter to A. Wetmore, in possession of the State Library of South Australia, Mortlock Library, Mountford-Sheard Collection, Publication Correspondence, 1949–1951, V.525/1, p. 63.

Mountford, C. P. (1951, December 4). Letter to Mr. Rene d'Harnoncourt, Director of the Museum of Modern Art in New York, in possession of the State Library of South Australia, Mortlock Library, Mountford-Sheard Collection, Publication Correspondence, 1949–1951, V.525, p. 135.

Mountford, C. P. (Ed.). (1956). *Records of the American-Australian Scientific Expedition to Arnhem Land, Vol. 1: Art, Myth and Symbolism.* Melbourne: Melbourne University Press.

Mountford, C. P. (1957, March 16). Cited in Setzler, F., June 26, 1957, Letter to Fred McCarthy, in possession of the Australian Museum Archives, Series 235, Central Correspondence Files 1949–1969, g70/513, Arnhem Land Expedition, Sydney.

Mountford, C. P. (Ed.). (1960). *Records of the American-Australian Scientific Expedition to Arnhem Land, Vol. 2: Anthropology and Nutrition.* Melbourne: Melbourne University Press.

Mountford, C. P. (1961). *Aboriginal art.* London: Longmans.

Mountford, C. P. (1963). Australia's Stone Age men. *Great adventures with National Geographic* (pp. 385–92). Washington, DC: National Geographic Society.

Mountford, C. P. (1966). *Worcester art museum exhibition catalogue.* Exhibition February 17–April 3, 1966, Worcester Art Museum, Worcester, MA.

Mountford, C. (1975). Report on expedition for the National Geographic Society. *Great adventures with National Geographic.* Washington, DC: National Geographic Society.

Mountford, C. (1976). *Before time began.* Melbourne: Thomas Nelson.

Mountford, C. P., and Specht, R. (Eds.). (1958). *Records of the American-Australian Scientific Expedition to Arnhem Land, Vol. 3: Botany and Plant Ecology.* Melbourne: Melbourne University Press.

Muensterberger, W. (1994). *Collecting, an unruly passion.* Princeton, NJ: Princeton University Press.

Mulvaney, J. (2004). *Paddy Cahill of Oenpelli.* Canberra: Aboriginal Studies Press.

Mulvaney, J. (2006). Personal correspondence. Archaeologist, Australian National University, Canberra.

Mulvaney, J. (2008). "Annexing All I Can Lay Hands On:" Baldwin Spencer as Ethnographic Collector, in Peterson, N., L. Allen, and L. Hamby (Eds.). *The Makers and Making of Indigenous Australian Museum Collections.* Melbourne University Press, Melbourne, pp. 141–62.

Mulvaney, J. and Calaby, J. (1985). *So much that is new: Baldwin Spencer 1860–1929.* Melbourne: Melbourne University Press.

Mulvaney, R. (1983). *From curio to curation: The Morrison collection of aboriginal wooden artefacts.* Unpublished BLitt Dissertation, Australian National University, Canberra.

Murphy, K. (1948, July 14). Letter to Frank Setzler, in possession of the Smithsonian Institution Archives, Accession File 178294, Washington, DC.

Murphy, K. (1955, May 23). Letter to Dr. J. W. Evans, in possession of the Australian Museum Archives, Series 235, Central Correspondence Files 1949–1969; G70/513, Arnhem Land Expedition, Sydney.

Myres, L. (Ed.). (1906). *The evolution of culture and other essays.* Oxford: Oxford University Press.

Nawirridj, W. (2002). Personal correspondence to Sally K. May. Artist, West Arnhem Land.

Nayinggul, J. (2002). Personal correspondence to Sally K. May. Senior Traditional Owner, West Arnhem Land.

Neale, M. (1998). Charles Mountford and the "Bastard Barks." In Seear, L., and Ewington, J. (Eds.), *Brought to Light: Australian Art 1850–1965.* Brisbane: Queensland Art Gallery.

Nietzche, F. (1974). *Thoughts out of season*, Part 2. New York: Gordon Press.

Northern Territory times and gazette. (1948, September 10). *Silent Men Back from the Silence of Arnhem Land.*

O'Hanlon, M., and Welsch, R. L. (Eds.). (2000). *Hunting the gatherers: Ethnographic collectors, agents, and agency in Melanesia, 1870s–1930s.* Oxford and New York: Berghahn Books.

Ortiz, G. (2003). Overview and assessment after fifty years of collecting in a changing world. In Robson, E., Treadwell, L., and Gosden, C. (Eds.), *Who owns objects? The ethics and politics of collecting cultural artefacts* (pp. 15–32). Oxford: Oxbow Books.

Pearce, S. (1992). *Museums, objects and collections.* Washington, DC: Smithsonian Institution Press.

Pearce, S. (Ed.). (1994). *Museums and the appropriation of culture.* London: Athlone Press.

Pearce, S. (1995). *On collecting: An investigation into collecting in the European tradition.* London: Routledge.

Pearce, S. (1998). *Collecting in contemporary practice.* Walnut Creek, CA: AltaMira Press.

Pearce, S. (1999). *Museums and their development: The European tradition, 1700–1900.* London: Routledge.

Rathje, W., and Schiffer, M. (1982). Artifacts and Behaviour. *Archaeology.* New York: Harcourt Brace Jovanovich.

Renfrew, C., and Bahn, P. (1996). *Archaeology: Theories, methods and practice*, 2nd ed. London: Thames and Hudson.

Reynolds, H. (1987). *Frontier: Aborigines, settlers, and land.* Sydney: Allen and Unwin.

Reynolds, H. (2006). *The other side of the frontier: Aboriginal resistance to the European invasion of Australia.* Sydney: University of New South Wales Press.

Roberts, R.G., R. Jones, and M.A. Smith. (1993). 'Optical dating at Deaf Adder Gorge, Northern Territory, indicates human occupation between 53,000 and 60,000 years ago,' *Australian Archaeology*, vol. 37, pp. 58–59.

Rose, F. (1960). *Classification of kin, age structure and marriage amongst the Groote Eylandt Aborigines: A study in method and a theory of Australian kinship.* Berlin: Akademie Verlag.

Rose, F. (1968). *Australia revisited: The aboriginal story from Stone Age to space age.* Berlin: Seven Seas.

Rosenthal, D. (2000, July 17). Personal correspondence. Collection Management, Museum of Natural History, Smithsonian Institution, Washington, DC.

Rowley-Conway, P. (2007). *From Genesis to prehistory: The archaeological three age system and its contested reception in Denmark, Britain, and Ireland.* Oxford: Oxford University Press.

Ryan, J. (1990). *Spirit in land: Bark paintings from Arnhem Land in the National Gallery of Victoria.* Melbourne: National Gallery of Victoria.

Ryan, J. (2000). Letter from the Senior Curator, Aboriginal and Torres Strait Islander Art, to Sally K. May with accompanying list of bark paintings from the Arnhem Land Expedition held in the National Gallery of Victoria, in possession of recipient.

Setzler, F. (n.d.). Memo to Mountford, in the National Anthropological Archives, Setzler Files, Box 7, folder 2 of 2, Washington, DC.

Setzler, F. (1947, September 1). Letter to Mountford, in possession of the National Anthropological Archives, Setzler Files, Box 7, Folder 4, Arnhem Land Correspondence 1948–1949, folder 1 of 2, Washington, DC.

Setzler, F. (1947, September 31). Letter to Mountford, in possession of the National Anthropological Archives, Setzler Files, Box 7, Folder 4, Arnhem Land Correspondence 1948–1949, folder 1 of 2, Washington, DC.

Setzler, F. (1948a). Label from Glass Plate Negative 64, in possession of the National Anthropological Archives, Setzler Files, Box 18, Folder 3, Washington, DC. [note: description of negative available in Vertical File Rm. 61-A, control number 36–3 of 7.]

Setzler, F. (1948b). List of Specimens Collected by F. M. Setzler, Australia, 1948, in possession of the National Anthropological Archives, Setzler Files, Box 22, Folder 1, Arnhem Ethno Objects, Washington, DC.

Setzler, F. (1948, January 6). Letter to Mr. Hoopes, National Geographic Society, in possession of the National Anthropological Archives, Setzler Files, Box 7, Folder 4, Arnhem Land Correspondence 1948–1949, folder 1 of 2, Washington, DC.

Setzler, F. (1948, July 12). Letter to A. Wetmore, in possession of the Smithsonian Institution Archives, Accession File 178294, Washington, DC.

Setzler, F. (1948, July 18). Letter to A. Wetmore, in possession of the Smithsonian Institution Archives, Accession File 178294, Washington, DC.

Setzler, F. (1948, August 29). Letter to A. Wetmore, in possession of the Smithsonian Institution Archives, Accession File 178294, Washington, DC.

Setzler, F. (1948, October 6). Letter to A. Wetmore, in possession of the Smithsonian Institution Archives, Accession File 178294, Washington, DC.

Setzler, F. (1948, December 21). Statement released through the Department of the Interior, in possession of the Smithsonian Institution Archives, Accession File 178294, Washington, DC.

Setzler, F. (1950, January 13). Lecture Notes, National Geographic Society presentation, in possession of the Smithsonian Institution Archives, Accession File 178294, Washington, DC.

Setzler, F. (1957, June 26). Letter to Fred McCarthy, in possession of the Australian Museum Archives, Series 235, Central Correspondence Files 1949–1969; G70/513, Arnhem Land Expedition, Sydney.

Setzler, F., and McCarthy, F. (1950). A unique archaeological specimen from Australia. *Journal of the Washington Academy of Science, 40,* pp. 1–5.

Simpson, C. (1951). *Adam in Ochre: Inside Aboriginal Australia.* Sydney: Angus and Robertson.

Smith, C. (2005). Decolonising the museum: The National Museum of the American Indian in Washington, DC. *Antiquity, 79*(304), 424–39.

Smith, M. (1988). *The pattern and timing of prehistoric settlement in central Australia.* Unpublished PhD Dissertation, University of New England, Armidale.

Smyth, R. (Ed.). (1878). *The Aborigines of Victoria: With notes relating to the habitats of the natives of other parts of Australia and Tasmania,* 2 vols. Melbourne: Government Printer.

Specht, R. (1948, April 22). Arnhem Land Expedition field diary, in possession of Raymond Specht, Brisbane, Australia.

Specht, R. (Ed.). (1964). *Records of the American-Australian scientific expedition to Arnhem Land, Vol. 4: Zoology.* Melbourne: Melbourne University Press.

Specht, R. (2002, September 12). Oenpelli Rock Art, Personal Correspondence. Online e-mail (e-mail address withheld).

Specht, R. (2006a). *American-Australian Scientific Expedition to Arnhem Land (1948), its long-range impact.* Unpublished report.

Specht, R. (2006b). Personal Correspondence. Expedition Botanist and Professor, University of Queensland, Australia.

Spencer, B. (1928). *Wanderings in wild Australia,* 2 vols. Melbourne: Government Printer.

Spencer, H. (1864). *The principles of biology.* London: Williams and Norgate.

Stanton, J. (2008). I Did Not Set Out to Make a Collection, The Ronald and Catherine Berndt Collection at the Berndt Museum of Anthropology, in Peterson, N., L. Allen, and L. Hamby (Eds.). *The Makers and Making of Indigenous Australian Museum Collections.* Melbourne University Press, Melbourne, pp. 511–36.

Sun (Melbourne). (1948, March 9). U.S. Allies for Assault on "Last Frontier."

Sutton, P. (Ed.). (1988). *Dreamings: The art of Aboriginal Australia.* New York: George Braziller/Asia Society Galleries.

Sydney Morning Herald. (1948, March 20). Scientists will probe mysteries of Arnhem Land.

Taçon, P. S. C. (1989). Art and the essence of being: Symbolic and economic aspects of fish among the peoples of western Arnhem Land, Australia. In Morphy, H. (Ed.), *Animals into art* (pp. 236–49). London: Unwin Hyman.

Taçon, P. S. C. (1989). 'From the "Dreamtime" to the Present: the changing role of Aboriginal rock paintings in western arnhem land, australia', *The Canadian Journal of Native Studies,* vol. Ix, 2, pp. 317–39.

Taçon, P. S. C. and Christopher Chippendale. (1994). 'Australia's Ancient Warriors: changing depictions of fighting in the rock art of Arnhem Land, N.T.', *Cambridge Archaeological Journal* 4(2), pp. 211–48.

Taylor, L. (1982). Bark painting in western Arnhem Land. In Cooke, P., and Altman, J. (Eds.), *Aboriginal art at the top* (pp. 24–25). Maningrida: Maningrida Arts and Crafts.

Taylor, L. (1988). New life for the dreaming: Continuity and change in western Arnhem Land bark paintings. In West, M. (Ed.), *The inspired dream: Life as art in aboriginal Australia* (pp. 26–30). Brisbane: Queensland Art Gallery.

Taylor, Luke. (1996). *Seeing the inside: Bark painting in Western Arnhem Land.* Oxford: Clarendon Press.

Thomas, M. (2007a). *Return to Arnhem Land.* ABC Radio, Australia.

Thomas, M. (2007b). Gerald Blitner interviewed by Martin Thomas [sound recording]. National Library of Australia, ID 4198706 (ORAL TRC 5851).

Thomas, M., and May, S. K. (2007). Raymond Specht interviewed by Martin Thomas and Sally K. May [sound recording], National Library of Australia, ID 3697066 (ORAL TRC 5662).

Thomson, D. (1935–36). *Interim general report of preliminary expedition to Arnhem Land, Northern Territory of Australia, 1935–36.* Canberra, Commonwealth Government Printer.

Thomson, D. (1949). *Economic structure and the ceremonial exchange cycle in Arnhem Land.* Melbourne: Macmillan.

Torrence, R. (1993). Ethnoarchaeology, museum collections and prehistoric exchange: Obsidian-tipped artifacts from the Admiralty Islands. *World Archaeology,* 24(3), 467–81.

Trigger, B. (1989). *A history of archaeological thought.* Cambridge: Cambridge University Press.

Trudgen, R. (2000). *Why warriors lie down and die: Towards an understanding of why the aboriginal people of Arnhem Land face the greatest crisis in health and education since European contact.* Darwin: Aboriginal Resource and Development Services.

Tuhiwai Smith, L. (1999). *Decolonising methodologies: Research and indigenous peoples.* Dunedin: University of Otago Press.

Vergo, P. (1989). *The new museology.* London: Reaktion Books.

Walker, H. (1949). Cruise to Stone Age Arnhem Land. *National Geographic,* 96(3), 417–30.

Walkom, A. B. (1948, January 19). Letter, in possession of the Australian Museum Archives, Series 10, Correspondence 1927–1956, 22/1948, Sydney.

Walsh, K. (1992). *The representation of the past.* New York: Routledge.

Warner, L. (1937). *A black civilization.* New York: Harper and Brothers.

Washington Post. (1975, February 20). Anthropologist Frank M. Setzler dies.

Weil, S. (1995). *A cabinet of curiosities: Inquiries into museums and their prospects.* Washington, DC: Smithsonian Institution Press.

West Australian (Perth). (1948, January 12). Expedition to unknown north.

Wetmore, A. (1945). Ethnological project for Australia. Unpublished report for Smithsonian Institution, in possession of the Smithsonian Institution Archives, Accession File 178294, Washington, DC.

Wetmore, A. (1946, December 24). Letter to Mountford, in possession of the Smithsonian Institution Archives, Accession File 178294, Washington, DC.

Wetmore, A. (1947, December 3). Letter to Bridges, in possession of the Smithsonian Institution Archives, Accession File 178294, Washington, DC.

Wetmore, A. (1948, January 8). Letter to Frank Setzler, in possession of the National Anthropological Archives, Setzler Files, Box 7, Folder 4, Arnhem Land Correspondence 1948–1949, folder 1 of 2, Washington, DC.

Wetmore, A. (1948, January 15). Letter to Mountford, in possession of the Smithsonian Institution Archives, Accession File 178294 Washington, D.C.

Wetmore, A. (1948, July 9). Letter to Setzler, in possession of the Smithsonian Institution Archives, Accession File 178294, Washington, DC.

Wetmore, A. (1948, August 10). Letter to F. Setzler, in possession of the Smithsonian Institution Archives, Accession File 178294, Washington, DC.

Wetmore, A. (1951). Letter to Mountford, in possession of the State Library of South Australia, Mortlock Library, Mountford-Sheard Collection, V. 525/1, Publication Correspondence, 1949–1951, p. 59.

Wilkins, G. H. (1929). *Undiscovered Australia.* New York: G.P. Putnam's Sons; London: Knickerbocker Press.

Wise, T. (1985). *The self-made anthropologist: A life of A.P. Elkin.* Sydney: Allen and Unwin.

Worsley, P. M. (1957). Review, *Man, 57,* 241.

Worsnop, T. (1897). *The prehistoric arts, manufactures, works, weapons, etc., of the Aborigines of Australia.* Adelaide: Government Printer.

Wright, R. (1979). A modicum of taste: Aboriginal cloaks and rugs. *A.I.A.S. Newsletter, 11,* 51–56.

Wylie, A. (1989). Archaeological cables and tacking: The implications of practice for Bernstein's "Options beyond objectivism and relativism." *Philosophy of the social sciences, 19*, 1–18.

Yamaguchi, M. (1991). The Poetics of Exhibition in Japanese Culture. In Karp, I., and Lavine, S. D., (Ed.), *Exhibiting cultures: The poetics and politics of museum display* (pp. 57–67). Washington, DC: Smithsonian Institution Press.

Yulidjirri, T. (October 12, 2002). Personal correspondence to Sally K. May. Senior Kunwinjku artist from Gunbalanya (Oenpelli).

Index

Aagaard-Mogensen, Lars, 29
ABC Weekly, 181
Aboriginal and Torres Strait Islander Commission (ATSIC), 184
Aboriginal art, 102; anthropological definition of, 127; as anthropology subject, 143; in Art Gallery of South Australia, 117, *118–19*, 120; as "authentic," critical response to, 144; critical context for, 126–27, 144, 155, 157; cultural significance of, 150–51; as fine art, 155, 157, 194; Mountford on, 179–80; Mountford selling of, 117, 120; ownership of, among Aboriginal culture, 153; on paper v. bark, *145*; in private art galleries, 114–15, 117, 144–45, *145*; religious themes in, 143, 193; rock art, 57, *58*; Spencer, B., and, 154. *See also* bark paintings; paintings, from Arnhem Land Expedition; rock art
Aboriginal artists, 163, *164*, 165, 168, *168*, 170, 173–74

Aboriginal culture: Arnhem Land Expedition and, political importance of, 7–8, 16, 181–94; Australian government collection policy for, 103–4; body art in, *83*; collecting philosophy for, 95–97; cultural death of, 104; Darwin on extinction of, 96; definition of, 17n1; drawings in, 38; ethnographic collection themes for, 12; filming of, 63; loss of authenticity of, 97, 104; Mountford and, early contacts with, 36; Mountford's expectations of, 96–97; myth and symbolism of, 74–75; Native Americans and, ethnological comparisons to, 25; social views on longevity of, 96; socioeconomic status and, 16; sound recordings of, 63; worldwide interest in, 21
"Aboriginal Rain-Makers and Their Ways" (McCarthy, F.), 9
Aborigines: during Arnhem Land Expedition, as participants in,

217

182–83; under assimilation policy, 81; body art by, *83*; CMS and, 55, 81; cultural significance of paintings for, 150–51; education policy for, 81; exploitation of, 56; filming of, 63; food-gathering techniques of, 56; human remains returned to, 185, 191; near Umbakumba camp, 55; plaster casting of, 58–59, *61–62*, 68n1; social treatment of, 16; sound recordings of, 63

Adam, Leonard, 155

Adam in Ochre (Simpson), 84

Adnjamatana people, 39

Altman, Jon, 151

Amagula, Thomas, xviii

Ancient Monuments of the Mississippi Valley (Squier/Davis), xii

Andrews, Roy Chapman, xii

antiquarians, 25–26

Aranda people, 39

Arctic Studies Center (ASC), xiii–xiv

Arnhem Land: formation of, xii; Setzler in, prior knowledge of, 100

"Arnhem Land Baskets" (McCarthy, F.), 9

Arnhem Land Expedition, 1–2, 21; aboriginal culture collection and, as microcosm of, 7–8; Aborigines and, as participants in, 182–83; academic works on, 10; Art Gallery of South Australia and, artifacts in, *132*; artifact collection and, 95–105; artists encountered during, 163, *164*, 165, 168, 170, 173–74; Australian Museum and, artifacts in, 7, 108–9, 113, 135–37, 141; bark paintings collected during, 64–65, 108, *162*, 162–63; basket artifacts, 139, *140–41*; CMS

and, 186–87; collection policy during, from government, 98–99; collection restrictions during, 99; collection strategies during, of expedition members, 102–3; competitive collecting during, 66–68; cultural institutions influenced by, 143–47; cultural significance of, 181–94; documentation of, 10; early aims of, 36, 42–43; ethnographic collections from, 8, 11–12, 45, 92–93, 125–47; exploitation of Aborigines during, 56; fiber objects from, 103; fieldwork component of, 91; filming during, 63; funding for, 6, 41–42; human remains collected during, 183–84, *190*; literary references to, 9; media coverage of, 9, 69; Milingimbi Island and, 139–41; missing artifacts from, *116*; Mountford removed as head of, 70–72; Mountford's promotion of, 51; in museums, 10, 13, 143–44, *176*; National Museum of Australia and, artifacts in, 112–13, *132*, 136, *136*, 143; nutrition research during, 56, 73, *74*; paintings from, *113*, 113–14, 157, 159, *159–60*, 161; political importance of, 4, 7, 16, 35–36, 43, 92; as political propaganda, 4–5; public ownership of artifacts from, 120; regions visited during, 3; religious missions and, 186–87; remains from, return of, xix; sacred artifacts from, 120; sexism during, 73; Simpson on, 84, 90; Smithsonian Institution and, artifacts in, 7, 13, 43–44, 108, 113, 131, *131*, 137, 143; Smithsonian Institution

commission of, 7, 13; sound
recordings during, 63; South
Australian Museum and, artifacts in,
108–9, *130*, 143; specialist collections
during, 99–100; specimen collection
during, 8; string figure artifacts from,
133–34; weapons collected during,
76, 108; worldwide distribution of
artifacts from, 107–21. *See also*
Calwell, Arthur; Groote Eylandt, base
camp in; McCarthy, Frederick;
Mountford, Charles; Oenpelli, base
camp in; Setzler, Frank; Yirrkala, base
camp in
art galleries. *See* private art galleries,
Aboriginal art in
Art Gallery of New South Wales, 144
Art Gallery of South Australia, 117,
118–19, 120; Arnhem Land artifacts
in, *132*, 144
ASC. *See* Arctic Studies Center
Ashini, Daniel, xv
assimilation policy, for Aborigines, 81
ATSIC. *See* Aboriginal and Torres Strait
Islander Commission
Australia: Aborigines in, social treatment
of, 16; assimilation policy in, 81;
collecting of artifacts in, 20–21,
32–33; collecting policy, for
Aboriginal culture, 103–4; common
world view of, in late 18th-19th
century, 21; FACSIA, xix;
immigration policies in, 41; Northern
Territory in, *3*; "White Australia
Policy" in, 41. *See also* Arnhem Land
Expedition
Australia Institute of Anatomy, 112, *112*;
bark paintings in, 114

Australian Museum, 7, 98; Arnhem Land
artifacts in, 7, 108–9, 113, 135–37,
141; bark paintings in, 175;
McCarthy and, 108–9
"Australia's Stone Age Men"
(Mountford), 9

Baird, Spencer Fullerton, xiii
bark paintings, 5, 14–15, 57, 64–65, 108,
113, 149–51, *150*, *156*, *158–60*, *162*; in
Art Gallery of South Australia, 117,
118–19, 120; in Australia Institute of
Anatomy, 114; in Australian
Museum, 175; "bastard barks," 115; as
ceremonial, 153; development of,
151–53; in dwellings, 153; early
collectors of, 154; economic value of,
100, 154; execution of, 153; from
Groote Eylandt, 5, 127–28, *128*, 130,
156, 177, *178*; history of, 151–52;
McCarthy's collection of, 66–67, 134,
138, 162–63, *163*; from Milingimbi
Island, 154; Mountford's
commissions of, 11, 65–66, 126, 183;
in National Museum of Australia,
177; at Oenpelli, 82, 170; ownership
of, among Aborigines, 153; paper v.,
145, 161—162; payment and trade
for, 64–65, 101, 155, 182–83; in
private art galleries, 114–15, 117,
144–45, *145*; public perceptions of,
15–16; role of, 152–53; in South
Australian Museum, 114, 129–30,
176, 178; Spencer, B., commissions
of, 183; from Yirrkala, *127*, 127–28,
154
Barnett, Homer Garner, 46
Barton, Ralph, 81

Barunga (rock art site), xvi

baskets, as artifacts, 139, *140–41*, 141

Bassett-Smith, Peter, *49, 52*, 53–55, 77, 83

"bastard barks," 115

Beagle (ship), xii

Bennett, T., 30

Berndt, Catherine, 47, 82, 93n1, 170, 173; as collector of Aboriginal art, 155

Berndt, Ronald, 47, 82, 93n1, 155, 170, 173; as collector of Aboriginal art, 155

Bickerton Island, 72

Billington, Brian, *52, 87–88*

The Birth of the Museum (Bennett), 30

A Black Civilisation (Warner), 44

Blitner, Frederick Charles, 63

Blitner, Gerald, 63–64, 68, 189

body art, *83*

Bray, John, *52*, 72, *89*, 107

"Bush Toys" (Hagen), 10

A Cabinet of Curiosities (Weil), 30

Cahill, Patrick "Paddy," 79–82, 173; Oenpelli and, 79–82; poisoning of, 173

Calwell, Arthur, 36, 38–43, *40*; early life of, 40–41; political career of, 41–42; "White Australia Policy" under, 41

Cardinal, R., 30

Chapin,. James, xii

Chaseling, Wilbur, 82, 154

Chifley, Ben, 43

Childe, Vere Gordon, 24

Church Missionary Society (CMS): Aborigines and, 55, 81; Arnhem Land Expedition and, 186–87; Oenpelli and, 79, 81

Clarke, Annie, 10

CMS. *See* Church Missionary Society

Coates, Howard, 47, 56, 67–68, 72

Coates, Ian, 11

Cole, Keith, 80, 81, 187

Collecting: An Unruly Passion (Muensterberger), 30

collecting, of artifacts, 20–31; age system for, 23; Arnhem Land Expedition and, 95–105; of art, 26; in Australia, 20–21, 32–33; biases in, 178–79; classification of human culture and, 20–21, 24, 28; as competitive, 66–68, 100–102, 104–5; definition of, 20; desire for, 20–25; of exotic material, 26; "Great Chain of Being" and, 24; of historical material, 26; intercultural relations and, 35; "modernity" and, 22–23; motivation of sponsors and, 103; by Mountford, origins of, 37; of natural history, 26; Pitt-Rivers' influence on, 24; political rationality in, 24–25; as refined form of hunting, 25–26; social attitudes of, 95; Social Darwinism and, 26, 95–97; theory of natural selection and, 26. *See also* ethnographic collections

collections: from Arnhem Land Expedition, cultural significance of, 7–8; ethnographic, 8; museum theory and, 12; studies of, 12; as supra-artifact, 12

The Constellation of Orion and the Pleiades, 156

Cordon, Keith, 72

"Cruise to Stone Age Arnhem Land" (Walker), 9, 53

The Culture of Collecting (Elsner/Cardinal), 30

Cummings, Eileen, xvi
Curtin, John, 43

Daily Mirror, 53
Daily Telegraph, 120
Daniels, Glyn, 32
Darwin, Charles, xii, 23, 25; on
    Aboriginal culture, extinction of, 96;
    theory of natural selection, 22
Davis, Edwin, xii
Deignan, Herbert G., 43, 48, *49*, *52*, *62*,
    62–63, 91; biological collections of, at
    Oenpelli, 82
Descent of Man (Darwin), 25
d'Harnoncourt, Rene, 117
Dodd, Tara, xvi
Dominguez, Virginia, 33
Driver, Arthur Robert, 70
Drucker, Philip, 46
Dyer, Alf, 81–82, 155
Dyer, Mary, 81

education, of Aborigines, 81
Eggleston, Frederic, 42
Elkin, A.P., 46–47, 67, *67*, 72
Ellemor, Arthur F., 75–76, 139; bark
    paintings collected by, *162*;
    ethnographic collection of, *125*
Elliott, Craig, 9–10
Elsner, J., 30
ethnographic collections, 31–33; of
    Aboriginal culture, themes for, 12;
    analysis of, 123–25; from Arnhem
    Land Expedition, 8, 11–12, 45, 92–93,
    125–47; artifacts for trade and, 75; of
    bark paintings, 57; classification
    changes as result of, 14, 31; cultural
    inferences as result of, 124;

development of, 96; of Ellemor, A.F.,
    125; evolutionary theory and, 23–24;
    fiber objects, 103; hunting
    implements in, 76; of McCarthy, 57,
    125, 133–41, *134–36*, *139–42*, 146–47;
    from Milingimbi Island, *142*; of
    Mountford, 11, 18n3, *125*, 125–33,
    126, *128–29*; plaster casting in, 58,
    61–62, 68n1; of rock art, 57; of
    Setzler, 57–58, *125*, 137–41, *138–42*;
    Social Darwinism and, 19;
    typological system for, 31; weapons
    in, 76. *See also* bark paintings;
    paintings, from Arnhem Land
    Expedition; weapons, in
    ethnographic collections
Evans, J.W., 109, 137
evolution, theories of, 22–24;
    ethnological collections and, 23–24.
    See also Social Darwinism
*Exhibiting Cultures: The Poetics and
    Politics of Museum Display*
    (Karp/Levine), 30
exploitation, of Aborigines, during
    Arnhem Land Expedition, 56
"Exploring Stone Age Arnhem Land"
    (Mountford), 9, 22

FACSIA. *See* Families Community
    Services and Indigenous Affairs
Families Community Services and
    Indigenous Affairs (FACSIA), xix
"F.D. McCarthy's String Figures from
    Yirrkala: A Museum Perspective"
    (Florek), 10
Fforde, Cressida, 186
Fife, G., 30
Fisher, Irene, xvi

Florek, Stan, 10
Flynn, Barney, 80
food-gathering techniques, 56
Forde, Francis, 43

Gordon, Keith, *49*
"Great Chain of Being," 24, 32
Grey, Fred, 55–56, 155
Griffiths, Tom, 95, 103–4
Groote Eylandt, base camp in, 1, 51–68;
    bark paintings and, *5*, 127–28, *128*,
    130, *156*, 177, *178*; competitive
    collecting at, 66–68; daily life in,
    56–57; expedition equipment for, 53;
    McCarthy at, collections from,
    134–35; medical workstation in, 62;
    Mountford at, collections from, *127*,
    127–28; paintings from, 157, 159,
    161; RAAF support in, 53; reasons for
    selection as camp, 51–52, 55; Setzler
    at, 45; Umbakumba camp as part of,
    52, 55
Grosvernor, Gilbert, 6–7, 44, 47
Gumurdul, Donald, xviii, 188
Gunbalanya. *See* Oenpelli, base camp in

Hagen, Claudia, 10
Hale, Herbert, 112
Harney, Bill, 35, *67*, 71–72, *72*, 86, 90,
    189
Harris, Dick, 187
Henry, Joseph, xiii
Hipsley, E.H., 111, 114
Hodges, Kelvin, *52*, *87*
Hollow, Reginald, 72
Hooper-Greenhill, Eilean, 27
human remains, as anthropological
    artifacts, 183–89, *190*; at Oenpelli,

187–88; removal of, 186–89; return to
    Aboriginal community, 185, 191; at
    Smithsonian Institution, 190–91
Hunter, Richard, xvi
hunting implements, in ethnographic
    collections, 76

immigration policy, in Australia, 41
"The Incredible Kangaroo" (Johnson,
    D.), 9
Indigenous Australians, xvii; FACSIA,
    xix; Mountford and, research on, 39;
    remains of, returned by Smithsonian
    Institution, xviii–xix
indigenous cultures: cultural property
    ownership of, 182, 191–94; definition
    of, 17n1; under Social Darwinism,
    32–33, 193
Injalak Hill, 86
Isaacson, Ken, xvi

Jackson, Clarence, xi
Johnson, David H., 9, 43, 48, *49*, *52*, 62,
    77
Johnson, William, 80
Johnstone, William, 80
Jones, Chris, 10

Karp, I., 30
Kumutun (Aboriginal artist), 82, 84,
    168, 170, *170–72*, *171–72*; Cahill and,
    poisoning by, 173; paintings by, *174*
Kunwinijku, Wulkini (Aboriginal artist),
    84, 165, *166*
Kuru (ship), 76

Lamshed, Max, 36, 48
Lang, Herbert, xii

Larida (Aboriginal painter), 84

"The Last Frontier? Acquiring the American-Australian Scientific Expedition Ethnographic Collection 1948" (May), 10

Levine, S., 30

Loring, Stephen, 12

Lumley, Robert, 30

Macklin, Jenny, xix

Manabaru, Peter, xvi–xvii

Mankind, 46

Maralngurra, Gabriel, 186, 188

Marika, Mawalan (Aboriginal artist), 73, *102*, 165, 168, *169–70*, 170

Marika, Wandjuk (Aboriginal artist), *102*

Mason, Otis Tufton, 31

Mataranka (rock art site), xvi

Mathews, M., 155

May, Sally K., xii, xviii, 10

McArthur, Margaret, 10, *52*; as nutritional anthropologist, 56, 73, *74*, 86; sexism and, 73

McCarthy, E. Doyle, 28–29

McCarthy, Frederick, 4, 9–10, 36, 45–47, *49*, *52*, *57–58*, 64–65, *85*, 92, 108–9, 133–41, 149; on Aboriginal authenticity, 97; artifacts for trade by, 75; Australian Museum and, 108–9; bark painting collecting by, 66–67, 134, *138*, 162–63, *163*; collaboration with Setzler, 75; collection restrictions on, 99; collection strategy of, 133; competitive collecting by, 68; on distribution of Arnhem Land artifacts, 108–13, 117, 175; ethnographic collections for, 57, *125*, 133–41, *134–36*, *139–42*, 146–47;

expedition aims of, 46; in Groote Eylandt, 134–35; human remains collected by, 183–90; on Milingimbi Island, 139–41; Mountford and, tension with, 73–74, 110–12; as museum representative, 133; in Oenpelli, 135, *135*; paintings collected by, 114; physical anthropological research by, 84–86; Setzler and, combined collections of, 138–41, *139–42*; in Yirrkala, 134–35, *135*

McDonald, S., 30

Milingimbi Island, 139–41; bark paintings from, 154; ethnographic artifacts from, *142*

Miller, Robert, 43, 48, *49*, *52*, 62; biological collections of, at Oenpelli, 82–83

Minimini Numalkiyiya Mamarika, 65, *65*, 120

"modernity," 22–23; metanarratives in, 23; "primitive" cultures and, 23; theory of natural selection and, 22; theory of unilineal progress and, 22

Morphy, Howard, 16, 82, 150, 154–55

Mountford, Bessie, *49*, *52*

Mountford, Charles, 1, *5*, 6, 9, 22, 36–39, 44, 46, *49*, *52*, 56, 92, 107, 125–33; on Aboriginal art, 102, 179–80; Aboriginal myth and symbolism for, 74–75; Arnhem Land Expedition promotion by, 51; bark painting commissions by, 11, 65–66, 126, 183; collecting history of, 37; competitive collecting by, 68, 100–102, 104–5; distribution of Arnhem Land artifacts by, 108–14, 117, *129–30*, 146;

doubts about training of, 47–48; early Aboriginal contact with, 36; early life of, 36; early work history of, 37; educational background of, 37; ethnographic collections for, 11, 18n3, *125*, 125–33, *126*, *128–29*; expectations of Aboriginal culture, 96–97; as filmmaker, 4, 38–39, *83*, 83–85; in Groote Eylandt, *127*, 127–28; indigenous people and, research history on, 39; McCarthy and, tension with, 73–74, 110–12; in Oenpelli, 79, 128–29, *129*; as photographer, 37–38; record keeping by, 73; removal as head of expedition, 70–72; rock art collection by, 83–84; selling of Aboriginal art by, 117, 120; South Australian Museum and, 108–10; tension with Setzler, 90–91; in Yirrkala, *127*, 127–28

Mountford, Ken, 37

Muensterberger, Werner, 20, 30

Mulvaney, John, 80, 180n3

Murphy, Kevin, 70, 114, 137, 157, 191

Museum of Modern Art, 117

museums, 26–31; Arnhem Land Expedition and, collections in, 10, 13, 143–44, *176*; collecting biases, 178–79; decolonization of, 32–33; development of, 26–29; enclosing nature of, 33; literary works on, 30–31; modern view of moral improvement and, 28; "new museology" and, 29–30; Ptolemaic mouseion, 26; as public, 27–28; research for, 29–31

museum theory, collections and, 12; age system and, 23

The Museum Time Machine (Lumley), 30

Nadel, George H., 111

NAGPRA. *See* Native American Graves Protection and Repatriation Act

Nanawanda, 66

Nangapiana (Aboriginal artist), 165, *167*; art by, *168*

Nanyin (Aboriginal artist), *102*

Naritjbambulan (rock art site), xvi

Narritjin Maymuru, 73

National Gallery of Victoria, 144

National Geographic Magazine, xii, 6, 43

National Geographic Society, 6, 9, 42, 58–59, 92, 96

National Museum of Australia, 13; Arnhem Land artifacts in, 112–13, *132*, 136, *136*, 143; bark paintings, *177*; establishment of, 191

National Museum of Natural History. *See* Smithsonian Institution

National Museum of the American Indian Act (1989) (U.S.), xiv

Native American Graves Protection and Repatriation Act (NAGPRA) (1990) (U.S.), xiv

Native Americans, Aboriginal culture and, ethnological comparisons to, 25

natural history, 26

naturalists, 25–26

natural selection, theory of, 22; collecting of artifacts and, 26; Social Darwinism and, 22

Nawirridj, Wilfred, 187–88

Nayinggul, Alfred, xviii

Neale, Margo, 10, 115, 157

Negaocol technique, for plaster casting, 58

"new museology," 29–30

The New Museology (Vergo), 30

Ngkalabon people, xvi
nutritional anthropology, 56, 73, *74*, 86

"Oenpelli" (Harney), 86, 90
Oenpelli, as mission, 79–83; assimilation policy in, 81; CMS and, 79, 81; education policy for, 81; population of, 81–82
Oenpelli, base camp in, 2, *2*, 52, 79–93; bark painting collecting at, 82, 170; biological collections at, 82; Cahill and, 79–82; CMS and, 79, 81; establishment of, 79–81; film production in, *83*, 83–85; human remains at, 187–88; Injalak Hill at, 86; Kumutun in, 82, 84, 168, 170, *170–72*, 173, *174*; McCarthy at, collections from, 135, *135*; medical research at, 86; Mountford at, collections from, 79, 128–29, *129*; paintings from, 157, 159, 161; removal of human remains from, 187–88; Sprecht at, collections from, 82–83
On the Origin of Species (Darwin), 23
otherness, 33

paintings, from Arnhem Land Expedition, *113*, 113–14; in Art Gallery of South Australia, 117, *118–19*, 120; as artifact category, 15–16; distribution of, 114–15; from Groote Eylandt, 157, 159, 161; McCarthy's collection of, 114; Mountford's collection of, 162–63, *163*; from Oenpelli, 157, 159, 161; on paper, 113–14, *145*, *152*; paper v. bark, *145*, *161–62*; in private art galleries, 114–15; provenance of, 157, 159, *159–60*, 161; from

Yirrkala, 157, 159, 161. *See also* bark paintings
paper paintings, from Arnhem Land Expedition, 113–14, *145*, *152*; bark v., *145*
Pearce, Susan, 7, 29, 123
Petrie, Flinders, 32
The Phantom (ship), 77
Phoenix (barge), 53, 56, 69
"The Phoenix Never Came In," 53–55
Pitjantjatjara people, 39
Pitt-Rivers, Augustus Henry Lane-Fox, 24
plaster casting, of Aboriginal people, 58–59, *61–62*, 68n1; Negaocol technique for, 58; in Smithsonian Institution, 59
politics, Arnhem Land Expedition and, 4, 7, 16, 35–36, 43, 92
Powell, John Wesley, xii–xiii
"primitive" cultures, modernity and, 23
Principles of Biology (Spencer), 23
private art galleries, Aboriginal art in, 114–15, 117, 144–45, *145*; bark paintings, 114–15, 117, 144–45, *145*
Ptolemaic mouseion, 26
public museums, 27–28
Pularumpi community, xvi
Purnell, Florence, 37
"Purse-Net Fishing in Arnhem Land" (McCarthy, F.), 9

Queensland Art Gallery, 144

RAAF. *See* Royal Australian Air Force
Records of the American-Australian Scientific Expedition to Arnhem Land, 110, 162
Records of the Australian Museum, 46

religion, in Aboriginal art, 143, 193
The Representation of the Past (Walsh), 30
Richardson, Lori, xviii
Robinson, E.O., 80
rock art, 57, *58*; collection of, by Mountford, 83–84; dating of, 151; portable v., 151
Rose, Frederick, 155
Royal Australian Air Force (RAAF), 53; transport by, 76–77, *77*
Ryan, Judith, 10, 82, 140, 154–55

Scougall, Stuart, 145, 157
Seibert, Elvin, 70
Setzler, Frank, 4, 9, 36, 43–46, 48, *49, 52, 57*, 69–70, *85*, 92–93, 137–41; artifacts for trade by, 75; bark paintings collected by, *162*; collaboration with McCarthy, 75; competitive collecting by, 68; on distribution of Arnhem Land artifacts, 117; ethnographic collections for, 57–58, *125*, 137–41, *138–42*; excavation techniques of, 85; at Groote Eylandt, 45; human remains collected by, 183–89; knowledge of Arnhem Land prior to expedition, 100; McCarthy and, combined collections of, 138–41, *139–42*; on Milingimbi Island, 139–41; physical anthropological research by, 62, 84–86; plaster casting by, of Aboriginal people, 58–59, *60–61*, 68n1; Smithsonian Institution and, 43–44; tension with Mountford, 90–91
Setzler, Paul, 45

Setzler, Susan Perkins, 45
sexism, during Arnhem Land Expedition, 73
Simpson, Colin, 9, 79; on Arnhem Land Expedition, 84, 90
Smith, Claire, xv–xvi, 12
Smith, F.A., 173
Smith, Linda Tuhiwai, 25, 33
Smithsonian Institution, xii–xv, 98; Arnhem Land Expedition artifacts in, 7, 13, 43–44, 108, 113, 131, *131*, 137, 143; Arnhem Land Expedition commissioned by, 7, 13; ASC in, xiii–xiv; collection focus of, xiii; curators for, 31; expansion of, xiii; human remains from Arnhem Land Expedition at, 190–91; Indigenous Australian remains returned by, xviii–xix; linguistics in, xiii; materialist bias in, xii–xiii; plaster casts in, 59; Setzler and, 43–44
Social Darwinism, 22–23; collecting of artifacts and, 26, 95–97; ethnographic collection and, 19; indigenous cultures under, 32–33, 193; theory of natural selection and, 22; theory of unilineal progress, 22
South Australian Museum, 13; Arnhem Land artifacts in, 108–9, *130*, 143; bark paintings in, 114, 129–30, 176, 178; Mountford and, 108–10
Spencer, Baldwin, 154, 173; commission of bark paintings by, 183
Spencer, Herbert, 22–23; evolution theories of, 22–23
Sprecht, Raymond, *49, 52*, 56–57, 66, 72, 75, 165, 186; biological collections of, at Oenpelli, 82–83

Squier, Ephraim, xii
Strehlow, T.G.H., 38
string figure artifacts, 133–34
Sun, 47
supra-artifacts, 12
Sutton, Peter, 144
swaggies, 36–37, 49n1

Taylor, Luke, 151, 183
Theorizing Museums (McDonald/Fife), 30
Thomas, David Hurst, 25
Thomson, Donald, 154, 187
Tindale, Norman, 37, 96, 155, 176
Tjurunga, 38
Triumph (barge), 76, 91, *91*
Tuckson, Tony, 145, 157

Umbakumba camp, 52, 55, 100; Aboriginal people near, 55
unilineal progress, theory of, 22; Social Darwinism and, 22
"A Unique Archeological Specimen from Australia" (McCarthy, F./Setzler), 9
United States National Museum. *See* Smithsonian Institution

Vergo, Peter, 29–30
Victory (ship), 76–77

Walkabout, 38
Walker, Howell, 9, 48, *49*, 53

Walkom, Arthur Bache, 98
Walsh, K., 30
Warner, Lloyd, 44, 154
Warnindilyakwa people, 65
weapons, in ethnographic collections, 76, 108
Webb, Theodore T., 82, 154
Weil, S., 30
Wells, Edgar, 82
Wessan, Jimmy, xvi–xvii
Wetmore, Alexander, 6, 42, 44–45, 69–70, 90–91; on Arnhem Expedition collection policy, 98–99; on human remains collection, 185
"White Australia Policy," 41
Whitlam, Gough, 43
Wilkins, George Hubert, 20, *153*
Willey, Gordon Randolph, 46
Willirra (Aboriginal painter), 84
Wondjuk, Marika, 73
Wuramara, Joaz, xviii
Wye Oak, xviii

Yankunytjatjara people, 39
Yirrkala, base camp in, 1, 52, 69–77; bark paintings from, 154; McCarthy at, collections from, 134–35, *135*; as Methodist Overseas Mission, 69; Mountford at, collections from, *127*, 127–28; paintings from, 157, 159, 161; Yolgnu people at, 69
Yolgnu people, 69

About the Author

Sally K. May is a lecturer in heritage, museums, and material culture at the Australian National University. She is also convenor of the Cultural and Environmental Heritage stream of the Graduate Program in Liberal Arts. Previously Sally was an ARC Postdoctoral Fellow based at Griffith University (Queensland) and a lecturer in the Department of Archaeology at Flinders University (South Australia). She works closely with Indigenous communities around Australia on projects relating to museum collections, repatriation, archaeology, anthropology, and cultural heritage management.